Freedom in Captivity

How do borderland dwellers living along militarised frontiers negotiate regimes of state security and their geopolitical location in everyday life? What might 'freedom' mean to those who do not resist captivity engendered by borders? Focusing on the predicaments of a double-minority, *Freedom in Captivity* examines the affective attachments, political imaginaries and ethical claims-making among the Shi'a Muslims of Kargil in the union territory of Ladakh, India. In contrast to calls for freedom in the Kashmir Valley, Shi'as on the frontiers of Kashmir have sought belonging to India. Yet they do not entirely succumb to its hegemonic ideological boundaries. Departing from the dominant focus on physical cross-border mobility, this book is an invitation to re-imagine borderlands as cartographies of ideas, cutting across spatial scales. Based on original ethnographic research conducted between 2008 and 2021, the book offers a unique *longue-durée* insight into the lives of people residing at the intersections of the biggest states in Asia.

Radhika Gupta is Assistant Professor at the Institute for Cultural Anthropology and Development Sociology, Leiden University, Netherlands. Her research interests include anthropology of religion (especially Islam), borderlands, post-colonial politics, urban anthropology, environmental humanities and critical theory.

SOUTH ASIA IN THE SOCIAL SCIENCES

South Asia has become a laboratory for devising new institutions and practices of modern social life. Forms of capitalist enterprise, providing welfare and social services, the public role of religion, the management of ethnic conflict, popular culture and mass democracy in the countries of the region have shown a marked divergence from known patterns in other parts of the world. South Asia is now being studied for its relevance to the general theoretical understanding of modernity itself.

South Asia in the Social Sciences will feature books that offer innovative research on contemporary South Asia. It will focus on the place of the region in the various global disciplines of the social sciences and highlight research that uses unconventional sources of information and novel research methods. While recognising that most current research is focused on the larger countries, the series will attempt to showcase research on the smaller countries of the region.

General Editor
Partha Chatterjee
Columbia University

Editorial Board
Pranab Bardhan
University of California at Berkeley

Stuart Corbridge
Durham University

Satish Deshpande
University of Delhi

Christophe Jaffrelot
Centre d'etudes et de recherches internationales, Paris

Nivedita Menon
Jawaharlal Nehru University

Other books in the series:

Government as Practice: Democratic Left in a Transforming India
Dwaipayan Bhattacharyya

Courting the People: Public Interest Litigation in Post-Emergency India
Anuj Bhuwania

Development after Statism: Industrial Firms and the Political Economy of South Asia
Adnan Naseemullah

Freedom in Captivity

Negotiations of Belonging along
Kashmir's Frontier

Radhika Gupta

CAMBRIDGE
UNIVERSITY PRESS

CAMBRIDGE
UNIVERSITY PRESS

Shaftesbury Road, Cambridge CB2 8EA, United Kingdom

One Liberty Plaza, 20th Floor, New York, NY 10006, USA

477 Williamstown Road, Port Melbourne, vic 3207, Australia

314 to 321, 3rd Floor, Plot No.3, Splendor Forum, Jasola District Centre, New Delhi 110025, India

103 Penang Road, #05–06/07, Visioncrest Commercial, Singapore 238467

Cambridge University Press is part of the University of Cambridge.

It furthers the University's mission by disseminating knowledge in the pursuit of education, learning and research at the highest international levels of excellence.

www.cambridge.org
Information on this title: www.cambridge.org/9781009201612

© Radhika Gupta 2022

First published 2022
Reprint 2024

Printed in India by Avantika Printers Pvt. Ltd.

A catalogue record for this publication is available from the British Library

ISBN 978-1-009-20161-2 Hardback

Contents

Figures

Acknowledgements

It has taken over a decade to bring this project to fruition. I faltered many times along the way, uncertain if I had anything of value to say. Had it not been for the faith reposed in me by family, friends and, above all, people in Kargil, I might not have persisted. When I embarked upon this research, everyone in Kargil was eager to tell their stories, for their voices to be heard. This book is a small gesture of gratitude for the immense learning, friendship and grace I have received from them over the years.

My introduction to Kargil was facilitated by the International Association for Ladakh Studies (IALS). I am indebted to the entire Munshi clan, especially Gulzar, Aijaz and Riaz Munshi, and Dr Fatima, for their hospitality and valuable insights into the region. The companionship of Stanzin, Lamo, Benazir and Asgar at the Munshi Habibullah School made fieldwork all the more fun. I am deeply grateful for the generous support offered by the Iqbal family who took me into their home in the cold wintertime as one of their own. I spent many joyful hours in the company of Shafiqa, Shakila, Iliaz, Mustafa, Hussain (Chandu) and Sajjad. On shorter visits, the staff at Caravan Serai kept me well fed. I will always carry with me the humour, wisdom and care of Bashir and Zahra Wafa, who have unreservedly kept the doors of their home open to me. Memories of apricot excursions with Zahra hold a special place in my heart. I benefitted enormously from Rahman *sahib*'s wisdom and encouragement to always think deeper and harder and have been touched by his family's warmth. Even after the initial months of assisting me with research, Jaffar continued to be a good friend and a source of many insights. Many thanks to Fayaz Husain for his kindness and shared research trips to several villages. Sajjad Kargili has been a bedrock of support. I am immensely grateful to him for sharing his knowledge, helping with organising my trip to Iran and the wonderful memories of journeys across the Kargil district. Thank you, comrade!

I have been fortunate to have many teachers in Kargil. Thanks to Sibte Kalim for language lessons. Along with Master Sadiq Hardasi, late Sadiq Ali Sadiq and Bashir Wafa, he also taught me much about Balti culture, helping me to imagine Baltistan. Tanvir *sahib*'s lessons in history were invaluable. Shaykh Rajai and Hajji Batul patiently explained several aspects of Islam and Shi'ism in a spirit of quiet friendship, as did Archo Fatima from Minji. I am also thankful for the time given to me by Hasan Khan, late Shaykh Ahmad Mohammadi, late Shaykh Zakiri (Imam Khomeini Memorial Trust), Agha Qasim (Saliskot), Shyakh Anwar, Nasir Munshi and Hajji Azgar Ali Karbalai. A brief stint of fieldwork in Iran in 2009 would not have been possible without the help and hospitality of Shaykh Lutfi, Hasnain and Rubab, Shaykh Zakiri, Javad *bhai* and Shahid *bhai*. The warp and weft of this book are also composed of conversations with Nazir and Ali Taq at the Jammu and Kashmir Cultural Academy, Abba Zakir, Ahmad Ali Payja (Apati), Ahmad Jawan (Drass), Akhon Fida (Sangra), Dr Raza, Hajji Mohammad Hussain and family (Latoo), Hajji Tahira, Mahdi (Poyen) Mahinder Singh and family, Malik (Chanegond), Master Ali Khan and family (Purgue), Master Baqir (Pashkum), Master Gulzar and family, Master Namgyal (Wakha), late Musa Chigtan, Parveen, Rokia and Hajji Zahra (Pashkum), Ustani Hamida, Wazir Ali (Shiliktse), Zakir Ali, and the students at Dar al-Quran, especially Jina, Sakina and Zahra. I am indebted to all of them and the many others who are not mentioned here by name for their hospitality and indulgence. Many names have been anonymised in the text to protect the privacy of views that are not in the public realm.

In Leh, I am deeply grateful to Tsewang Yangjor's family and Bicky at Padma Guesthouse for their care and friendship over the years. Tashi Morup has been an abiding friend; thank you for all the brief restorative escapes to beautiful, quiet spots in and around Leh. Much gratitude to Abdul Ghani Sheikh for generously sharing his knowledge. My work has also been blessed by John Bray's sustained interest, encouragement and resourcefulness. A warm thank you to Janet and Saiyid Rizvi for their enthusiasm surrounding my research.

This book has morphed out of my DPhil dissertation at the University of Oxford. A scholarship from the UK India Education and Research Initiative (UKIERI) generously funded my PhD. I am grateful to David Gellner and Fernanda Pirie for smoothly and diligently shepherding me through the doctoral process. At different stages of writing, I was fortunate to receive generous feedback from Faisal Devji, Mohammad Talib, Paul Dresch and Sondra Hausner. My time in Oxford was enriched by the camaraderie and intellectual support of Ammara Maqsood, Jelena Baranovich, Kabir Mansingh Heimsath, Linda Fibiger Martin Saxer, Masooda Bano, Melanie Griffiths and Sandeep Sengupta.

I was fortunate to receive postdoctoral fellowships at the Max Planck Institute and the Centre for Modern Indian Studies in Göttingen. Amidst starting new research in Bombay, I luxuriated in the time to read widely and slowly rethink and start revising my Kargil work. I am grateful to Aparna Nair, Ajay Gandhi, Dag Erik Berg, Lalit Vachani, Leilah Vevaina, Michaela Dimmers, Nandagopal Menon, Nate Roberts, Neena Mahadev, Patrick Eisenlohr, Peter van der Veer, Roschanack Shaery-Yazdi, Reza Masoudi Nejad, Sebastian Schwecke, Srirupa Roy and Weishan Huang for friendship and stimulating feedback on fragments of this work. A shared interest in Shi'ism made for lively conversations with Sarover Zaidi. Many of the arguments in this book were influenced by intense discussions over delicious food with Shaheed Tayob. Without these, life in a small German town might have been unbearable.

In Leiden, I thank Nira Wickramasinghe for her support in a system that can be overwhelming. A teaching relief grant for one semester from the Leiden Institute for Area Studies enabled me to finally wrap up this manuscript. Bindu Menon, Crystal Ennis, Erik de Maaker, Martijn Boven and Sanjukta Sunderason offered valuable feedback on portions of the manuscript. Walks in the neighbourhood with Sanjukta helped crystallise many ideas. Ajay and Nandu continued to read my work at critical stages and offered constructive feedback.

I am grateful to Qudsiya Ahmed and Anwesha Rana at Cambridge University Press for appreciating my scholarship and for their professionalism. It gives me great pleasure to publish with them. The completion of this book is also an opportunity to thank my teachers at the Department of Sociology, Delhi School of Economics, whose classes and scholarship have remained a source of inspiration.

Conversations with fellow borderland travellers and scholars, Sahana Ghosh and Farhana Ibrahim, linger throughout these pages. Their feedback along the way has been invaluable. Farhana has been integral to this project from its inception to completion. Along with her, Mijin, Rohini, Sonia, Prashant and Vinayak have stood by me through a long and sometimes bumpy journey. Aparna Balachandran's humour and support and Amit Ahuja's regular nudging and advice at critical moments were crucial in persisting with writing. I have been nourished by Ned Bertz's humour, gentle support and companionship. He has also patiently read and corrected messy portions of this manuscript.

Latika Gupta, my sister, has contributed to this book in every possible way: from sharing the love for Ladakh to discussing ideas, editing parts of the text, problem solving and, above all, enabling me to be so far away. It is joyous to share our mother's passion for the Himalayas. My parents' love has lit my path, always reminding me to stay grounded, value humility and retain perspective in life. I dedicate this book to my family.

Abbreviations

BADP	Border Area Development Programme
BCF	Baltistan Cultural Foundation
BJP	Bharatiya Janata Party
CAA	Citizenship Amendment Act
CEC	Chief Executive Councillor
FCR	Frontier Crime Regulation
FCRA	Foreign Contribution Regulation Act
IALS	International Association for Ladakh Studies
IB	Intelligence Bureau
IKMT	Imam Khomeini Memorial Trust
INTACH	Indian National Trust for Art and Cultural Heritage
J&K	Jammu and Kashmir
KASCO	Kargil Social and Cultural Organisation
KDA	Kargil Democratic Alliance
LAHDC	Ladakh Autonomous Hill Development Council
LBA	Ladakh Buddhist Association
LG	lieutenant governor
LoC	Line of Control
MLA	member of state legislative assembly
MP	member of parliament
NC	National Conference
NGO	non-governmental organisation
PDP	People's Democratic Party

SC	Supreme Court
ST	Scheduled Tribe
UT	union territory
VHP	Vishva Hindu Parishad
WIN	World Islamic Network
YMBA	Young Men's Buddhist Association

Notes on Transliteration

I have used John T. Platts' *Dictionary of Urdu, Classical Hindi and English*[1] to transliterate most of the Urdu and Hindi words. For words not found in the dictionary, I have transcribed phrases and terms in a way that best reflects the pronunciation in the Kargil region. Diacritical marks have not been used throughout the text for the sake of simplicity with the exception of *'ayn* and *hamza* (for examples, Qur'an, *shari'a*, and *'ulama*). All entries in the glossary use diacritical marks but omit emphatic consonants.

To reflect subcontinental and local pronunciation, *i* and *u* are used rather than *e* and *o* (for examples, 'Qur'an' in place of 'Qoran' and 'Muharram' in place of 'Moharram'). Exceptions have been made for constructions that approximate the Urdu pronunciation (for example, *yaum-e-azadi*).

Persian and Arabic words not found in Platts' dictionary have been transcribed following the *International Journal of Middle Eastern Studies* (*IJMES*) guidelines. Accordingly, words found in the *Merriam-Webster Dictionary* and the *Oxford Advanced Learner's Dictionary* have not been treated as technical terms and are therefore not italicised or marked with diacritics (for examples, 'abaya', 'agha', 'fatwa', 'hadith' and 'hijab').

Purigi, Ladakhi and Balti are Tibetan dialects. I have transcribed the words according to the local pronunciation as this varies between dialects. Purigi often includes words from Urdu, Persian and Arabic (for example, 'Hajji Mo'). Where the spelling is relevant, I have included the widely accepted Wylie transliteration of the Tibetan script[2] in only the glossary.

Notes

1. Digital Dictionaries of South Asia, http://dsal.uchicago.edu/dictionaries/platts (accessed on 20 July 2022).
2. Turrell Wylie, 'A Standard System of Tibetan Transcription', *Harvard Journal of Asiatic Studies* 22 (December 1959): 261–67, https://doi.org/10.2307/2718544 (accessed on 20 July 2022).

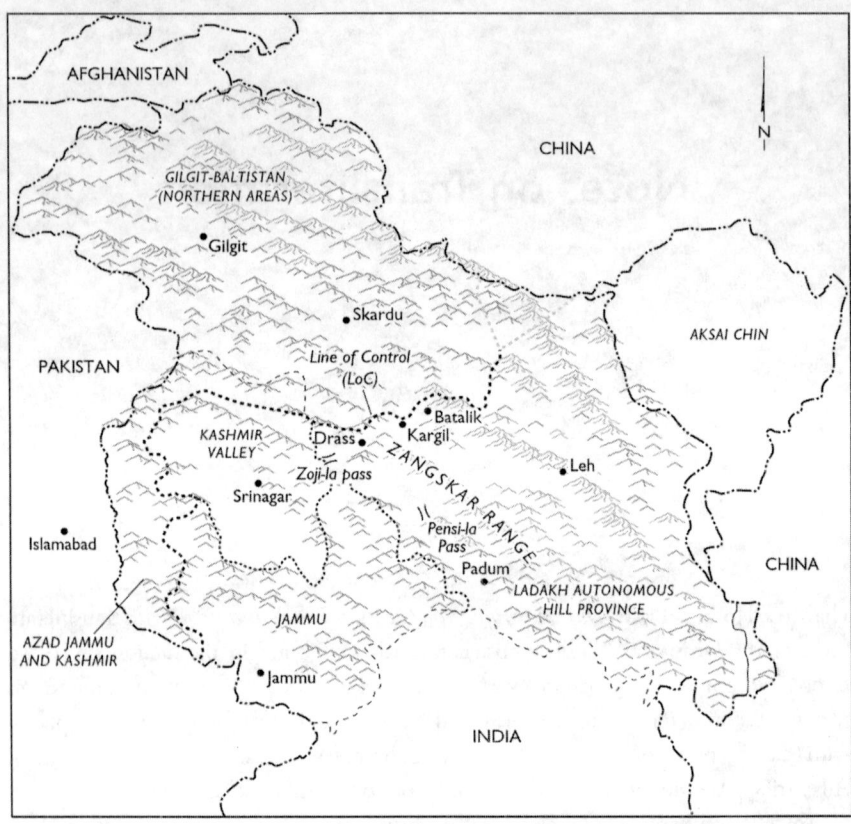

Map of Kargil and surrounding regions

Source: Reproduced from David N. Gellner (ed.), *Borderland Lives in Northern South Asia* (Durham, NC: Duke University Press), with the permission of Duke University Press. The map is drawn by William L. Nelson.

Note: Map not to scale and does not represent authentic international boundaries.

Introduction

Freedom in Captivity

> The traversals of freedom and subordination, sovereignty and subjection, and autonomy and compulsion are significant markers of the dilemma or double bind of freedom.
>
> —Saidiya V. Hartman[1]

Every year in the month of July, the otherwise sleepy town of Drass, a key site of confrontation in the fourth war between India and Pakistan, buzzes with activity. By this time of summer, the streams are gushing with snowmelt, and the mountainsides and pastures are a verdant green. Construction work has resumed for the season, and residents are busy tending to their fields of barley or travelling to Srinagar for errands that winter brought to a halt. Besides the greater traffic of tourists stopping for a cup of tea in the Drass bazaar on their way to Srinagar or Leh, the Indian army and district administration of Kargil are also gearing up to organise the annual Vijay Diwas celebrations to mark India's victory over Pakistan in the Kargil War (1999). This was the first war to be mediatised, beamed through national television directly into people's homes in India. Fought on the high mountain battlegrounds of Kargil – located along the *de facto* border in the far northwest frontier of Indian-controlled Kashmir – the Kargil War continues to have a long affective afterlife in the national imagination. Images of soldiers holding aloft the Indian flag on Tololing and Tiger Hill, the two peaks on this treacherous terrain which the Indian army recaptured from Pakistani incursions in 1999, are today household names. The war captivated the nation, and like legends told and retold, its enchantment has been sustained through Vijay Diwas celebrations.[2]

The tenth anniversary of the war demanded even greater pomp and splendour. Heavy security arrangements were in place for the high-profile nature of the event in 2009, for the guest list included army generals, the kin of martyred soldiers, Bollywood stars and the national media. Against a backdrop of rugged mountains with patches of melting snow, a hill slope etched with 'Tenth Anniversary, Op. [Operation] Vijay Divas' ran down to a vast ground prepared for the event with the neatness and precision of a cantonment area. Marquee-like tents had been erected for the dignitaries to watch a horse-polo match, a traditional sport in the region, and a cultural show. Sortie displays and a paragliding show by the military reinforced the region's repute as a war zone in the national imagination. Vijay Diwas was reminiscent of the national Republic Day parade celebrated every year in India's capital, reiterating that the exercise of power is always inseparable from its display.[3]

A few days before the event, I had bumped into a young Kargili journalist at a tea stall in the Kargil bazaar. When I asked him, 'What's the latest in the news?', Vijay Diwas came up, and he complained about the difficulty he was facing in obtaining a pass to enter the venue while the national media was to be flown up especially for the event. Resentful and annoyed in that moment, he let slip that Kargili reporters always had covered army programmes despite being warned against this by separatists in Kashmir, and yet such treatment was the reward for their allegiance to India. The journalist was echoing a common refrain among the people of this region about the insufficient recognition of their patriotism: Without them, they asserted, India could not have won the Kargil War. Civilians in this region have been written out of state narratives of heroic nationalism despite their sacrifices during the war.[4]

I was privileged to be able to access the venue a few days later with the help of the Jammu and Kashmir Academy of Art, Culture and Languages. It had organised cultural troupes from different ethnic groups of the region, which, along with the horse-polo teams, were the only officially solicited local participation. Others ringed the perimeter of the area as a paraglider descended to the ground (Figure I.1), while army *jawans* (foot soldiers) served refreshments to the dignitaries sheltered from the sun and dust.

Backstage, before the cultural show commenced, teenage boys in traditional costumes shared brief moments of jest with *jawans*, taking photos with and of them. Each troupe took to the stage in turn, performing song and dance, conforming to state-endorsed formats of collective ethnic representation. A Shina-speaking troupe dressed in cream-coloured *pathan* suits and their signature woollen cap, more commonly worn in Gilgit and Chitral in Pakistan, sang a song with a striking chorus: 'We don't want money or fame, we only want Hindustan/We don't want

Figure I.1   Vijay Diwas, 2009
Source: Photograph by the author.

Islamabad or Lahore, we only want Hindustan.' I had heard similar paeans to India in the poetry of the many established and budding poets in the region at the *musha'ira* (poetry gatherings) held by the Jammu and Kashmir Academy of Art, Culture and Languages. These performances of patriotism and expressions of the desire to belong to India did not reflect the backstage disappointments with the Indian state that I had heard in everyday conversations, such as the one with the young journalist I recount here.

The journalist's comment exceeded the feeling of routine frustration with the bureaucracy entailed in entering a highly securitised national event. It had a double valence. It simultaneously gestured to the desire for recognition by the nation state and the awareness among the people of this region of their potential to challenge its sovereignty. His all-too fleeting reference to resisting pressure from separatists in the Valley suggested awareness of a power held but not exercised. It reminded me of a stray comment by another young man who expressed his frustration with the state's failure to build a motorable road to his village: 'We could have easily taken up the Kalashnikov, but we did not.' The rhetorical flourish of this remark might appear out of proportion to the regular demand for roads by mountain communities everywhere. But in a village close to the Line of Control (LoC, the *de facto* border), it expressed a charged unrequited emotion – disappointment with the state for not returning the love that they, the guardians of the nation state's sovereignty, had extended to it.

Against the backdrop of these resentful emotions, how do we interpret the routine staging of patriotism along a heavily militarised, fraught frontier of Kashmir? Are such performances just another scene of subjection, of citizen-subjects on the peripheries of the nation state paying obeisance to it? Or does the backstage tell a story that is more complex than one of either resistance or submission? How do people make lives liveable when they do not consider resistance to state sovereignty a viable option and yet never feel wholly recognised by the state? Is it possible to sustain a measure of political agency, cultural and intellectual autonomy in non-resisting borderlands?

In contrast to the calls for *azadi* (freedom) from India by the majority of Muslims in the Kashmir Valley,[5] the people of Kargil have sought belonging in India. A Shi'a majority district in the trans-Himalayan region of Ladakh, Kargil has never extended support to separatist movements in the Valley. Yet it always sought to remain attached to Kashmir under the protection offered by Article 370 of the Indian Constitution that had granted Kashmir partial autonomy until 2019.[6] Muslim Kargilis never endorsed Ladakhi Buddhist demands for union territory (UT) status first raised in the early 1990s, but they also remain deeply anchored in Ladakh. Located thus in an interstitial space, the predominantly Shi'a Muslim inhabitants of Kargil have been struggling for recognition of their distinct political subjectivity and cultural identifications.

Pondering what constitutes a '"viable life", a life that is worth living', Ghassan Hage proposes the concept of 'bearable life', a life that hovers 'between the viable and non-viable'.[7] For Muslims in the Kashmir Valley, life under Indian control is non-viable and unbearable; dignity is denied to them even in death. In contrast, people living in Kargil had just enough space to continue to search for lives that were more than 'just-bearable'. State benevolence as a reward for fidelity to the nation is articulated within a liberal discourse of citizenship rights, one which Muslims in the Kashmir Valley have refused, but which the Shi'a Muslims of Kargil have sought. They have embraced small freedoms and continue to seek liberty and protection of democratic rights within a state of siege. This book explores what 'freedom' might mean for those who do not equate it with a quest for national sovereignty.[8] It shifts the gaze away from top-down security concerns to examine how borderland dwellers themselves negotiate regimes of state security and their geopolitical location in everyday life.

A Captive Borderland

I characterise Kargil as a captive borderland because the licit and illicit *cross-border* movement of goods and people that vitalise life along borders in other parts of South Asia and the world scarcely can be found along this frontier of Kashmir. The pervasive focus on physical border crossings in borderland scholarship did not offer me comparative conceptual resources to understand the dynamics of life in this region. Instead, the analytic of 'captivity' has been more productive to think with. It enables me to foreground how people living along impermeable geopolitical borders choose not to transgress them but rather consciously and tactically negotiate relations with the nation state.[9] Unlike the violent, invasive presence of the military in the Kashmir Valley, which has turned it into an open-air prison, people in Kargil do not encounter state brutality at every step in daily life. Rather, their entrapment is generated by this frontier's importance to a carceral state whose security relies on the docility of borderland dwellers to protect its sovereignty. This necessitates the sustenance of a particular relationship with the inhabitants of this region such that they accept living under the conditions of 'freedom in captivity'. If freedom, as Hannah Arendt has argued, primarily exists in action,[10] then how might we consider the politics of those who choose to act within captivity? How can we 'recuperate the category of "freedom"' to think about creative and improvisational politics?[11]

Forms of Captivity

In the wake of the partition and the three subsequent wars (1965, 1971 and 1999), India's *de facto* border with Pakistan has experienced growing militarisation and closure. From checkpoints, army cantonments, military vehicles and soldiers in the bazaar to Bofors guns on display along the national highway, infrastructures of militarisation are ubiquitous across Ladakh.[12] Each war rendered the border less porous. The harsh mountainous landscape aided the military on both sides to deter border crossings.[13] Offering a view from the other side, Cabeiri Robinson, too, points to the danger and difficulty of crossing the border in Azad Kashmir (a semi-autonomous region administered by Pakistan) after 1971, when the LoC was demarcated.[14]

It is important to note that encapsulation is a process. Borderlands are not homogeneous spaces. Villages located close to the LoC experienced inclusion into the nation state at a different pace from those farther away.[15] While 1947–48 was a foundational time in the biography of this frontier, it did not cast the ceasefire line in stone.[16] Villages (or parts of them) lying on the Pakistani side were abruptly incorporated into territory claimed by India during the 1965 and 1971 wars.

Despite territorial capture, these villages remained suspended in a liminal state for long after. Their stories show how belonging is negotiated on differential terms within a borderland. Histories of the encapsulation of particular villages into India after 1947–49 also open up the partition archive to its silent *longue durée* on the frontiers of Kashmir.[17] Narratives of cross-border settlers in Chapter 5 lend insight into processes of encapsulation in India through an ongoing dynamic between connection and disconnection that characterises freedom in captivity.

The direct overland route between Kargil and Skardu in Baltistan was already sealed in 1948. This made the entire Ladakh region almost entirely dependent on the Kashmir Valley for essential supplies, higher education, advanced medical care, bureaucracy and politics. The Zoji-la pass that connects Kargil to the Valley became its lifeline. Heavy snow, however, makes the pass untraversable for nearly five months of the winter every year, disconnecting Kargil, as Kargilis put it, 'from the rest of the world'. By the month of March, when winter stocks have run out, people become dependent on the army to airlift even basic commodities such as onions, tomatoes and eggs. An acute deprivation borne from this disconnection was affectively expressed as 'being jailed'.

Cross-border mobility at other places along this section of Kashmir's frontier is deterred not just by military presence, but also by the absence of the desire to go across illicitly. Growing sectarian violence in Pakistan since the 1980s, including in the neighbouring region of Gilgit–Baltistan, considered a bastion of Shi'i orthodoxy, also crucially underpinned Kargili belonging to India. An awareness of the persecution of Shi'as in Pakistan, the lack of political representation in Gilgit–Baltistan and prosaic material realities of life across the LoC formed a prism through which life on the Indian side was constantly refracted.[18]

Besides the confinement engendered by a heavily militarised border and the politics and practices of state security, Kargil has also been rendered captive by discursive representations of the region in the national public sphere. Physical cross-border immobility engendered by a state of siege has been consolidated through the discursive practices of a security state that are reproduced by popular media in India. Kargil has been suffocated by a 'cantonment perspective'.[19] It has been produced as a 'territory of desire'[20] for the Indian public, but very differently from the Kashmir Valley. In contrast to the erasure of military presence and state violence in popular, orientalist representations of the Valley as a sylvan paradise,[21] Kargil represents the ultimate vanquishing power of the Indian state. Indian hegemony is legitimised through a particular dynamic of militarisation: Kargil is positioned as 'peaceful' in opposition to the 'insurgent' or 'violent' Kashmir Valley.

Tourism has been another tool used by the state to encapsulate the region physically and discursively in a seemingly benign way. Since the late 2000s, a steady traffic of 'domestic tourists', as Ladakhis refer to Indian travellers, has plied to Kargil to see the War Memorial in Drass and borderland villages that no longer required an Inner Line Permit.[22] After the delineation of Ladakh into a separate UT in 2019, border tourism has been given a massive fillip by the Indian state. Ever-more integral to the politics of state security, borderland tourism is an unrecognised site within 'imperial fields of force'.[23] As participants in tourism infrastructure, borderland residents knowingly and unknowingly become conduits of information without directly working for the security apparatus. Tourism further depoliticises the region by conflating people's quest for recognition of their political subjectivity with their desire for economic development.[24] Encouraging Indian tourists to consume the spectacle of war through travel to the borderland also echoes colonial projects of mobility and the fixity engendered within them. Jingoistic tourists yearning to view Pakistan and experience the thrill of the border reproduce the national frame by reifying the border and fixating on borderland residents as ethnic objects.

Historically, Kargil had been subject to another kind of discursive captivity, when few tourists ventured there. As a junction between Leh, Zangskar and the Kashmir Valley, it was a dreaded one-night halt for travellers. Colonial depictions of a *mofussil* 'Mohammedan' town infested with bed bugs lingered for long after. Kargil evoked little interest, and Ladakh became synonymous with its Tibetan Buddhist inhabitants and culture. It was the veritable Shangri-la, for tourists and scholars alike.[25] Kargil was also neglected in academic scholarship on the region until the 1990s.[26] Long years of invisibility in image and text contributed to a yearning for recognition among the inhabitants of this region.

Despite the impossibility of physical cross-border mobility and growing entrapment, people living in this borderland nonetheless manage to sustain senses of place and modes of selfhood that are anchored within wider horizons that transcend its geopolitical boundaries. To understand the processes of creative calibration and negotiation that sustain these horizons, which I describe in this book, I argue that borderland studies need to go beyond the 'infrastructural perspective' that dominates this field to appreciate how the life-worlds of borderland dwellers are nestled within cartographies of ideas.

Cartographies of Ideas

Anthropological scholarship on negotiating border security has predominantly focused on movement and curtailments to mobility across national borders and contested boundaries between nation states. This focus can be traced back to studies of the US–Mexico border, which set the template for scholarship in many ways.

Decolonisation, post–Cold War fragmentations and post–9/11 'War Against Terror' displacements leading to the so-called 'refugee crisis' in Europe intensified statist concerns with hardening and securing borders. Explicit and implicit in this scholarship is an *infrastructural perspective* on borders and borderlands. This made important contributions towards expanding quotidian understandings of infrastructure beyond cement, brick and mortar to include a variety of materialities that are visible and invisible. Border(land) infrastructures range from barbed wire, electric fences and walls to prevent mobility, to checkpoints and documentation regimes to track legal and detect undocumented mobility, to agents of policing ranging from border guards, military, police and corporatised surveillance complexes and accompanying technologies.[27] Ethnographic attention to 'border work' along the edges of newly created states has lent insight into the complex, messy and contested processes entailed in putting these infrastructures in place to spatialise the state.[28]

Alongside these state infrastructures and impersonations of the state that materialise borders, scholarship has also focused on the infrastructure deployed by those who seek to cross borders, from vehicles (migrants on boats) to routes (smuggled in trucks or arduous journeys on foot), documents (passports and identity cards) and networks (agents, middlemen, kinship). This infrastructural perspective on borderlands is fundamentally grounded in the porosity of borders, underpinning both the desire to move (to seek refuge, to labour, to aspire for a better life) and the desire to curtail that movement through various bordering practices.

The effects of many of these infrastructures – checkpoints, border guards and passports – on the lives of Kargilis cannot be underestimated. An infrastructural perspective that confines scale to cross-border mobility, however, does not afford space to understand other routes through which people living in a captive borderland navigate closure and disconnections imposed by security states.

In his seminal work on borderlands, Willem van Schendel urged scholars to break out of area study silos and 'jump scale' to 'develop new concepts of regional space'.[29] He suggested that one way of doing this is to cross regional borders to study interregional linkages and proposed the concept of 'Zomia' – to refer to the highlands of the Southeast Asian massif – as one iteration of this re-scaling.[30] The study of borderlands and transnational flows of objects, peoples and ideas, and their collective overlap, he argued, would be two principal themes that would further this project. The burgeoning literature on migration and mobility in borderland studies has contributed immensely to expanding scale to cut across continents and underscore the value of the transregional. Yet its infrastructural perspective also firmly tethers it to *terra firma*, where demarcations by agents of state policing inevitably delimit scholarly horizons to studying bodies and commodities attempting to move across borders. In contrast to this approach, this book foregrounds the movement of ideas and ideologies that shape borderland dwellers' negotiations of belonging. I suggest a hermeneutics of borderlands as cartographies of ideas, cutting across spatial scales.

Reimagining borderlands as cartographies of ideas is an invitation to think about how borderland dwellers exercise agency without engaging in acts of resistance or cross-border transgressions. It is in the space between the border and the broader horizon, a space of friction, that negotiations of belonging take place through careful and creative acts of calibration. These acts – as ways of making life viable within captivity – belie analyses framed by dichotomies of legal–illegal, insurgent–subjugated, mobility–stasis that pervade borderland studies.

In places where cross-border mobility is practically non-existent, 'third-places' become key sites of flight. These are contact zones where people living on two sides of an impermeable border exchange objects, ideas and memories. Connections reactivated or forged in third-places lie outside the frames of long-distance nationalism, diaspora or exile. Third-places may enable only temporary face-to-face contact yet sustain horizons of belonging that nation states attempt to shrink. Seminary cities and pilgrimage sites in Iraq and Iran and the Hajj are important third-places where Muslims arbitrarily separated by borders can meet. These third-places are crossroads for the traffic of ideas and ideologies that feed into selfhood and politics back home in Kargil.

The anthropology of borderlands has examined cross-border cultural forms and networks that forge affective connections and sustain belonging across borders. However, barring some notable exceptions, the travel of transnational religious ideas and ideologies critical to shaping political and ethical subjectivities in post-colonial borderlands has hardly been explored.[31] Partition appears to have also effected a rupture in South Asian borderland scholarship which has not built on the rich histories of Muslim internationalism and trans-border traffic of ideas connecting South, Central and West Asia in the eighteenth and nineteenth centuries.[32] Furthermore, it is typically the figure of the cosmopolitan Muslim who draws upon Islam as an intellectual resource or progressive, Islamic socialists who have garnered interest for discussions of emancipatory politics forged through transnational connectivity. The tendency to dismiss 'orthodoxy' broadly construed is also reflected in the scholarly focus on connections wrought through Sufi networks, ideas and values.[33] A perhaps unintended effect of this has been that modernist discourses propagated by Islamic reformist movements scarcely feature in a positive way in discussions on the shaping of affective attachments, political imaginaries and ethical claims-making along post-colonial borders.

In the case of India, there is a latent assumption that Islamic ideologies along its frontiers either provoke 'fundamentalist' resistance and insurgency or are suppressed or dissimulated when there is an investment in the nation state. Kargil tells a story to the contrary.

Contours of Fieldwork

When I embarked upon fieldwork in Kargil in 2008, friends in Delhi and Leh expressed reservations. 'Isn't it a dangerous place?' folks in Delhi asked, while Buddhist friends in Leh warned me about the 'conservatism' of the Shi'as and the dirt and bedbugs in Kargil town. These reactions only affirmed the problem of representation that had sparked my interest in the region. I visited Kargil for the first time in 2005 to participate in a conference organised by the International Association for Ladakh Studies (IALS). Although I had been working and travelling in Ladakh for non-governmental organisation (NGO) research for some years, I had not ventured beyond the Lamayuru monastery, which marks the implicit border between Buddhist and Muslim Ladakh. Like most visitors to Ladakh, I too had ended up travelling mostly in Buddhist Ladakh. At the IALS conference, a prominent intellectual from Kargil town rightly chastised me for titling my paper 'Traditional Irrigation Practices of Ladakh', peeved that I had generalised my findings to Ladakh even though the research was conducted only in villages in Leh district. People in Kargil, particularly the elite, were acutely aware of the representational lacuna that besieged Kargil. I was thus welcomed with open arms when I started long-term research. One of the highlights of the conference was the excitement and joy surrounding the presence of a well-known poet from Baltistan, Hasan Hasni, who was among the small delegation of Baltis that had managed to visit Kargil for the first time since 1948.

It was during this trip that I first encountered turbaned and cloaked Shi'i clerics in the bazaar. I was also struck by images of Ayatollah Khomeini, and his successor Khamenei (Figure I.2), and Ayatollah Sistani openly displayed across the militarised landscape.

A neighbourhood called Bagh-e-Khomeini and Khomeini Chowk in the bazaar of Kargil town, the district headquarters, further sparked my curiosity. Why are these figures, globally associated with 'fundamentalist' Islam, tolerated by an insecure state along Kashmir's frontier? In a place where people are under heightened surveillance and their extra-territorial links immediately ignite suspicion and interrogation, why do the Shi'a Muslims of this region not feel the need to dissimulate their religious connections? I wondered what routes, media, and negotiations facilitated this immersion of Kargil in a wider constellation of places.

Figure I.2 Signboard with images of Khomeini and Khamenei, 2009
Source: Photograph by the author.

This melange of impressions piqued my curiosity about Kargil, a place whose history has been occluded within multiple representational frames. It led me to focus my future research on Kargil district (excluding Buddhist majority Zangskar) and its predominantly Shi'a Muslim inhabitants. I was based in Kargil town, the district headquarters. The town also served as the head office of politico-religious organisations that exert enormous influence in all facets of life across the district and beyond. Akbar Ahmed points to the value of taking the intermediary level of the district as a unit of study despite its colonial origins for it enables access to three distinct spheres of leadership: traditional leaders, official representatives of the established state authority and religious functionaries.[34] Indeed, being based in the district headquarters allowed me access to these spheres of authority. Through the course of my research, I frequently travelled to and stayed for shorter spells in various sub-regions such as Drass, the Suru Valley, Chigtan and Sot, following leads I heard in Kargil town of events, people and stories. My fieldnotes thus followed less the administrative demarcation of sub-regions, and more their contours with reference to longer histories of petty kingdoms, conversion to Islam, sacred and environmental geographies, and agriculture. These continue to pervade everyday conversations and structure marital exchange, kinship support networks and intra-regional rivalries. This led me to understand 'how past spatial orders inflect the present'.[35] From this perspective, the administrative boundaries of the region became less salient.

Kargil also emerged and morphed as a region through its connections and disconnections with places afar, sites that could be no longer reached by travelling overland, whether to third-places in West Asia or locations a few hundred kilometres away in Baltistan. In situating Kargil within these wider political, religious, cultural and imaginative horizons, this ethnography slides across scales such that the referential contours of the region change depending on the issue at hand. My efforts to track Shi'i networks between Kargil and West Asia also led me to a short spell of fieldwork in Iran in 2009 among Kargili scholars studying in Qum and then in 2012 to Mumbai, where important institutions mediating contemporary transnational Shi'i linkages are based. The capaciousness of Kargil as a region thus transcends both internal administrative boundaries and external political borders while always remaining conditioned by them.

Patriotism beyond Performance

All through my fieldwork, when people learnt that I was from Delhi, they would exclaim, 'Wonderful, you are from the *dil* [heart] of Hindustan, from Dilli [Delhi].' And then they would add with a hint of pride, 'We are the *sar* [head] of Hindustan.' In this 'enchanted mapping of the nation's geobody',[36] they placed themselves at the crest of national territory, using the metaphor of the crown of the national body as an expression of their proud loyalty to it. This patriotic self-representation was another site for the constitution and enactment of border subjectivity.[37] But beyond this performance of patriotism was another cartographic imagining with political referents.[38]

According to a prominent activist of Purigi culture, Master Hussain of Silmo village, in folklore, historically Ladakh was divided into three parts, ruled by three kings: The area ruled by the king of Leh was called *stang lha yul*, referring to the upper land of the gods, the higher region; Kargil or Purig was called *zan yul* (probably derived from *btsan yul* or beings of the middle world), or the middle area; and Skardu (Baltistan) was known as *lhu yul* (again probably derived from *klu yul* or the deities of the subterranean world), or the lower region.[39] Drawing upon Bon and Tibetan Buddhist beliefs, the 'motif of height' (verticality) and the 'layering of the world', which are common in trans-Himalayan geographical representations we see in this depiction of ancient Ladakh, are also deployed in the enchanted mapping of the nation in Kargil.[40]

In Ladakhi, *yul* is an 'abstract category and a contextual reference point for various locales'.[41] On the most intimate level, it refers to the immediate boundaries of one's village or the place of one's dwelling. The resilience of identification drawn from the village one belongs to was reflected in the popular use of the name of the village as a suffix to the first name of people active in local politics and on the social media of Ladakhis. Thus, someone from the village of Hardas may call himself so-and-so Hardasi or someone from the village of Kaksar may call herself so-and-so Kaksari. *Yul* could also have broader territorial referents, sliding in scale to stretch to sub-regions within Ladakh and even beyond to region and nation. A historical examination of people's identifications with *yul* reveals that cartographic imaginations predated the imperative of patriotism to the nation state.

The historian Christopher Bayly employed the term 'patriotism' to refer to the sense of loyalty to regional homelands that predated the nationalist movement or even the pre-colonial period in the subcontinent. These 'popular patriotisms', he argued, can be discerned in vernacular conceptual realms that implied rootedness in a particular territory. Hindustani words such as *watan*, for example, which referred in their earlier meanings to the domain of particular ruling dynasties, reflected pride in belonging to particular territories and were in use long before their incorporation into the nationalist lexicon.[42] The word *yul* holds this valence in Ladakh. It symbolised loyalty to and rootedness in homelands defined by the boundaries of petty kingdoms among which sovereignty was dispersed until the Dogra annexation of Ladakh in 1842.

Patriotism and nationalism have been conflated in the modern era of the nation state. I suggest that understanding patriotism through an indigenous semiotic – as an embodied attachment to place – steers clear of the danger of methodological nationalism. It offers a possibility to underscore people's attachment to their regional homelands, which is not available to them in the language of nationalism, especially when defined in majoritarian terms. There is little scope within the language of territorial nationalism to rescue attachment to place from the nation. Perhaps patriotism should not simply be reduced to the conceptual categories of modern-day nationalism.

Liberal theorists such as Alasdair MacIntyre, in analysing patriotism as a virtue, have contributed to congealing the association of patriotism with the nation state. MacIntyre argues that while power and government can be criticised by a patriot, the conception of the nation 'as a project ... somehow or other brought to birth in the past and carried on' must be exempt from criticism.[43] In this vein, if patriotism is understood primarily as according legitimacy to the nation, it detracts from the complexity of the conditions of belonging that Kargili Shi'as have to negotiate, given their location between an Islamic state (Pakistan) that challenges the Muslim status of its sectarian minorities and a failing, nominally secular state (India) that nonetheless affords them some freedom to practise faith. By yoking patriotism to the nation, MacIntyre also writes out its foundational violence. This silences a past that particularly haunts the lives of borderland dwellers.

Gilgit–Baltistan, on the other side of the LoC, reverberates deeply for all Muslim Kargilis. Repeatedly expressing deep anguish at being separated from family and friends across the LoC is an emotional response to the political violence of arbitrary border delineations. The post-colonial desire to belong to India, however, manifests in a reluctance to speak about this foundational violence.

Silence and Surveillance

One day I confided my frustration with the difficulty in eliciting partition narratives to a Balti friend, especially in villages close to the LoC. With a tinge of sarcasm, he teasingly remarked, 'Well, one never knows who may be a spy!' His response was understandable not only because I was from Delhi, but also because of the tricky resemblances between anthropological modes of enquiry and intelligence work that make the anthropologist 'sound very like a spy'.[44] My experiences resonated with those of other researchers who have done fieldwork in geostrategic areas. Nosheen Ali writes of feeling hurt when some of her close interlocutors in Gilgit–Baltistan suspected her of being untrustworthy. She rightly points out that such suspicion 'was more structural than personal', a 'characteristic of conflict zones more generally that have become engulfed with spies and surveillance'.[45] But the fear of intelligence agencies appeared to also deter confiding in kin. My friend's relatives in Turtuk (Leh district), which was annexed by India in 1971, were hesitant to speak about their lives in Pakistan even to him.

Unsurprisingly, both researchers and borderland dwellers are solicited to take on the role of local informer for intelligence agencies, a legacy of anthropology's colonial origins. On a preliminary visit to Kargil in 2007, when I had not yet embarked on a longer stint of fieldwork, Intelligence Bureau (IB) personnel visited the guesthouse where I was staying and requested the title of my thesis and notes. Later, when I became a familiar figure sauntering around Kargil, I began to recognise some intelligence agents even in their plain clothes. One morning as I was rushing to the bus stand, one of them waved to me and jovially asked, 'Madam, where are you going today?' I replied in jest, 'It is your work to know that, you tell me!' Even though suspicions lurk that the anthropologist is a spy, over time these usually diminish as locals get used to her presence, as Katherine Verdery notes in her reflection on fieldwork in communist Romania.[46] While Verdery speaks of her interlocutors getting used to her, this could also be true of the informers themselves, going by my experience of such jesting exchanges.

Like the exercise of research, perhaps surveillance is also a zone of serendipity, where tracking those being surveilled is not as systematic an operation as it is made out to be. My travel in the region was borne from hubris: As an Indian passport holder from Delhi, at the time I felt I had little to fear. Such foolish confidence was perhaps a luxury that privileged researchers could risk until 2019. This was never the case for borderland dwellers, especially those who travelled to Pakistan and subsequently attracted magnified surveillance. For them, suspicion by the state often bodes consequences more serious than interrogation. A mule runner for the army in an LoC village was refused business without any explanation upon his return from a visit to Gilgit–Baltistan, depriving him of his basic livelihood. Yet others, who were not dependent on the army for sustenance, navigated this regime of surveillance with a touch of bravado.

Imtiaz from Latoo – a village that was encapsulated into Indian territory in 1971 – recalled being approached by Pakistani intelligence in Skardu on a trip to Baltistan: 'But they did not trouble me as they were our own people,' he related with a lightness of touch. Instead, he mocked Indian intelligence for not doing its job properly: 'What is the need to come and ask me about the military posts in Baltistan when everything shows up on Google Earth these days?' He told the Indian agents that he went there to meet friends and relatives, not the military. They asked him to become an informer, offering to pay for his travel to Baltistan. Imtiaz refused. Another Balti interlocutor related, while laughing, that when intelligence agents came to enquire why he received so many phone calls from Pakistan, 'I told them, the calls are not from terrorists but from my friends.' Such humour laced with bravado is an affective mode of negotiating encounters with the security state while living under its constant gaze.

Horizons of Belonging

The Kargil War became a critical event for the inhabitants of Kargil for it afforded them a platform to make material and symbolic claims for recognition by the state. Negotiating belonging has, however, not only been a matter of external recognition. It is also animated by an internal liberatory politics. Undergirding claims for recognition is an emergent articulation of a place defined by a distinct political subjectivity and cultural identifications. Kargili Shi'as have sought to carve out a space for themselves that was neither subsumed within Kashmir nor overshadowed by Buddhist Ladakh. Freedom, here, holds different meanings. It has been attached to the sustenance of social imaginaries that for long have been nourished by being simultaneously anchored within a transnational Shi'i universe and a trans-Himalayan ecumene.

Shi'i Internationalism

Modes of selfhood grounded in Shi'i ethics have been foundational to liberatory politics in Kargil. Twelver Shi'i politics in India historically has drawn upon a political theology of suffering and waiting for the return of the Twelfth Imam from occultation to render justice. This passive stance towards the experience of injustice by Shi'i minorities around the world was transformed in varying degrees, and not without internal debate, after the Iranian Revolution (1979). The revolution became a critical discursive resource for the propagation of a more activist form of Shi'i politics that had an enormous influence in Kargil, too. Contrary to geopolitical representations and analyses, the export of Khomeinist ideologies did not foment Shi'i radicalism. In Kargil, the shift to more active engagement with the immanent world to address injustice and oppression offered idioms to challenge legacies of colonisation and negotiate Indian secularism and democracy. In order to assert difference from the adversarial politics in the Kashmir Valley, a strand of Shi'i ethics was selectively invoked to foreground a political theology of non-violence, but which did not assume suffering in silence. There is little dissimulation of religious identity and practices in Kargil's public sphere. The many images of Ayatollah Khomeini and Khamenei and even symbols of the Hizbollah are evidence of this. There is no doubt that structural subjection forced the maintenance of a low political profile; Kargilis have been hyper-cautious to avoid any action that might appear seditious to the state. This has not, however, translated into internalised modes of suppressed religious identity and practice in the public sphere that Nosheen Ali observes in her analysis of sectarian politics across the LoC in Gilgit–Baltistan.[47] Kargil's public sphere is instead a carefully calibrated arena that straddles the desire for recognition within the nation state without entirely succumbing to its hegemonic ideological boundaries. I must clarify, lest I be misunderstood, that this is not a functionalist account of the straightforward role that religion plays in consolidating belonging within the terms set by the nation state. I argue that it is a site for creative agency.

A striking example of these calibrations was the construction of a discursive frame that brought together Khomeini and Gandhi to articulate an anti-colonial political ethics. For the purveyors of Khomeini's ideas and ideologies in Kargil, the Iranian Revolution represented the coming into being of an active, critical consciousness, an *inqilabi nazariya* (revolutionary outlook), that might hold the power to challenge existent hierarchies locally, if not nationally. It was a kind of liberation theology.[48] Such discursive connections are paradigmatically repeated globally across other regional locales with a presence of Twelver Shi'as. In Dar es Salaam, Tanzania, for instance, I saw posters of Gandhi, Khomeini and Mandela placed alongside each other during Muharram 2019, outside the main Twelver

Shi'a mosque in the city, articulating decolonisation in African countries. For many Shi'as around the world, the 1979 revolution was a defining moment of 'freedom', offering an alternative locus of modernity and political ethics. Such discursive connections and symbolic frames must be acknowledged as part of the broader horizons of anti-colonial and post-colonial internationalism that have been predominantly defined by histories of left socialism in modern South Asia.

Revolutionary discourse was a 'traveling theory' that was creatively and selectively appropriated and modified to respond to the perceived demands of a context at a specific historical conjuncture.[49] Events in West Asia, just preceding my long stint of fieldwork between 2007 and 2009, contributed to the anti-imperial fervour of transnational Shi'i solidarity. After the fall of Saddam Hussein in Iraq, Ayatollah Sistani's insistence on democratic elections to protect the country's sovereignty in the context of the American occupation in 2005[50] and Hizbollah's war with Israel in 2006 were not distant political events. These events contributed to the confidence in Shi'i identity kindled by the Iranian Revolution. We need to understand the value of the 1979 revolution through not just its 'export' by Iran as a geopolitical tactic, but also the meaning it came to acquire for ordinary Shi'as around the world.

Places like Kargil bring to light historical trajectories of plebeian religious personages who did not hail from urban centres and are relegated to the periphery in mainstream Islamic and Shi'i Studies.[51] These figures, circulating along twentieth-century Shi'i networks within a wider 'Muslim cosmopolis',[52] lived in the shadows of both empire and nation but contributed to shaping ethical and political subjectivities that fed into tactical negotiations of national belonging.

Kargil was connected to West Asia since the late nineteenth century through scholars who sailed from Bombay to Basra to study in seminaries in the shrine cities of Iraq.[53] Some of the most renowned *'ulama* (clerics) in the region hailed from Baltistan, as evidenced by the extant corpus of Balti (a dialect of classical Tibetan) religious poetry and local hagiographies.[54] Historically, the de-privileging of Shi'i centres in the heartlands of India was tied to linguistic differences. Rather than labouring in Urdu, scholars preferred to train in Persian and Arabic, the classical languages of Islamic learning. As elderly Shaykh Hasan, who had studied in Najaf in the 1960s, explained to me, 'In Lucknow the *'alim* [teacher] is not so proficient in Arabi and Farsi. In India there was no *mujtahid*, someone who has studied all the books and then gives free lectures without the aid of a book, someone who is a *khariji* [studied beyond *darz al-kharij*].'[55] Till date, those who can afford it prefer to go to Iran and Iraq for higher religious education.

The region's embedding within transnational Shi'i horizons, however, became increasingly evident only from the late 1980s onwards. After Saddam Hussein expelled foreigners from Iraq in the late 1970s, students from Kargil shifted to studying in Iranian seminaries in Qum and Mashhad, where they became exposed to the ideals and ideologies of the 1979 revolution. Just as Muslim holy men and religious *émigrés* in the age of empire were exposed to Islamic intellectual hubs in the Mediterranean world[56] and elsewhere, foreign students studying in Iranian seminaries absorbed the intellectual currents that coalesced in the revolution. In 1989, following Khomeini's death, an institution called the Imam Khomeini Memorial Trust (IKMT) was established with the proclaimed aim of keeping alive his legacy in Kargil. The founding of the IKMT, as I will discuss in Chapters 2 and 3, was a turning point. It instigated significant transformations in practices of piety, public space and politics. The IKMT confronted the religious bastion of the region, the Islamia School that had been established in the early 1950s. The Islamia School and the IKMT became decisive mediators of political life in the region.[57] The Indian state had to enter into implicit dialogue with them in order to govern or rule the region.

I am aware that it is important to be cautious of overstating the influence of Iran in Kargil. Many people across the region, especially those aligned with the Islamia School, questioned the value of guidance from the Islamic Republic, particularly its relevance concerning political affairs in a secular country. Despite the fault lines that emerged out of this schism, Shi'as across Kargil unequivocally shared the sentiment that the biggest influence in Kargil of the *inqilab* (revolution) – an Urdu word integral to the lexicon of Indian anti-colonial resistance – was to impart a new confidence in Twelver Shi'i identity. The gradual embrace of a more confident sense of self in Kargil must be understood in relation to historically resilient pejorative attitudes towards Shi'as held by Sunnis of the Kashmir Valley and Buddhists in Leh, which I describe in Chapter 1. Frantz Fanon argued that one of the most powerful tools of colonial subjugation was to impose derogatory images on subjects.[58] He asserted that the colonised must rid themselves of self-perceptions fostered by this denigrative subjugation in their struggle for freedom. The moral and ethical project of rehabilitating individuals and society through transnationally inspired discourses of Islamic reform was integral to the struggle to change self-perceptions in Kargil. Shi'i Kargilis' renewed confidence in the sense of self could be interpreted as a kind of inner freedom, a reckoning with an externally triggered inferiority complex.

Shi'i modernist reform in Kargil intervened on the level of both the individual and the collective. A cornerstone of its propagation was the emphasis placed on the honing and use of *'aql* (intellect) by the individual believer in striving to build a just political community. While embedded within a Shi'i theological, jurisprudential and philosophical tradition, and resonating with the *akhlaq* (ethics) tradition of reformist thought in colonial India,[59] modernist reform in Kargil directly drew upon 'theorizations of Shi'i rationality by clerics and intellectuals allied with the state' in post-revolution Iran.[60] For instance, the deployment of *'aql* for the crafting of moral citizens who would contribute to the well-being of society echoed the ideas of Sayyid Ahmad Khan, the founder of the Aligarh Muslim College,[61] but instead claimed inspiration from Iran. An exception to this orientation in Kargil was seen in references to the poet and philosopher Muhammad Iqbal.[62] Kargilis critical of reformist dogmatism invoked Iqbal's critique of religious tutelage as encumbering human freedom, abstracting his thought from its deployment in sectarian polemics in Pakistan.[63]

On the level of the individual, I foreground the reception of reformist discourses through the quotidian understandings and application of *'aql* by common people, especially the youth. For many people in Kargil, freedom was articulated in the opening up of space to make choices based on critical reflection, ultimately independent of clerics. *'Aql* was deployed to reflect upon not only ritual practices but also everyday ethical sensibilities. Many Kargilis more consciously pondered how to live as a pious modern Shi'a Muslim among those of different religious persuasions in a non-Islamic state. While these relational ethics drew upon the Islamic discursive tradition, in being articulated as 'common sense' they were not bound by it, illustrating the blurred boundaries with 'ordinary ethics'[64] that are based on practical wisdom and action.

Over the years, religious leaders and friends from different walks of life frequently blessed me with *du'a*s (supplications) for pursuing the 'quest for knowledge'. Within this deep embrace, there was awareness, on both their part and mine, that I was a 'Hindu' woman from Delhi, the centre of power. This filtered into our interactions in myriad ways. In the early days I was asked often when I would write articles for newspapers to raise the problems that Kargil faces. Just as I was interested in Shi'ism, so were many people curious about 'my religion'. Some friends asked me about Hinduism, intrigued by the belief in rebirth or the logic behind the worship of several gods. A lady cleric, Hajji Amina, who you will meet in Chapter 2, for instance, asked me, 'Is the Gita to the Hindus as the Qur'an is to Muslims?' Women were particularly curious about the system of marriage and festivals like Diwali and Holi, their impressions shaped by depictions in Hindi soap operas on television. Such curiosity must be recognised as integral to leading an ethical relational life. I always would be asked at meals whether I eat meat. When responding in the affirmative, my hosts would clarify that the meat being served was of the 'small' animal and not the 'big' one – that is, mutton and not beef. As time passed, 'So what do you think about Shi'ism?' was a question that was increasingly posed, mostly casually and in passing, reiterating the concern with outsiders' perceptions.

Muslims in the Trans-Himalayan Ecumene

Islam came to Kargil via Baltistan and Kashmir through preachers who travelled overland from Khorasan (present-day Iran) from the fourteenth century onwards.[65] Despite the gradual and peaceful conversion from Tibetan Buddhism to Islam, Kargili Muslim senses of self and place have remained firmly anchored in a *trans-Himalayan ecumene*. The simplest and a common visual image of this rootedness in place are the ceremonial scarves called *khatak* used across the Tibetan trans-Himalayas – to honour people, sacred places and deities – tied around the pillars of mosques and shrines in Kargil. This meeting of religion and region was particularly striking to me in a photograph that a friend had taken of a *khatak* placed around an image of Ayatollah Khamenei in a Shi'i mosque in Chuchot in Leh district.[66]

Stretching from Tibet in the east to Gilgit–Baltistan in the west, the trans-Himalayan ecumene, as I conceive it, refers to a space that has been defined by the rain-shadow ecology of the trans-Himalayas and Bon and Tibetan Buddhist belief systems. Historically, it was knit together by the mobility of traders, preachers, pilgrims and petty sovereigns who not only went to war with each other but also exchanged wives. Despite the drawing of national borders and the hardening of religious boundaries, the cultural habitus of people who dwell in this land continue to share affinities. In contradistinction to the concept of 'cosmopolis' shaped by linguistic and textual modes of circulation and transmission, ecumene foregrounds *everyday regional cultural practices* that cut across contemporary religious and linguistic boundaries in the trans-Himalayas. Ranging from healing traditions to seasonal rituals and material culture, many regional practices in Ladakh can no longer be essentialised to its Tibetan Buddhist inhabitants.[67] Kargili Shi'i assertions of their Ladakhi, trans-Himalayan identity are integral to their negotiations of belonging.

Debates on the differences between 'religious' and 'regional' culture animated conversations among Kargili intellectuals and young people. Besides reflecting an instrumental desire for recognition in terms acceptable to the national public sphere, these debates, discussed in Chapters 4 and 5, direct our attention to the dynamic encounter between Tibetan Buddhism and Islam in the trans-Himalayas. The traces of this encounter can be found in material culture (such as Tibetan floral motifs adorning old mosques), language (such as Persian and Arabic loan words in the Tibetan dialect that predate the conversion to Islam) and everyday off-stage practices (such as the rare Muslim oracle achieving an altered state of consciousness through Shi'i liturgy). While underscoring the historical interaction between Indo-Persian and Tibetan cultural realms in the western Himalayas, these practices illustrate ongoing calibrations between the Buddhist past and the Islamic present. They articulate a sense of place that constitutes an important language of belonging on this frontier – a language that muddies any neat temporal or socio-spatial classifications that borders attempt to write.

The political subjectivity of Kargili Shiʻas and their transregional cultural horizons belie any easy encompassment into a generalisable Muslim minority. Their negotiations of belonging undoubtedly reflect a Shiʻi post-colonial imaginary of the Indian nation that consolidated its difference from the Sunnis in the colonial period.[68] These negotiations, however, have to be contextualised within a regional history of their affiliations *and* differences with both the Kashmir Valley and Buddhist Ladakh. Squashed between two other minorities in the nation state – Sunnis and Buddhists – border subjectivity in this captive frontier points to the conceptual limits of 'minority' as an analytical category for understanding post-colonial predicaments of belonging.

Double Minority

The discursive reproduction of the invisibility of Kargil and its predominantly Shiʻa Muslim inhabitants is also a reflection of the overdetermination of politics by the framework of communalism in South Asia, underpinned by homogeneous categories of Hindu and Muslim. Post-colonial politics and state security agendas in India have strategically sustained and manipulated colonial representations of the subcontinent. Historians trace the minority rights discourse back to the colonial period when categories such as minority–majority or native–outsider (Hindu–Muslim) entered 'popular common sense', in part, through various classificatory systems.[69] Gyanendra Pandey argues that even though nationalist discourse attempted to reposition this by presenting India as consisting of several communities, 'the proposition about a majority religious community living alongside a number of minorities remained in place'.[70] Muslims in post-colonial India have been trapped in an artificial binary opposition between secular nationalism and religious communalism. Among all minorities, Muslims in particular have been forced to don secular credentials to prove their allegiance to India. Although Indian secularism espoused its own variant of political secularism which was premised not on the strict separation of religion and state but on selective state intervention that was not against religiosity,[71] it nonetheless conformed to the 'modular form' that the regulation of religious difference in the modern liberal state takes across geographical boundaries.[72] Through her analysis of the structural challenges that Coptic Christians faced in their struggle for equality as a minority in Egypt, Saba Mahmood points to the fundamental paradox inherent in political secularism: its foundational promise of civil and political equality and its failure to fulfil this promise precisely because it is a doctrine that *creates* religious difference.

Rather than taming the power of religion, its regulation under secularism ends up making it ever more germane to the identity of majority and minority populations.[73] Drawing upon Talal Asad, she analyses secularism as a 'discursive operation of power' that generates boundaries between the public and private, upon which the 'political rationality of the modern state is predicated'.[74] In India, too, public performance by minority religious communities is legitimate only under the rubric of culture,[75] as we saw with the habitation of the ethnic slot by Kargili performers during the Vijay Diwas celebrations. Minority religious communities continue to struggle with straddling the often contingent and shifting boundaries between the public and private and the space available to them within forms of political secularism to negotiate belonging through religious identification.

I take inspiration from Mahmood's argument to examine how structural challenges faced by minorities are negotiated by the Shiʿas on Kashmir's frontiers *through* their religious affiliations. I suggest, however, that it is important to recognise that the modern nation state does not treat all minorities equally in its management of religious difference. The Shiʿa Muslims of Kargil are a minority within the majority Sunni Muslims, who are a minority vis-à-vis Hindus in India.[76] I argue that the category of the minority itself needs to be disaggregated because longer and particular histories of disenfranchisement and discrimination are erased in the creation of equivalence between different minorities. The political and social power of different minorities is historically unequal and not simply exchangeable or amenable to easy solidarities. Articulating the issue as the problem of majoritarianism and the minority question does not address the predicaments of double minorities. It allows the state to propose a level playing field for different minority groups for political bargaining and expressing cultural identities without taking into account the entanglements of specific minority identities with other vectors of representation, recognition and belonging, such as region, caste and sect. The play of equivalence between different minorities also enables the state to detract from its partisan positioning towards particular minorities through their incorporation into a broad majoritarian identity while also strategically manipulating sectarian differences in its politics of security. For a double minority positioned between two other minorities and geopolitically located literally in the interstices of nation states, as an analytic the category of minority – unless critically unpacked – does not go far enough to understand the complexity of the negotiations of belonging for Kargili Shiʿas, or other locations that are home to multiple minorities.

Kargil's Shiʿas have always been caught between a rock and a hard place. Hindu nationalists courted Ladakhi Buddhists as part of an agenda of saffronising the nation since the 1980s, when the Hindu-right party, the Bharatiya Janta Party (BJP), became a significant presence in the national political field. The deployment of communal idioms in the struggle for UT status by radical Buddhists since the 1990s[77] led the Shi'a Muslims of Kargil to seek a sense of psychological security in their ties with Kashmir. But the rise of insurgency in the Kashmir Valley in 1989 also led them to foreground their differences from the Valley to make clear their allegiance to India. Anxieties of being clubbed with the Valley Muslims, as they had often been before the Kargil War when their loyalty to India was still suspect, led to an emphasis on their territorial and cultural identification with Ladakh. The apparent 'lack of integrity' in the category of minority,[78] then, lends itself to manipulation by the Indian state. Regional differences between the Valley and Ladakh have been strategically exploited through a kind of sectarian divide and rule. In turn, Kargili Shi'as themselves have adopted the generalised framing of Shi'as as the 'good Muslims' as opposed to the Sunnis as 'bad Muslims'. Feeding the projection of Kargil as 'peaceful' in contrast to the Kashmir Valley is advantageous for it confers the concession of certain freedoms by the state.

Negligible Freedom

While Muharram processions were banned in the Valley, these were permitted across Ladakh. Under the watchful eyes of the police, over the years processions moved through the main bazaar of Kargil town on both the ninth day of Muharram and Ashura (Figure I.3).[79] Ritual condemnations of imperial powers were not censored on this and other occasions. 'There is *mazhabi azadi* [religious freedom] in Hindustan' was one of the first things that Kargili clerics studying in Iranian seminaries, returning home for Muharram preaching, pointed out to me, before heaping praise on Iran as an exemplar of Islamic modernity. Hindustan was consistently evoked as a superior *watan* (nation). 'Hindustan is ahead of everyone else in *adab* [etiquette] and *akhlaq*. There is peace here, unlike Saudi or Pakistan, because different religions thrive here,' gushed one cleric.[80]

Echoing the stance of Shi'as across India and globally, in Kargili parlance Wahhabism became a metaphor for Sunni fundamentalism. Although it was seldom mentioned, this sense of religious freedom was likely heightened because of an awareness of its absence in the Valley. Two years after the separation of Ladakh from Jammu and Kashmir (J&K), as frustration with their UT status mounted, during Muharram in 2021 a few Kargili Shi'as spoke of Muharram in the Valley. They expressed disappointment when a Muharram procession in Srinagar that had been granted permission after decades eventually met with violence. I heard rumours that the Indian administration had given this permission at the bidding of a co-opted Shi'i leader in the Valley, suggesting that it was a sectarian

Figure I.3   Muharram procession, Kargil Bazaar, 2009
Source: Photograph by the author.

tactic of placation. Reticence to openly express their views on politics in the Valley did not mean that Kargili Shi'as were unaware of the divisive practices of the state. At first, I thought the praise for India was a cautious response given to a non-Muslim researcher from the heartland, necessitated by a culture of suspicion in a region under heightened surveillance. Its refrain over time made me realise that this was one manifestation of freedom in captivity that characterises the conditions of belonging on this frontier of Kashmir. Why, then, did the ideal of political secularism and its promise of equality continue to hold an important place in the social imaginary of Kargili Muslims?

As Mahmood rightly qualifies in her work, we must not dismiss the value of 'negligible freedom'. In an atmosphere of increasing persecution of Muslims in India, being able to publicly commemorate Muharram illustrates the paradox of political secularism: 'its regulatory impulse and its promise of freedom as being thoroughly entwined'.[81] As if to express gratitude for this freedom in captivity, people in Kargil regularly celebrated India's Independence Day and Republic Day to display their patriotism to the nation state, while Muslims in the Kashmir Valley boycotted these events. Negotiations of belonging in Kargil lend insight into the *practice of secularity*, wherein 'a secular state does not guarantee toleration; it puts into play different structures of ambition and fear'.[82] Gratitude then becomes a sublimated expression of fear: the fear of losing even basic freedoms as witnessed in the Kashmir Valley. In places where structural violence shifts between the visible and the invisible, indeterminacy and insecurity are heightened. For a captive borderland such as Kargil, 'war' is embedded within 'peace'. Each time violence against Muslims in the Valley became ever more brutal, an unspoken but palpable fear engulfed Kargil. It manifested in quotidian concerns such as internet shutdowns or the inability to travel to Srinagar for medical treatment. Gratitude may not diminish backstage resentment, but it sustains negligible freedom and the ability to continue to negotiate belonging.

I argue that sectarian identification and contestation in Kargil was simultaneously a source of emancipatory critical consciousness and a reflection of a state of subjection. The rise of a separatist insurgency in the Kashmir Valley and the Indian state's concomitant framing of all Kashmiri youth as 'militants' supported by Pakistan roughly coincided with public manifestations of Iranian influence in Kargil in the early 1990s. At a time when the theocratic state in Iran came to be reviled globally and resisted internally, was India's toleration of links with it simply about not interfering in the religious life of its citizenry so long as it remained non-political? Some of my interlocutors in Kargil speculated that appeasing religious institutions that channelled influences from West Asia also was part of the strategy to counter Islamising influences from Pakistan. In the absence of archival evidence, and in light of the difficulty of broaching this sensitive topic in a region swarming with intelligence agents, it is plausible to suggest that the state patronised the Islamia School and the IKMT. Allowing religious life to flourish along this frontier of Kashmir has been part of a counterinsurgency strategy to cultivate allies.[83] It would have been in the Indian security state's interest to cultivate nascent sectarian divides between the Valley and Kargil to forestall the possibility of political solidarity across the Zoji-la pass. As Ann Stoler has argued, imperial logics 'depend on the differential allocation of resources and rights'.[84] This strategy has structured the Indian state's approach to Kashmir's frontiers, in aid of its violent colonisation of the Kashmir Valley, and has also been applied *within* the frontier to consolidate power.

The embrace by a double minority of negligible freedoms shows us how subjection operates within freedom by structuring its inherent possibilities and limits of agency. On an instrumental level, it sustains a space for manoeuvre – one of give-and-take between a security state and its subjects – who could but have not challenged its sovereignty. On an affective level, it sustains sociocultural horizons of self and place that cannot be contained by geopolitical borders.

In the chapters that follow, this book seeks to lend some insight into how the lives of borderland dwellers are shaped by 'a dialectic of mobility and confinement, motion and rest, freedom and incarceration, and agency and coercion'.[85] Instead of engaging in a politics of resistance, belonging in Kargil is negotiated through creative calibrations across scales: local, regional, national, transregional – offering no easy relapse into state territoriality while always being conditioned by it.

Notes

1. Hartman, *Scenes of Subjection*, 115.
2. See Zins, 'Public Rites', on the forging of a new icon of the 'hero-martyr' in the national imagination through public rituals surrounding the repatriation of the bodies of dead soldiers from the Kargil War.
3. Hartman, *Scenes of Subjection*, 7.
4. See Rashid, *Dying to Serve*, 23, on how similar state spectacles of commemoration in Pakistan 'shape and discipline citizens' perception of the military and its role'.
5. Kanth, *Seeking Futures, Shaping Pasts*, challenges the representation of a 'unified Kashmiri political community', especially in the pre-1990s period perpetuated by the paradigm of conflict resolution. Since the 1990s, however, alienation from India has grown among Muslims in the Kashmir Valley.
6. Article 370 of the Indian Constitution granted semi-autonomous status to J&K to acknowledge that the accession to India by the maharaja of the Dogra princely state was conditional upon a plebiscite being held for Kashmiris to determine their own political destiny. Along with Article 35A, it prevented those who were not 'state subjects' from purchasing land and settling in the region. Both these articles were illegally revoked by the Indian state in August 2019. The Epilogue discusses Kargil's response to this.
7. Hage, 'Bearable Life', 81–83.
8. I draw inspiration here from Wilder, *Freedom Time*. Through his analysis of the writings of post-war thinkers, Aimé Césaire and Leopold Senghor, Wilder urges us to question how concepts such as freedom and sovereignty have been made synonymous with each other. He argues that it is erroneous to assume 'that anticolonialism must be oriented toward national independence' (p. 20). Decolonization for these thinkers entailed 'the reconfiguration rather than the elimination of imperial domination' (p. 8). There was never any predetermined understanding of what freedom would entail.
9. I draw here upon O'Neill and Dua, 'A Forum on Captivity', 493, and 'Captivity', 8.
10. Arendt, 'What Is Freedom?'

11. Wilder, *Freedom Time*, 46.
12. See Bhan, *Counterinsurgency, Democracy and Politics of Identity*, 171, on the land occupied by the army in Kargil.
13. De León, *Land of Open Graves*, 43.
14. Robinson, *Body of Victim, Body of Warrior*, 54.
15. See Khosravi, 'What Do We See', on temporal aspects of bordering practices that include 'waiting' and 'delaying' as mechanisms of subordination.
16. The unfinished business of partition also unfolded along the India–Bangladesh border, as evidenced by the problem of 'enclaves', pieces of sovereign territory that remained surrounded by the other country. These enclaves were finally exchanged and absorbed into either India or Bangladesh in 2015. See Cons, *Sensitive Space*.
17. The violence and mass exchange of populations that occurred over a short period of six months in Punjab in 1947 was an exception rather than the norm for the course of the partition. In all other parts of the subcontinent, partition was long drawn out. Chatterji, 'Partition Studies', 310. Ladakh has received hardly any attention in the historiography of the partition.
18. See Fuchs, *In a Pure Muslim Land*, ch. 1, for a historical account of the reservations expressed by Shi'as in the years prior to the partition about their potential fate in a Sunni Islamic state, and the growing drift between the All India Shi'a Conference (AISC) and the Muslim League.
19. van Schendel, *The Bengal Borderland*, 366.
20. Kabir, *Territory of Desire*, 2009.
21. Zia, *Resisting Disappearance*, 2019, 21.
22. Inner Line Permit is a document of the legacies of colonial-era surveillance to control the movement of 'dangerous populations'. Breda, 'Managing Dangerous Populations', 628.
23. Stoler, *Duress*, 15. Promotion of tourism is included in the Border Area Development Programme (BADP), a significant source of funds for infrastructure development along various sectors of India's borders.
24. Robinson, 'The Dangerous Allure', 2014.
25. Aggarwal, *Beyond Lines of Control*, 9–10; van Beek, 'Dangerous Liaisons', 195; van Beek and Pirie, *Modern Ladakh*. The orientation to Tibetan Studies may also have partially contributed to neglecting the historical study of ties between Ladakh and the Islamic world. See also Digby, 'Travels in Ladakh', 303. From the 1990s, Martijn van Beek, Ravina Aggarwal and Mona Bhan have made influential contributions towards orienting Ladakh towards the nation state rather than as a mere extension of Tibet.
26. An exception was Nicola Grist, a pioneer in the study of Kargil.

27. There is a vast literature on borderland infrastructures, mobility and policing. See, for example, Andersson, *Illegality Inc.*; Bornstein, 'Military Occupation'; de Genova, 'Migrant "Illegality"'; de León, *Land of Open Graves*; Fassin, 'Policing Borders'; Ghosh, 'Cross-border Activities'; Ibrahim, *From Family to Police Force*; Sur, *Jungle Passports*.

28. See Reeves, *Border Work*.

29. van Schendel, 'Geographies of Knowing', 647.

30. 'Zomia', in van Schendel's definition, was a large region that 'lacked strong centres of state formation' and was therefore marginalised in academic scholarship shaped by the carving up of area studies after the Second World War.

31. See, for example, Robinson, *Body of Victim, Body of Warrior*, on the fluidity between the categories of victim, warrior and refugee in relation to jihad on the Kashmir borderland; Ibrahim, 'Islamic "Reform"', on the intersections of transnational Islamic reform and neoliberal development discourses in shaping Muslim women's subjectivity in Kutch (Gujarat); Mostowlansky, 'Development Institutions'.

32. See, for example, Green, 'Trans-Border Traffic'; Alavi, *Muslim Cosmopolitanism*.

33. See, for example, Aras, 'Naqshbandi Sufis', on networks across the Turkish–Syrian border; Henig, 'Crossing the Bosphorus', on networks of Dervish brotherhoods in post-socialist southeast Europe; Marsden and Henig, 'Muslim Circulations', on the land-based mobility of Sufis in West Asia.

34. A. Ahmed, 'Islam and the District Paradigm', 78–79.

35. Reeves, *Border Work*, 19.

36. Ramaswamy, 'Visualizing India's Geo-body', 154.

37. Aggarwal, *Beyond Lines of Control*.

38. Ramble, 'Gaining Ground', 83.

39. Discussion with Master Hussain, Silmo village, September 2007 and September 2015.

40. Ramble, 'Gaining Ground', 85.

41. Aggarwal, 'At the Margins of Death', 552.

42. Bayly, *Origins of Nationality*, 4.

43. MacIntyre, 'Is Patriotism a Virtue?' 9–13.

44. Dresch, 'Wilderness of Mirrors', 112; Verdery, *Secrets and Truths*, 140.

45. Ali, *Delusional States*, 19.

46. Verdery, *Secrets and Truths*.

47. Ali, *Delusional States*, 143.

48. As Ghamari-Tabrizi, *Foucault in Iran*, 17, points out, in Iran the 'revolutionary moment' must be regarded 'as the realization of a condition of possibilities'.

49. Said, 'Traveling Theory'.

50. Otterman, 'Iraq'.

51. Marsden and Henig, 'Muslim Circulations', make a similar point regarding the intellectual peripheralisation of 'Muslim Asia' by Islamic studies and area studies. My use of West Asia serves to not only re-scale the region geographically, but also underscore its value as an analytical category that breaks the imperial and orientalist boundaries within which academic disciplinary boundaries continue to remain embedded.

52. Alavi, *Muslim Cosmopolitanism*.

53. Bombay became an important gateway to Mecca, Istanbul, Cairo and other cities in the Middle East for Muslim scholars in the mid-nineteenth century. Alavi, *Muslim Cosmopolitanism*, 3. With the establishment of printing presses, it also became a key site for the dissemination of religious material across the subcontinent and the Indian Ocean. Green, *Bombay Islam*. Many Kashmiri scholars and clerics upon their return from the shrine cities would spend periods of time in Bombay, servicing the mercantile Twelver Khoja community. As Kargil became more connected to mainland India in the post-colonial period, Bombay became an important site mediating their linkages with Iran and Iraq.

54. To this day, many influential Shi'i *ulama* in contemporary Pakistan are from Gilgit–Baltistan. Fuchs, *In a Pure Muslim Land*, 11.

55. *Darz al-kharij* denotes studies at a higher level beyond the 'strict sequence of textbooks'. Fischer, *Iran*, 63. It is usually imparted by a specific teacher of choice. Mervin, 'The Clerics of Jabal 'Āmil'. Most students from Kargil do not study beyond this level.

56. Alavi, *Muslim Cosmopolitanism*, 4.

57. Intra-Shi'i factionalism instigated by the setting up of new organisations after the Iranian Revolution was not unique to Kargil. It has been also noted in Pakistan. See Fuchs, *In a Pure Muslim Land*; Abou Zahab, 'Politicization of the Shia Community'.

58. Fanon, *Wretched of the Earth*.

59. For a historical overview of Islamic reform and modernities in South Asia, with a focus on Sunni sects, see Robinson, 'Islamic Reform'. See Tayob, 'Decolonizing the Study of Religions', 18–19, on taking seriously the intellectual labour of modernist Muslim thinkers to the 'Muslim discourse of religion'. He argues that Muslim reformists must be treated not only as an object of study, but also as 'developers and participants of a discourse of religion'. The oppositional stance taken by Shi'i modernist reform to the secular west is better analysed from this perspective to avoid confusing its empirical propagation with its discursive formation.

60. Doostdar, *The Iranian Metaphysicals*, 5.

61. For a succinct account of Sayyid Ahmad Khan's ideas on civilising the individual through the cultivation of virtues and emotions founded on *akhlaq* that link individual to nation, see Pernau, 'Space and Emotion'.

62. Some youth also referred to Syed Javad Naqvi of Pakistan, a proponent of the concept of the Guardianship of the Jurisprudent. That his books reached Skardu might also explain his appearance in Kargil. Fuchs, *In a Pure Muslim Land*, 146–47.

63. Devji, *Changing Places*, 171.

64. Lambek, *Ordinary Ethics*.

65. See Bray, *Readings on Islam*, for an overview of the historiography of Islam in Ladakh.

66. Thanks to Abeer Gupta for sharing this image with me.

67. It is often presumed that all Tibetans are Buddhists, making Muslims seem like an anachronism in the wider Tibetan culture sphere. Atwill, *Islamic Shangri-La*.

68. In the late colonial period, Shi'as in India consolidated their distinction from the Sunnis, rejecting efforts to harmonise the differences between the two sects. There is a general agreement on this in historical scholarship even if there is a debate on whether the Shi'as succeeded in establishing a 'freestanding religion'. See Fuchs, *In a Pure Muslim Land*; Jones, *Shi'a Islam in Colonial India*.

69. For a succinct summary of the creation of the Muslim minority in colonial India, see Sherman, *Muslim Belonging*, 3–4.

70. Pandey, *The Construction of Communalism*, 18.

71. Bhargava, 'Reimagining Secularism'.

72. Mahmood, *Religious Difference*, 2.

73. Mahmood, *Religious Difference*, 12.

74. Mahmood, *Religious Difference*, 5.

75. Hansen, 'Predicaments of Secularism', 258.

76. Fuchs, *In a Pure Muslim Land*, 9, too, uses the term 'double minority' to point to the complex choices that the Shi'as faced in the late colonial period.

77. van Beek, 'Identity Fetishism', 'Public Secrets', 'The Art of Representation'.

78. Devji, *Changing Places*, 176.

79. Ashura is the tenth day of the Islamic month of Muharram. It commemorates the martyrdom of Imam Husayn, the grandson of Prophet Muhammad, at the Battle of Karbala at the hands of the army of Yazid, descendant of the Umayyad dynasty, which denied political succession to the family of the Prophet. It became a foundational event for the birth of Shi'ism in 680 CE. Performing rituals of lamentation on Ashura is believed to earn the reward of intercession. As a ritual of re-enactment and remembrance, it reinforces the religious and social community of Shi'i Muslims.

80. In Pakistan, the 'thinking Shi'a' were in favour of a secular state which would allow them to follow their beliefs and practices unhindered, as compared to a Sunni Islamic state. Keddie, *Iran and the Muslim World*, 14. Indeed, the Shi'as

of Kargil often remark upon their good fortune of living in India, as they despair over the sectarian violence that Pakistan is mired in.

81. Mahmood, *Religious Difference*, 21.
82. Asad, *Formations of the Secular*, 5–8.
83. Funds for the modernisation of *madrasa* education are allocated as part of the BADP to prevent Islamic fundamentalism. The Islamia School and the IKMT both run *madrasas*. See GoM, *Report*.
84. Stoler, *Duress*, 21.
85. Hage, 'Bearable Life', 81–82.

Genealogies of Political Consciousness

Rescuing Place from Territory

When rendering their history, people in Kargil usually divided their past into ancient (*qadim*) and modern (*jadid*) eras (*zamana*) in Urdu. The ancient period referred to a *longue durée* stretching from the time of the early settlement of the region during the ninth and tenth centuries CE to the period of princely Dogra rule, beginning in the mid-nineteenth century. The modern period corresponds to Kargil's incorporation as part of the erstwhile state of J&K into post-colonial India when Hari Singh signed the instrument of accession to India in October 1947. In my first conversations with many people, some of whom later became my friends and steady interlocutors, I noticed an eagerness to relate fragments of Ladakh's ancient history. They urged me to read historian Kacho Sikandar Khan Sikandar's book, *Qadim Ladakh* (1987), praising it for being a definitive account of the region's history. Although only some Kargili intellectuals had read parts of this book, it was widely known. Even people who had not read it first-hand invariably directed me to *Qadim Ladakh*. Sikandar Khan's book in turn draws upon the Dogra administrator Hashmatullah Khan's *Tarikh Jammun, Kashmir, Ladakh aur Baltistan* (History of Jammu, Kashmir, Ladakh and Baltistan) (1939).[1] Both these books serve as significant historical sources on Kargil and Baltistan. Written by administrator-turned-local-historians at very different points in time, both these sources are in Urdu. As Daniela Bredi has pointed out, both works are quite different from the 'usual Indo-Muslim' historical accounts for they hardly rely on previously written histories. Rather, information was collected from official papers, observations of the landscape and oral accounts.[2] These renditions of history have been readily reproduced in contemporary constructions of a collective regional memory.

Copies of *Qadim Ladakh* were no longer easily available in Ladakh by the time I started fieldwork. My access to this book was mediated by a much-respected local historian and poet, Abdul Hamid Tanvir, a Sunni Muslim of Kashmiri origin whose ancestors had settled in Kargil during the Dogra period. Even though he was in his seventies and struggling with poor eyesight, Tanvir *sahib* insisted on giving me 'classes' in the history of Kargil. He spent hours over many sessions literally dictating passages from the book, bringing it close to his eyes to decipher the words. He would periodically check if I was taking proper notes, nudging me to drink up the cup of thick milk tea turning cold as I scribbled furiously. Tanvir *sahib* would embellish this written account of the Dogra period with titbits of his own recollections, blurring the lines between the written word and oral history. This emic distinction between the ancient and modern periods is important for it situates the representational occlusion of Kargil within a *longue durée*. It illustrates the layers of historical oppression and its perpetrators and the continued legacies of colonisation that have fed into the emergence of a regional and sectarian consciousness. This chapter traces the genealogies of place and self underlying this consciousness.

The early history of 'ancient Ladakh' relates the migration and settlement of the Mongols from Tibet in the east and the Dards from Gilgit and surrounding areas to the west of Kargil and Baltistan, the cessation of warfare between them around the tenth century CE and the subsequent ethnic inter-mixing.[3] A significant portion of the present-day Kargil district was referred to as Purig. In ancient times, Ladakh, Baltistan and Purig were a conglomeration of small kingdoms under Dard or Mongol rulers. The history of the interaction between these three regions is largely one of conquest and predation between these petty kingdoms.[4] Each sought to expand and consolidate its territory, cross-cut by marital alliances, shifting the boundaries of sovereignty at different points in time. Predation and protection were central to the maintenance of the legitimacy and authority of these kingdoms, which demonstrated a high level of political development.[5] The history of Purig in particular is marked by a series of conquests, predations and alliances. Unlike Baltistan, which was under the three large ruling families of Skardu, Shigar and Khaplu for most of its history, and Ladakh, which began to be consolidated under the Namgyal dynasty from the fifteenth century, Purig was always fragmented into smaller chiefdoms with recurrent infighting. These small chiefdoms often had to seek the aid of either the rajas of Baltistan or the king (*gyalpo*) of Ladakh for protection, who then attempted to extend their sovereignty

over parts of Purig. They were eventually incorporated into the kingdom of
Ladakh by the mid-seventeenth century.[6] This could partially account for the
fact that it did not retain a strong, singular identity compared with Ladakh and
Baltistan. Purig's incorporation into Ladakh left it politically marginalised and
impoverished.[7] Over time Ladakh became synonymous with Leh, its capital,
and Purig became relatively invisible.

Growing ethnic competition in contemporary Kargil instigated by post-
colonial classifications accounts, in part, for the excavation of Purig from the
annals of history by Purigi activists in Kargil. The geographical boundaries of Purig
and linguistic politics with Baltis were frequent topics of discussion, especially
among local intellectuals.[8] Such discussions reflected an emergent consciousness
of regional (Kargili) identity in relation to Baltistan, Buddhist Ladakh and the
Kashmir Valley. Legacies of the old chiefdoms remain salient in the everyday social
and political lives of people in Kargil even today. Within the district, people self-
identify as Sot-pa, Chigtan-pa, from the Suru Valley or Drass. These are sub-regions
that correspond to the broad contours of the erstwhile petty kingdoms. Such self-
designations encode social histories, people's own senses of place and time. While
Sot is where a lot of powerful shaykhs hail from, the Suru Valley is known to be
the land of the aghas and religious conservatism.[9] Chigtan, due to its geographical
proximity to Leh, is considered more educated and modern than other parts of
Kargil, and one can still find relics of the Tibetan Buddhist past there. Renditions
of ancient Ladakh are thus 'time filled by the presence of the now'.[10]

The enthusiasm to narrate Ladakh's ancient or pre-modern history serves
to reinstate Purig (Kargil) in external imaginations of Ladakh which became
synonymous with its Tibetan Buddhist inhabitants. This was reflected in the
writings of explorers, missionaries and colonial officials from the nineteenth century.
It is also a narration of the history of *place* rather than *territory*, foregrounding
people's memories and legends of their land in contrast to nationalist narratives in
which Kargil is predominantly a strategic border.[11] As the long partition came to
bear down more strongly on the region, the shift from place to territory became
entrenched in nationalist historiography. The more capacious sense of place
that was ironically intact even under colonial Dogra rule was sundered with the
drawing up of the LoC and the fragmentation of the frontier areas of Ladakh and
Gilgit–Baltistan into the time-space of the post-colonial nation states of India and
Pakistan. Pre-modern trans-Himalayan histories of mobility and exchange have
been politically suppressed in the time of the post-colonial nation.[12] The break
between the *longue durée* of ancient Ladakh, including the Dogra period, and the
relatively short span of the modern era reflects the attenuation of histories that
narrate a sense of place. Narrations of pre-modern Ladakh are thus effectively

'rescuing history from the nation'.[13] Yet the ancient past was not recalled only in idyllic terms: As sovereignty became concentrated in the Dogra princely state, new social and spatial hierarchies emerged. Freedom for common people in Kargil necessitated challenging these legacies of colonisation in the modern era.

Hierarchies of Colonisation

When Kargilis speak about the colonial past, they refer to both British colonisation and Hindu Dogra rule. The legacy of social and spatial hierarchies engendered by Dogra colonial rule in Kargil shaped its relationship to both the Kashmir Valley and Buddhist Ladakh in the post-colonial or modern period.

Prior to the partition of the subcontinent in 1947, Leh, Kargil and Baltistan together constituted the Ladakh *wazarat* (province) in the princely Dogra state. These regions were encompassed into a single province with the invasion of Ladakh by General Zorawar Singh, who served Raja Gulab Singh of Jammu, a feudatory of the Sikh Durbar in Lahore, in 1834.[14] After the victory of the British in the first Anglo-Sikh War (1845), Gulab Singh was installed as the maharaja of all countries to the east of the Indus and west of the Ravi rivers – J&K, Ladakh and Baltistan – in return for his allegiance to the British during the war.[15] The princely state of J&K was established under the Treaty of Amritsar in 1846. The demarcation of three clear-cut provinces of Jammu, Kashmir and Ladakh by the Dogras replaced the 'layered and overlapping sovereignties' that had characterised pre-colonial India.[16] Within these boundaries, areas were mapped into distinct units of governance, primarily to facilitate revenue collection. The three provinces were subdivided into a number of *tahsil*s (revenue jurisdictions). The Ladakh *wazarat* comprised the *tahsil*s of Leh, Kargil and Skardu. The rotation of the administration between the winter headquarters in Skardu and the summer in Leh made Kargil inconsequential in administrative terms. Governance under Dogra rule thus reinforced the spatial hierarchy that already existed between Ladakh (Leh), Purig (Kargil) and Baltistan in the era of dispersed sovereignty. Kargilis often attributed their sense of 'backwardness' to Leh and Skardu having acquired a more extensive and sophisticated administrative machinery and infrastructure early on in the Dogra period.

Each of the *wazarat*s was presided over by a *wazir-e-wazarat* (minister) and under him *tahsildar*s (revenue officers) and *naib tahsildar*s (deputy revenue officers). *Patwari*s (village registrars) at the village level maintained land records. Revenue collection and taxation under the reign of Maharaja Gulab Singh (1846–56) and Ranbir Singh (1856–85) became an entirely predatory affair. An old man in Kargil recalled, 'People were treated like animals and had to pay *malya* and *res* [taxes]. A petty clerk used to rule like a *tahsildar*. *Malya* had to be paid according to land ownership and in addition people also had to give *jinsi* in *nas* [barley] and *kro* [wheat].' The British condemned the practice of *begar* (forced labour) imposed upon people for the provision of free labour for state public works, transport and carriage. But, characteristically, they took advantage of it themselves for the expeditions of foreign explorers and colonial officials. A favourite anecdote of old men in Kargil was that even the dogs of the *memsahib*s had to be carried in palanquins.[17] Musa Chigtan (d. 2021), a prominent elderly political activist from the Chigtan area and a staunch supporter of the National Conference (NC) party, proudly told me that his first experience of political activism was at the age of sixteen when he raised his voice against the *zildar* (native officer in charge of an administrative unit of land) system of the Dogras. He recalled, 'There used to be one *zildar* for eleven villages in our area. After fighting for fourteen years, I was made the *nambardar* [village headman]'. Recollections of Dogra rule by elders in Kargil indicate that such was the oppression (*zulm*) under the Dogras that they even turned to the supra-coloniser, the British, for help.

By the late seventeenth century, the British had begun to suffer losses as their efforts to take control of the trade in *pashm* (cashmere) with Tibet were thwarted by the maharaja. Already anxious about Afghan and Russian threats on the northwest frontier in the Great Game, they used the excuse of Dogra oppression to intervene directly in the maharaja's court. By the time Pratap Singh (1885–1925) ascended the throne, a British resident officer was deputed in Kashmir.[18] This was followed by land settlement operations, which were conducted between 1889 and 1895, creating classificatory systems such as Land Settlement Records (*bandobasti*).[19] Colonial governmentality further empowered revenue officials.

The lower echelons of the Dogra revenue establishment were predominantly composed of Hindu Pandits from the Kashmir Valley. This had contributed to the grievance among the Muslims in the Valley of being discriminated by their Hindu rulers, triggering a sense of solidarity and territorial consciousness among them. The ongoing Dogra oppression eventually led to the call to 'Quit Kashmir' in 1931.[20] In Ladakh, however, a number of Sunni Muslims from the Valley were placed in these bureaucratic positions. Along with the Sunnis, Sikh and Hindu families also lived in Ladakh, as either traders or officials in the administration.[21] Few Kargilis qualified for these administrative positions due to low levels of literacy. In hindsight, people in Kargil blamed the agha *zaat* or sayyids, descendants of preachers from Khorasan, who had settled there historically for poor education among the Shi'as.[22] They were criticised for keeping their followers in darkness to retain their power over them. Thus, important administrative posts, such as the keepers of land records, were occupied by Khachul-*pa* (Khachul – Kashmir; *pa* – people), people of Kashmiri origin, many of whom subsequently settled in Ladakh.

Five Sunni families – Mir, Wani, Bhatt, Lone and Kakporis – are said to have originally migrated from Kashmir. Fragmented into several households over time, different branches of these families can be found in Kargil town, Drass and Leh. The Wani family, for example, who trace their ancestry to two brothers – Aziz Munshi and Amir Munshi – came to Kargil during the reign of Maharaja Ranbir Singh (1856–85) as *kothidar* (storekeeper) and *thanedar* (police inspector). They were given revenue land to settle on and over the years also acquired large landholdings allegedly bought cheaply from the largely illiterate local population. As a young Shi'i man, once teasing his Sunni friend who was a descendant of one of these families, sardonically put it, 'Your forefathers bought off our land at the price of a cigarette.' Over time many of these families started businesses in Kargil and occupied important government posts in the post-colonial administration. These Sunni families continued to be among the wealthiest in the region and lived in big houses concentrated in the upper areas of Kargil town, in a neighbourhood called Khache Grong, away from, as they said, 'the bustle and dirt of the bazaar'.[23] Located in a narrow alley leading down from the main bazaar to the Suru River, the Sunni mosque is adjacent to the Sikh *gurdwara* (temple). The piercing, unforgettable voice of its muezzin rises up to Khache Grong, calling this small community to prayer, five times a day. Some Sunni families in Kargil town are also the descendants of traders in *pashmina* who travelled between Tibet, Changtang and the Kashmir Valley. Over time these families of Kashmiri origin identified themselves as Ladakhis. They speak the local Tibetan dialect fluently and often even prefer to marry within Ladakh if a suitable Sunni spouse can be found within the region due to cultural differences from the Valley. Sunni–Shi'a marriages are also not unheard of. Their wedding ceremonies are an amalgam of Kashmiri and Ladakhi traditions.

A prominent clan of Sunni Muslims of Kashmiri origin is the Munshis, who converted to Shi'ism at some point in time after living in Kargil. Their ancestors migrated to Kargil town from the Kishtwar region of Kashmir about four generations ago. The family traced its history in Kargil to Munshi Aziz Bhatt. Businessman, moneylender and affidavit writer, Aziz Bhatt is said to have owned seven shops and a *sarai* (caravansary) in Kargil, where traders would spend the night and exchange various goods. Ledgers that kept a record of loans given have been preserved by his grandsons and show the vast patronage network that their grandfather had spawned, extending across the district. If wealth begets wealth, then this was certainly the fortune of the Munshi family. Aziz Bhatt also served the Dogra regime as a *patwari*. Many Kargilis alleged that he exploited this position to acquire extensive landholdings in different parts of Kargil. Aziz Bhatt's son, Munshi Habibullah, further consolidated the family's wealth and power over time. He continued his father's mercantile business for a few years after his death before joining the NC party to enter politics. Munshi Habibullah was the first politician from Kargil to hold the position of a cabinet minister in the J&K state assembly for several consecutive terms. His legacy was reflected in the tremendous influence the family continued to exert on political dynamics in Kargili society. Perhaps the fame of the Munshi clan is best summed up by the nickname of the most charismatic son of Munshi Habibullah, 'Kingi', inscribed on the number plates of all his cars. Along with his brothers, Gulzar Munshi became a key mediator between local intellectuals and the outside world, introducing Kargil to many researchers, including myself. Munshi Habibullah's three wives begot several offspring, who were entered into strategic marital alliances with influential families in Kargil, such as the different Kacho clans.

Families of Kashmiri origin that settled in Kargil during the reign of the Dogras thus came to constitute a new elite in the region's extant social hierarchy. Until then power was concentrated in the hands of the Kachos – an honorific title prefixed to the name to mark royal patrilineage.[24] By the time the Dogras started ruling Ladakh in the mid-nineteenth century, power in the region was primarily divided between the kingdoms of Sot, Pashkum and Chigtan. These clans intermarried over several generations, presumably to both preserve the purity of lineage and concentrate land and political power among themselves. Despite the loss of sovereignty, power continued to be vested in these royal families. The Kacho family of Chigtan, for instance, retained the position of the *nambardar* across generations. They also enjoyed other privileges such as being exempt from *dak-begari* (obligatory porterage) during Dogra rule.[25] People in Ladakh, as in the rest of the J&K state, historically relied on agriculture and pastoralism as the primary source of livelihood. Although the levels of landlessness in this region were negligible compared to other parts of India, common people owned mostly small pieces of land yielding enough for subsistence. Large areas of land were owned either by the royal classes or by monasteries (in the case of Buddhist Ladakh) and were given out on lease to peasants on a sharecropping basis. In Kargil this meant that whole villages would come under the patronage of the royal family and were beholden to them to sustain their livelihoods. As a result, despite owning small pieces of land themselves, many peasants in Kargil continued to work as tillers on the lands of the Kachos. A young woman from Sot told me that the Kacho of Sot, for instance, received as much as 50 per cent of crop share from lands leased out even in 2009, demonstrating the resilience of social hierarchies that became a target of reformist discourses of injustice. Besides land, the Kacho family continued to enjoy other traditional privileges. Sot is drought-prone, and like other water-stressed areas in Ladakh, water was allocated according to a carefully laid out system of turns known as *chu res* (*chu* – water; *res* – turn). In the village of Yurbaltak, the ancestral home of the Kacho of Sot, people complained that the family continued to receive a disproportionate share of water.

The old and new elite entered into social and political alliances with each other through intermarriage, remaining at the helm of political and economic affairs until their power slowly began to be challenged in the 1990s. In comparison to the J&K *wazarat*s, the frontier areas – which included the Ladakh *wazarat*, Gilgit Agency and the vassal states of Hunza and Nagar – retained a 'semi-autonomous feudatory status within the princely state'.[26] Consequently, the Dogra kings were able to establish only limited administrative control in these regions. These clans thus became mediators between the princely state and the common people in its far-flung regions. The descendant of one such clan told me that his elders used to say that the time of the Dogras was not oppressive. For the common people, however, Dogra rule was unequivocally recalled as a period of colonial oppression across Ladakh and Kashmir and left its imprint in resilient social hierarchies. Despite such oppression, the Dogra period did not mark a rupture. It was probably included in the long span of 'ancient times' for under it Ladakh retained a unity that was geographically and politically severed by the partition of the subcontinent, converting the frontier region into a contested 'border' between two nation states. The era of the princely state was simultaneously remembered as a time of great oppression but also a time when borders did not separate Ladakh from Gilgit–Baltistan. Freedom from colonial rule was thus bittersweet: One kind of servitude was exchanged for another form of captivity.

Although the end of Dogra rule held the promise of freedom for both Ladakh and Kashmir, in the decades to come, freedom came to hold different meanings for the Valley and Ladakh. The political horizons of these regions did not overlap even though the seeming dawn of a new era came with new forms of subjection for Ladakh. For Shi'as living on the frontiers of Kashmir, 1947–49 remained uncertain years. As the desire to belong to India congealed over time, their aspirations of freedom were articulated *within* captivity in stark contrast to the Kashmir Valley.[27]

'Modern Times': From Partition to Post-colonial Governance

The fragmentation of the frontier areas after the partition led to a shift from *place* to *territory*. In nationalist history, places like Kargil were reduced to a remote border location. It was ironical that in a place that was to become so significant for the sovereignty of the nation state, people living there were oblivious to the first stirrings of partition. It was only with the advance of the Gilgit Scouts (a paramilitary force originally raised by the British in the Gilgit Agency in 1913) into Ladakh that the significance of the events dawned upon people in Kargil. As the British hurriedly split the subcontinent between India and Pakistan, the question of the fate of the princely states came up. The majority acceded to India or Pakistan by the time of the 'transfer of power' in August 1947, with the exception of Hyderabad, Junagadh and J&K. Both Hyderabad and Junagadh had Muslim rulers with a largely Hindu population, while J&K had Hindu rulers over a majority Muslim population. Gilgit, which had been on lease to the British, was reverted to the rule of the Hindu maharaja in June 1947 without consulting the people of this region, the majority of whom were Muslim. Resentment against this move simmered. Thus, while the maharaja ruled, de facto it was the Gilgit Scouts who are said to have held real power in the region.[28]

Political ferment in the Dogra princely state can be traced back to the early twentieth century, when people started raising demands for protection from the arbitrary rule of the Dogra maharajas. In response, between 1912 and 1932, the Dogra regime created legal provisions for extending the 'hereditary state subject' status to its subjects. This granted rights to government office, land use and ownership to 'the people of the land', which emerged as an administrative category in the Kashmiri Nationals' Law of 1912. This law subsequently became the basis of the special constitutional protection accorded to J&K in post-colonial India.[29] Following the agitation for legal recognition of proprietary rights in 1931, two major groupings – the NC and the Muslim Conference – came into existence. Both were opposed to the ruling Dogra dynasty, and their agitation had produced a certain degree of constitutional development leading to the promulgation of the Jammu and Kashmir Constitution Act (1934) and the establishment of the first legislative assembly known as the Praja Sabha (state assembly) on the recommendation of the Glancy Commission. Elected constituencies were created in the Praja Sabha for Hindus and Muslims from the J&K valleys, while Ladakh could only nominate members.[30] The representation of Ladakh by Buddhists in the assembly implicitly neglected the presence of the sizeable Muslim population. The support of the Kashmiri Pandits for the Buddhists also indicated an implicit coalescing of a non-Islamic against Islamic block, when read within the wider politics of J&K.

Alastair Lamb classifies public opinion in J&K over the issue of accession to India into four broad categories: The Hindus in Jammu and Hindu-Brahmin pandits of the Kashmir Valley supported the Dogras. In Ladakh, a new Buddhist political consciousness had begun to crystallise which tilted towards being with the Hindus.[31] The Muslim Conference represented the bulk of the Muslims in Jammu; they and the more 'hard-line' Muslims of the Valley were opposed to the idea of joining the Indian union. The NC, which proclaimed a secular outlook, preferred an independent Kashmir.[32] Gilgit *wazarat*, Baltistan and Kargil do not figure in this classification, prefiguring the subsequent deafness to their political voices in Pakistan and India. From an ethnographic perspective it is impossible to state how Kargilis might have envisioned their future in 1947 as memories of the past have been filtered through their present desire to belong to India. When recalling the partition, Kargili Shi'as do not betray any hint of being votaries of Pakistan in contrast to the position of the Shi'i-dominated area of Zaidibal in Srinagar where a session of the Muslim Conference was convened in July 1947.[33] The shared experience of Dogra oppression did not unite Shi'as on Kashmir's frontier with those in the Valley.

Kargil was in the eye of the storm in the months following August 1947. Soon after Hari Singh signed standstill agreements with both India and Pakistan on 12 August 1947, the Gilgit rebellion led by the Gilgit Scouts broke out in October 1947. When unrest against Dogra rule erupted in Poonch (Jammu), too, the maharaja appealed to Indian political leaders for military assistance. Most historical sources have focused on the initial advance of the 'invaders' towards the Kashmir Valley and the capture of Baramulla. But it was the frontier regions of Baltistan and Ladakh that came to be occupied for a few months. A branch of the maharaja's army rebelled in Skardu (Baltistan), and groups of pro-Pakistani Gilgit Scouts entered Kargil, Nubra, Sham and Zangskar in the Ladakh *wazarat*. As Tanvir *sahib* related these events to me:

> The Gilgit Scouts first captured Gilgit town and then, crossing Rong-*yul*, moved towards Skardu in January 1948. The maharaja of Skardu was besieged in Kharpocho, the fort at Skardu, and as the fighting continued there, a segment of the Gilgit Scouts moved towards Kargil. At this time, a thousand men of the Indian army came via Kashmir to Kargil.

Recalling the time as one of great hardship, as the road to Kashmir was closed when the Indian army fought the Gilgit Scouts, Tanvir *sahib* continued:

> On 5 May 1948, Kargil was attacked. The Indian army was small, and the men fled to the Suru Valley, facilitating the movement of the Gilgit Scouts towards Leh. During this time many Hindu and Sikh trading families settled in Kargil fled to Punjab and other areas in India, fearing the possibility of Ladakh's absorption into Pakistan. However, after several months of battle, the Gilgit Scouts were forced to retreat, and a ceasefire line was drawn up, fragmenting 'Greater Ladakh' between the two nations of India and Pakistan.

Annual 'Day of Victory' (*yaum-e-fateh*) celebrations organised by the Indian army in Kargil have memorialised the retreat of the Gilgit Scouts as the liberation of Kargil and incorporated it into nationalist history. *Yaum-e-fateh* marks the day the Indian army entered Kargil via the Zoji-la pass on 21 December 1948. In 2015, a memorial to Harka Bahadur – a Gorkha soldier who is said to have 'killed many Pakistani soldiers', as a Kargili friend put it – was under construction by the side of the national highway en route to Drass and the Zoji-la pass, with a plaque inscribed 'saviour of Kargil in 1948'. This memorial is one of several mnemonic reminders by the Indian state of its victory in recapturing this region, followed by its gradual enclosure by India. When I asked elderly Kargilis if the 'raiders', as they are often referred to in the region, received any support from the locals, they responded equivocally. A man from Hanu village in Chigtan, descendant of a family that got split between Baltistan and Kargil in 1948, told me he had heard that when the Gilgit Scouts attacked Kargil, they recruited many locals as porters. Many of these recruits fled to Pakistan when the Indian army forced the Gilgit Scouts to retreat. That is how his uncle ended up on the other side of the LoC. It was unclear if the people who aided the Scouts did so by choice or were coerced.

With the advance of the Gilgit Scouts into Ladakh, Sardarni Amarjeet Kaur was among the Hindu and Sikh trading families who fled to Punjab and other areas in the Indian plains. She was one of the few oldest surviving members of the Sikh families who continued to live in Kargil after the partition. Her father-in-law's father came as a *girdawar* (inspector) to Kargil during the Dogra regime. When the Gilgit Scouts approached Ladakh in 1948, she remembered the *wazir* telling all Punjabis to leave Kargil. Vividly recalling that time, she related:

> At the time of the *kabali* raid, we left for Punjab. It was the month of January. I was eight years old then. We stayed in Srinagar for a month. On 30th January 1948, the day Gandhiji [M. K. Gandhi] died, we left in an army vehicle and reached Pathankot from where we went on to Punjab, where we had relatives who had come from Pakistan as refugees. There were forty people in the *kafila* [caravan]. We had to spend a month in Drass as there was so much snow. The people there left us till the Zoji-la pass. They were very helpful ... it was almost like a picnic. We managed to reach without any *dahshat* [violence]. The *kabiliya* came from the mountains. They looted a lot and took the copper and vessels of the Pandits. They stayed in Kargil for six months in our house, we learnt from the locals upon our return. They looted people a lot – took their chickens and even asked for girls. They ran away in May when the Indian army arrived.

Amarjeet Kaur's family stayed in Punjab for seven to eight years after leaving Kargil in 1948. When work did not pick up there, they decided to return to Kashmir.

In Kargil they found their homes left in the care of friends intact: 'They kept them like their own precious possession [*amanat*]'. Her father opened a general store (ration shop) in Kargil. Unlike the Sunni families of Kashmiri origin or the descendants of the princely chiefdoms, the Sikh families that settled in Ladakh as administrators in the Dogra regime did not amass significant wealth or landholdings. Aside from acquiring land for a small Sikh *gurdwara*, they continued to live in rented accommodation in the Kargil bazaar. This rankled the younger generation, who did not always agree with their elders' representations of unblemished inter-communal relations in the region.[34]

The legacy of the princely state thus strongly lingered in the decades to come in this frontier region, shaping the imaginaries of freedom of those who did not benefit from Dogra rule. Despite the loss of the positions they held in the Dogra administration after the partition, the elite of Kargil remained wealthy and powerful even after the region's incorporation into the state of J&K. Besides large landholdings and wealth acquired through trade, they were also much ahead of the vast majority of Shi'as in terms of educational qualifications. Their descendants were therefore among the first to hold coveted positions in the new post-colonial governmental apparatus and acquire professional degrees. Although the old feudal relation between royal families and common people diminished over time, they continued to enjoy traditional privileges arising from land ownership and exploited these to their political advantage, compelling people to vote for them in elections to maintain their leases. The old elite sought to maintain their power by entering mainstream politics. The Sot and Pashkum Kacho families, for instance, became the local representatives of the two major political parties – the NC and the Congress – respectively. Despite becoming staunch political opponents, they continued to forge marital alliances with each other to maintain their status.

Not only did social power continue to remain vested to a large degree with these elite families in Kargil, the post-colonial administrative setup of the Indian state also reinforced the existent spatial hierarchies between the Kashmir Valley, Leh and Kargil. The Ladakh *wazarat* comprising Leh and Kargil was incorporated into J&K as one district (sub-provincial level), with the district headquarters housed in Leh. This led to the development of a more extensive administrative and developmental infrastructure in Leh. People in Kargil had to travel all the way to Leh for bureaucratic work, such as getting state subject paperwork or even a simple road permit, and for other needs, such as treatment at the district hospital. In turn, both Leh and Kargil became dependent on the state administration housed in Srinagar during the summer and Jammu in the winter season for allocation of funds, administrative approvals and better-quality health and education facilities.

Ladakh became the remote backwater of the state of J&K, and within it Kargil became the poor cousin of Leh. In the years to come, Kargilis partially attributed their relative 'backwardness' to this spatialisation of post-colonial governance, contributing to the emergence of a nascent regional consciousness.[35]

Given the large geographical area, it was difficult for a single district commissioner based in Leh to effectively cover all of Ladakh. Kargil was subsequently delineated as a separate district in 1979 at the behest of Sheikh Abdullah, leader of the NC party. Although the delineation of the Kargil district broadly followed the administrative division between Leh and Kargil *tahsils*, it mapped onto a communal divide: Kargil became a Muslim majority district, with Zangskar a Buddhist minority area within it.[36] Sheikh Abdullah is said to have visited Kargil in 1975, a year after signing the Kashmir Accord with Indira Gandhi. According to the NC-aligned Kargili politicians, this enabled the NC to really make inroads into the region. This was also the time when Munshi Habibullah of the Munshi family had joined the party. He subsequently won the state assembly elections in 1977 on an NC ticket and became a member of the legislative assembly (MLA) in the J&K parliament. Even before this formal electoral victory of a Kargili politician, Agha Sayid Haider from the Suru Valley had been a close associate of Sheikh Abdullah. His support was critical to Munshi Habibullah's victory in the elections; he is said to have taken 1,500 men from Kartse to Srinagar as a show of support for Habibullah.[37] Explaining the popularity of the NC in Kargil, staunch NC politician Qambar Ali Akhone, a close associate of Agha Haidar, who was also elected MLA in the 1990s, told me: 'People in Kargil prefer a local Kashmir party. Further, they liked the programmes and policies of the NC.' One of the policies that people in Kargil frequently cited were the extensive land reforms that were initiated in the entire state by Sheikh Abdullah. The passage of the Big Landed Estates Abolition Act in 1950 in J&K placed a general ceiling on the extent of landownership, and ownership rights were transferred to the tiller. Erstwhile royal families in Kargil lost large tracts of land in this process. This likely contributed to support for the NC even though the power of the elite families only diminished partially; loopholes in the Act enabled them to retain large holdings by making fictitious transfers of land within the network of kin. It explains why predominantly agricultural areas like the Suru Valley scarcely wavered in their support for the NC over several decades. Colloquially referred to as the 'Land of the Aghas', the Suru Valley is a bastion of aghas, who remained loyal to the NC. The relatively poor peasantry supported political leaders or parties that were backed by their powerful aghas. Another reason for the sustained popularity of the NC in Kargil relative to Leh must be understood in the context of growing Buddhist–Muslim antagonism in Ladakh since the 1980s.

The Kashmir Conflict and the Communalisation of Ladakh

The relationship between the NC leadership in the Kashmir Valley and the Congress party, which was politically dominant in Delhi well into the 1980s, was always tentative and problematic. Sheikh Abdullah was arrested in 1953, soon after he became the prime minister of J&K. His political career in India continued to be punctuated by long years in prison, and with each release he compromised the autonomy of the state within India granted to it under Article 370. The Nehru–Abdullah 'Delhi Agreement' (1952) and the Abdullah–Indira accord (1974) were seen by many in the Valley as a betrayal. Yet large parts of Kargil remained staunch supporters of the NC. Abdullah's visit to Kargil in 1975, then, coincided with growing disenchantment with the NC in the Valley. Abdullah is said to have toyed with the idea of a 'Greater Kashmir' that would include the district of Kargil.[38] This never came to fruition and was seldom mentioned in Kargil, where some aspired instead for 'Greater Ladakh', which would reunify Ladakh with Baltistan.

By the late 1980s, growing economic and political dissatisfaction among Kashmiri Muslims in the Valley led to a popular insurgency (*tehreek*), calling for freedom from India. Allegations of rigging in the J&K state elections in 1987, which brought the NC to power again, was the final straw for the *tehreek*, leading to the escalation of conflict in 1989.[39] These events coincided with the rise of the Hindu right in national politics. The concomitant intensification of Hindu communalism placed Muslims across India in a vulnerable position but with more acute consequences for Kashmir, which had already seen the mass murder of Muslims in Jammu in 1947 with the aid of the Rashtriya Swayamsevak Sangh (RSS).[40] Victoria Schofield conjectures that suspicions among the Muslims of Kashmir regarding their status within secular India may have contributed to separatist movements gaining additional support.[41] This created a vicious cycle as the loyalty of all Kashmiri Muslims to the nation, regardless of their own political viewpoint, began to be questioned across the country.

Ongoing violence and the resulting absence of 'normalcy' in the Kashmir Valley cast a shadow over other parts of J&K, including Ladakh. As the conflict in Kashmir intensified, Ladakhi dissatisfaction with the state government mounted, erupting in a struggle for regional autonomy in Leh. Led by the Ladakh Buddhist Association (LBA), political leaders in Leh raised a demand for UT status for Ladakh, which would place it directly under the jurisdiction of the central government. In a detailed and nuanced analysis of this struggle, Martijn van Beek examines how the LBA sought the attention of the central government by couching their appeals in a communal framework. Supported by the Bharatiya Janata Party (BJP) and the Vishva Hindu Parishad (VHP), it played upon the 'Muslims versus others' opposition, which had become a common political strategy within the wider national political field.[42] In 1989, the LBA ordered a boycott of all Muslims in Ladakh; Buddhists were banned from entering economic and social exchanges with them. The boycott lasted for three years. Although it was primarily targeted at Kashmiri Muslims who had captured a large part of the tourism and other lines of business in Leh town, it fostered Muslim solidarity in Ladakh. Responding to an appeal for help from the Sunnis, the Shi'as united with them to form the Ladakh Muslim Association. This elicited a negative reaction from the LBA, which then turned against both.[43]

Even though the boycott of Muslims in 1989 was not directly extended to them, it left, as many Kargilis put it, 'a bitter taste in our mouths too'. A Kargili intellectual recounted how his childhood was filled with stories in which elders would recall the times of great mingling and cultural exchange between Muslims and Buddhists. He lamented that now their friendship (*nyering*) was much weaker. The decline in inter-religious marriages was perhaps the clearest indicator of this. If a young man in Kargil falls in love with a Buddhist girl, he has to seek special permission from a cleric who would be willing to help the girl convert to Islam before they are allowed to marry. Young people often hid relationships for fear of social censure in both Leh and Kargil. I became privy to stories of moral policing and hunting of inter-religious couples, particularly by Buddhist organisations in Leh.[44] Buddhist women who married Muslim men were often written off as being the 'leftovers' of society in Leh, and in Kargil, despite converting to Islam, some felt a sense of incomplete acceptance within the husband's community.

As communal antagonisms between Buddhists and Muslims flared in the late 1980s, some Buddhists alleged that the demarcation of Kargil as a separate district was a tactic on Sheikh Abdullah's part to secure further allegiance of the Muslims of Kargil to his party. Many people blamed him for implicitly instigating the communalisation of the region. It intensified the perception in Kargil of being discriminated against by virtue of being Muslim. This was reflected in their sustained refusal to support Leh's demand for UT status for Ladakh as part of their agitation for autonomy since the 1990s. Although Kargilis shared the grievance that Ladakh was marginalised within J&K, they feared even greater neglect if clubbed together with the Buddhists in a single administrative entity. Kargili politicians had for long attributed their perceived backwardness and marginalisation to the economic and political dominance of Leh.[45] They alleged that the central government had historically favored Buddhists over Muslims. The refusal to open the Kargil airport to civilian traffic, the presence of central government offices and infrastructural apparatus in Leh, the difficulties Muslims faced in getting recruited into the Indian army, and the tardiness in approving the construction of a tunnel across the Zoji-la pass in comparison with the initiation of work on similar infrastructure at the Rohtang Pass connecting Leh with Himachal Pradesh, were some of the repeatedly voiced examples of systemic discrimination of the Muslim-dominated area of Ladakh.[46] Even though they sought to distance themselves from politics in the Kashmir Valley, a shared religious identity with its Muslim population offered Kargil a psychological sense of security.

Yet the relationship with Kashmir has never been an easy one for Muslims in Kargil. Despite grievances vis-à-vis Buddhist Ladakh, Kargil needed to be recognised on its own terms, as distinct from the Kashmir Valley. Subsumed under a pan Kashmiri–Muslim label, the nationalist sentiments of Shi'as in Kargil, too, were subject to suspicion, despite their consistent condemnation of the separatist movements. This spilled into other kinds of discrimination: Many were refused hotel accommodation in Delhi, and had difficulty obtaining visas to travel abroad or clearance for the Foreign Contribution Regulation Act (FCRA) permit that allows non-governmental organizations (NGOs) to accept foreign funding; the latter was due to state suspicion that this might act as a cover for funding separatist activities. Until the extremely violent repression of civilian protests against the killing of the iconic militant youth leader, Burhan Wani, in the Valley by the Indian state in the summer of 2016, Kargilis had largely remained aloof, at least publicly, from the cycle of violence and disaffection in the Kashmir Valley. But they could not look away from the maiming of civilians in the Valley by pellet guns.[47] Denouncing this violence as fundamentally inhumane, religious leadership in Kargil unequivocally and publicly condemned the Indian state even as they continued to perform patriotism.

The Muslims of Kargil have thus been entangled in a web of simultaneous allegiance and alienation from both the Kashmir Valley and Buddhist Ladakh (Leh) since the partition. Straddling both sides continues to haunt their negotiations of belonging in the aftermath of the revocation of Article 370 and the bifurcation of J&K, as I will discuss in the Epilogue.

The history of the political marginalisation of Kargil must be read in conjunction with a social history of sectarian prejudices and pejorative communal representations of Shi'a Muslims in Ladakh. Both fed into a growing consciousness of a sense of place and self in the region.

Sectarian Prejudices and Stereotypes

In contemporary Ladakh, Shi'ahs are regarded as the poor 'other' and sometimes treated with a degree of contempt and fear. In Leh *tahsil*, the name *balti* is used both for Shi'ahs and Muslim Kargilis in general. This term both has derogatory connotations and also implies that they are outsiders, as the name refers to neighbouring Baltistan.[48]

This characterisation of Buddhist attitudes to Shi'a Muslims in the 1980s by Nicola Grist stood true even decades after. The Shi'as were routinely referred to as dirty, barbaric and uncivilised. Sometimes the compliment of being 'simple-minded' was extended – a euphemism for 'primitive'. Pejorative stereotypes of Shi'as were often linked to their everyday habits and ritual practices by Sunnis and Buddhists alike. A Buddhist lady in Leh joked and then mimicked how 'people in Kargil sit crudely with their legs apart', while her mother-in-law expressed pity for me, for having to work among such 'dirty people'. They expressed dread at having to stay overnight in Kargil when travelling to Srinagar, deriding the 'filth in the bazaar' and the inevitability of getting bitten by bed bugs.

Buddhists and Sunnis often disparaged the Shi'i practice of *chattu* (*tse-tu*). Some Shi'as believe that the touch of a non-Muslim on anything wet (*sherpa*) as opposed to dry (*skambo*) is considered polluting. Those who practise *chattu* strictly translate this into a rule of commensality and do not accept food prepared by a non-Muslim. This does not, however, preclude hospitality to non-Muslims in people's homes. Sunnis do not believe in *chattu* and alleged misinterpretation of the Qur'an by Shi'as. Buddhists from Leh or other parts of Ladakh, living in Kargil, often lamented that when they finished drawing water from a handpump, Kargili women frantically muttered 'bismillah, bismillah' to purify it. I must add that as a non-Muslim, I never experienced this. In the first month of fieldwork, I lived in a room that was not connected to piped water, necessitating regular trips to the nearby handpump. Some college-going boys and girls who would come to my room to learn English in the evenings would, however, politely refuse offers of tea but shyly ate biscuits because these are a dry and packaged product. Though unlikely to do solely with the practice of *chattu*, Muslims and Buddhists would also typically eat at different restaurants (*dhabas*) in both the Kargil and Leh bazaars and while journeying along the Leh–Kargil–Srinagar highway. The Shi'i eating joints were recognisable by the posters of Iranian or Iraqi ayatollahs and the Buddhist ones by photos of the Dalai Lama. Some Kargilis travelling from Leh to Kargil would prefer to journey in a shared Kargil taxi, a practice I, too, came to adopt as I scoured the taxi stand for the JK07 (the Kargil number plate) vehicles.

Another Twelver Shi'i practice that raised eyebrows was the legitimacy accorded to temporary marriage (*nikah al-mut'a*). In contrast to a permanent marriage contract (*daimi*), *mut'a* allows a Shi'i man to marry a consenting woman for a duration ranging from a few hours to several years.[49] Bound by fewer obligations, temporary marriage is said to legitimately channel the sexual desire of men. Sunnis and Buddhists in Ladakh and the Kashmir Valley often cited the practice of *mut'a* to condemn the Shi'a Muslims as promiscuous. Talk of temporary marriage customs often provoked further stereotypes in Leh of the Shi'a 'breeding like rabbits', a common trope expressing the demographic anxiety among non-Muslims, globally. It betrayed the growing insecurity among Buddhists in Ladakh of being outnumbered by Muslims. The LBA and the Mothers Group (Ama Stsogspa) in Leh discouraged contraception in order to increase the Buddhist population. This anxiety sustained despite the fact that even though the Shi'a Muslims may have had larger families in the past, this was no longer the case, with growing acceptance of contraception in Kargil.

The prejudices of Sunnis from the Kashmir Valley first became evident to me on journeys between Kargil and Srinagar in shared taxis with Kashmiri schoolteachers who were posted in the Kargil district for a few years. Until the early 2000s, most teaching posts in Kargil's government schools were occupied by Sunnis from the Kashmir Valley or Hindus from Jammu as the locals, mostly uneducated, could not meet the qualifying criteria. Most teachers from Kashmir had little stake in Kargil and considered the posting as a punishment; not only did some of them work half-heartedly but they were also condescending towards Kargilis. Their numbers may have declined over the years as Kargilis acquired education, but the attitude remained unchanged. 'These people in Kargil eat meat in an almost raw form. This gives you tapeworms,' a Kashmiri teacher once remarked to me. Another comment that I heard several times was that the Shi'as are barbaric enough to even cut up human beings and eat them, referring to the bloodshed during flagellation, a ritual during Muharram. David Pinault mentions the 'disjunction between the public and private discourse' he found in the reactions to the rituals of Muharram among the Buddhists and Sunnis in Leh in the 1990s.[50] Although on the face of it both were respectful and even participated in some aspects of the festival, opinions expressed in private were disparaging. This disapproval of bloody flagellation reflected widely held colonial and post-colonial perceptions in India of the Shi'as as being 'intrinsically riotous and rebellious'. However, outside of ritual contexts, in everyday life, the Sunnis of Ladakh not only shared an amicable relationship with Shi'as but sometimes also harboured reservations about Kashmiri Sunnis. A sense of trans-Himalayan identity cut across sectarian boundaries.

Kargili Shi'as were extremely conscious of such pejorative representations of their community and religion. Many of them started following the ban on bloody flagellation imposed by Ayatollah Khamenei in Iran to counter, as they explained it to me, negative impressions of Shi'ism globally, provoked by scenes of flagellation during Muharram. Many people, especially young men, who had been educated outside Kargil, expressed shame and embarrassment at some of these practices. They criticised the practice of *chattu*, arguing that only the 'narrow-minded' continued to follow it. Others felt compelled to offer theological explanations for the provision of temporary marriage in Shi'ism or clarified that it was no longer widely prevalent. A common criticism with respect to temporary marriage that I came across was through rumours circulating about certain powerful aghas in the Suru Valley, who allegedly exploited the belief that their touch is sacralising to have illicit sex with young girls, legitimised by *mut'a* contracts. Internal critique of *mut'a* marriage was, then, also a critique of religious leadership, integral to the context within which modernist reformist ideas gained traction.

Shame and defensiveness were, however, not the only response of Shi'as in Kargil to these prejudices and stereotypes. Rather, these made them more conscious of their sectarian identity and led them to a search for more distinct and confident senses of self and place. At a more immediate level, this was expressed in counter-representations of Buddhists and Sunnis. In a discussion on Muslim–Buddhist elopements, and the policing of inter-religious marriages in Ladakh, a Shi'i friend was horrified by the perceived intolerance of Buddhists. In 2015, she related a rumour that was circulating at the time about how a Muslim woman who had run away with a Buddhist man and converted to Buddhism was forced to drink *chang* (local alcohol brewed from fermented barley) to prove her conversion. Muslims, in contrast, she explained to me, accepted a woman of another religion if she just recited the *kalma* (Muslim confession of faith). Some Shi'as remarked that Buddhists are dirty because they 'eat dead meat', referring to the consumption of meat not slaughtered according to Islamic norms of halal. Another example was the criticism of the custom of polyandry among Buddhists even though this had for long been outlawed. It was used to cast aspersions on Buddhist women as being of a loose moral character. Buddhist teachers in Kargil were conscious of this stereotype and, in turn, criticised the Muslims for being conservative and backward.

Kargili Shi'as also reproduced popular impressions in India of the Muslims of the Valley as being wily and greedy. In 2014, the Kashmir Valley experienced the worst floods in decades. In Kargil, rumours circulated of Shi'as being thrown off rescue boats in the Valley. Small trucks carrying aid on behalf of different religious and youth voluntary groups in Kargil left for the Valley every night, and families offered *niyaz* (a form of Islamic charity) in neighbourhood mosques to pray for the waters to recede. Kargilis were extremely sympathetic to the plight of people in the Valley. Yet in private many (across the religious spectrum – Shi'as, Sunnis and Buddhists) also commented that Kashmiris were bearing the punishment of their own sins (*gunah*), 'for always being after money'. Similar comments were made about Buddhists when a cloudburst wrecked immense damage in Leh in 2010. While reflecting shared cosmologies of sin and punishment across religious traditions, these mutual prejudices laced through the search for respect among Kargili Shi'as – to be free of an inferiority complex that had been internalised over a long period of time vis-à-vis their other minority neighbours. As I have argued in the previous chapter, equivalence should not be created among minorities if we are to take seriously longer histories of marginalisation perpetuated through consecutive eras of colonialism. But the struggle to overcome the internalised perceptions engendered by these histories echoes across minorities. It manifests as a race to become more 'modern', leading to mimesis and competition between minorities.

Thus, a pervasive trope that seemed to capture this search for self-respect in Kargil was the repeated use of the word 'modern': 'Leh is more modern than us' was almost like a chorus in conversations, especially with young people. Kargili imaginaries of modernity, however, reflected pan-Indian aspirations.[51] Becoming modern at the level of the region meant infrastructural development – roads, electricity, running water. As Kargil town and its peripheries became more urban in character, new fast-food cafes opened, and young women experimented with light make-up and heeled shoes, much to the chagrin of clerics, and young men from richer families cruised in the bazaar in the evening, sporting funky hairstyles and dark glasses. To be modern meant the embrace of new lifestyles and desires for consumption. The most substantive index of modernity was an education in English – a means to all these other ends, a 'passport to the future'.[52]

A euphemism for 'modern education' or 'worldly education' (*duniya-i 'ilm*), an education in English afforded access to government employment, which continued to be a highly coveted occupation in the region. It held the promise of enhanced status, long-term security and other benefits, such as pensions and the not-so-implicit opportunities for making some extra money on the side. The prestige associated with a government position, especially in the early days when few people were educated, was seen in the prefixing of the title of the position held to a person's name. The title lingered on long after retirement. For example, one of the first women to make a name in the region by becoming a senior official in a central government ministry in Delhi was Kaneez Fatima from the Munshi family. She was commonly referred to as 'TEO Kaneez Fatima', harking back to the early days of her illustrious career when she was the Tahsil Education Officer (TEO). Upon retirement, government servants in Kargil were given a lavish farewell. They were escorted home on their last day of work in a cavalcade of cars blaring *qasida* music,[53] with a large metallic urn carrying farewell gifts securely tied to the top of the vehicle. This spectacle of a parade of vehicles snaking its way through the town was also a common sight in the Hajj season, when those fortunate to be able to travel to Mecca were grandly sent off on this holiest of journeys. To be escorted in a parade of cars is a measure of honour in Kargil.

With rising education levels, greater numbers of Kargilis were able to apply for government jobs. This slowly posed a challenge to the traditional social hierarchy within the district. It has also enabled Kargilis to take up positions such as that of government schoolteachers. Rising in bureaucratic hierarchies indexed freedom from servitude. Perhaps more significant than these material accruements was the confidence at the level of both the individual and the community that modern education imparted: a confidence to stand up to their neighbours and traverse the wider world. It was typically the educated woman, often a teacher, who seemed to walk with a distinctly self-assured stride through the Kargil bazaar with her handbag on her way home from 'duty'. While travel and new media brought images and conceptions of modernity into people's homes and minds, it was the presence of these in Leh that most deeply influenced Kargil. Yet Kargil did not merely mimic Leh. Its search for a distinct sense of self and place was anchored in an alterity defined through religious and sectarian difference.

Sectarian and Regional Consciousness

Expressing a widespread but often inchoate sentiment that captured the psychic effects of a long history of political and economic marginalisation, a prominent political leader and one of the founders of the IKMT, Asgar Ali Karbalai, in an interview with me vociferously proclaimed:

> There is an inferiority complex in our *qaum* [community]. They feel they can't compete with either Leh or Kashmir here. This is because they have been oppressed by Kashmiri teachers and similarly by the people of Leh. Since after 1947, Leh has been dominating. Even the Hindus have dominated. Our whole *qaum* has become prey to an inferiority complex. The greatest impact of the Iranian Revolution has been to remove this complex. It has imparted confidence to people. The revolution is very valuable just for this.

While the imaginaries of modernity in Kargil reflected pan-Indian aspirations, it was the sense of pride in their Shi'i identity derived from the success of the Iranian Revolution (1979) that lent impetus to the process of articulating a distinct sense of self and place. Conceptions of modernity in the region were deeply influenced by the ideological landscape of modernist Islamic reform inspired by the Islamic Republic of Iran since the 1980s. Hidden below their public politics of recognition, Kargilis began to reflect on their own failings and shortcomings.

They did not lay sole blame on the state for their backwardness. The need for an education in English emerged as a trope for overcoming their lack of confidence. The discourse of Islamic reform gained legitimacy because it tackled some of these issues headlong. The emphasis of Islamic reform on modern education and social reform as being essential to Kargil's progress resembled a similar thrust among Buddhists in Leh a couple of decades earlier. Discussing the 'local imaginaries of Ladakhi modernity' in Leh, Martijn van Beek notes that both education and social reform 'were deemed necessary to prepare Ladakhis for self-government and survival as a distinct, i.e., a Buddhist community, as well as to protect them against the corrupting aspects of modernisation'.[54] Nevertheless, even if the impetus for reform among both Muslims and Buddhists was expressed through narratives of remoteness and neglect of Ladakh, reformist discourse in Kargil was embedded in a distinctly Twelver Shi'ite epistemology and political theology.

Growing confidence was reflected in an emergent sectarian and regional consciousness. Expressions of pride in belonging to Kargil became more common. Though certain political and cultural imperatives subsumed Kargil within Ladakh, and others under Kashmir, identification with Kargil as a distinct place acquired increasing salience. It started coming into its own as a place defined as much by its geographical and geopolitical boundaries as by modes of Shi'i selfhood.

ᏣᏨ

This chapter has situated Kargil within a genealogy of its links with its neighbours – Buddhist Ladakh and the predominantly Sunni Muslim Kashmir Valley – to historicise the scene of its perceived subjection. I have traced the hierarchies between regions that manifested politically and socially. It was in this context that ideas and ideologies of modernist Shi'i reform found traction, fomenting articulations of a distinct sense(s) of place and self. Despite being hemmed in by the LoC in the *jadid zamana* (modern times), regional (Kargili) and sectarian (Shi'i) consciousness was invigorated by connections with places beyond the territorial boundaries of India.

Notes

1. Bray, 'Readings on Islam in Ladakh', 15.
2. Bredi, 'History Writing in Urdu', 6–7.
3. The Purig-*pa* (people of Purig) and Baltis (people of Baltistan) are said to be the mixed descendants of the Dards and Mongols, while the people in Leh–Ladakh are predominantly of Tibetan Mongoloid stock.
4. The main source used by historians and scholars to trace the history of Ladakh is the Royal Genealogy of Ladakh (*La-dvags-rgyal-rabs*), a well-known chronicle of Tibet. Petech, *Study on Chronicles*. However, it is said to be full of inconsistencies,

particularly for the period before the seventeenth century. Bray, *Ladakhi Histories*, 7.

5. Emerson, 'Charismatic Kingship'.
6. See Bray, *Ladakhi Histories*; Emerson, 'Charismatic Kingship'; Grist, 'History of Islam'.
7. Grist, 'Local Politics'.
8. R. Gupta, 'Importance of Being Ladakhi in Kargil'. Also see Chapter 5.
9. Shaykhs are clerics in Kargil who have studied in seminaries in Iraq or Iran and are entitled to wear a white turban. Aghas are descendants of the family of the Prophet and the Imams and wear a black turban.
10. Benjamin, 'Theses', 252.
11. I draw here upon the point made by Zutshi, *Kashmir's Contested Pasts*, 303, that nationalist narratives of Kashmir's history suppress people's memories and different groups of people who made this region their home over time.
12. On trading histories of Ladakh, see Rizvi, *Trans-Himalayan Caravans*.
13. Daura, *Rescuing History from the Nation*.
14. Bray, *Ladakhi Histories*, 16.
15. Rai, *Hindu Rulers, Muslim Subjects*. The British sold Kashmir to the Dogras for a sum of 750,00 rupees in 1846. Zia and Bhat, *A Desolation Called Peace*, 1.
16. Rai, *Hindu Rulers, Muslim Subjects*, 111; van Beek, 'Identity Fetishism'.
17. The memoirs of a man called Ghulam Rassul Galwan, who served colonial travellers on their expeditions through Kashmir and Central Asia, were compiled and published in English by his masters in 1924. Butz and MacDonald, 'Serving Sahibs', 182, rightly argue that such texts, which purport to record the authentic voice of the native, in fact, enable 'a somewhat discredited discourse of benevolent colonial labour relations'.
18. Zutshi, *Languages of Belonging*, 89.
19. The settlement reports of Ladakh included several components: records of individual and fallow landholdings, *girdawari* (twice-annual crop assessments), *jamabandi* (annual consolidated crop report), information on trees and livestock, fiscal history of villages, sources of miscellaneous income, and remarks pertaining to the scope for increasing or decreasing revenue. Zutshi, *Languages of Belonging*; Crook and Osmaston, *Himalayan Buddhist Villages*, 143; van Beek, 'Identity Fetishism', 108–10.
20. Rai, *Hindu Rulers, Muslim Subjects*, 150; Behera, *Demystifying Kashmir*.
21. See Sheikh, *Reflections*, 44, 61, 167–69.
22. The aghas, referred to as the agha or sayyid *zaat*, occupy the top-most rung of the local 'caste' hierarchy.
23. *Khache* is a generic term used for people of Kashmiri origin. *Grong* means neighbourhood in the local Tibetan dialect.

24. *Ka* is a generic Ladakhi term used to address elder men with respect. When combined with *cho* (king), it refers to the male descendants of royal families and cuts across age status.

25. Grist, 'Use of Obligatory Labor'.

26. Robinson, *Body of Victim, Body of Warrior*, 36.

27. For Kashmiris in the Valley, 1931 represented an epochal break in modern history. The earliest martyrs' graveyard dates to the massacre of Muslims by the Dogras in response to the popular uprising. Junaid, 'Epitaphs as Counterhistories', 256.

28. Hassnain, *Gilgit*, 114.

29. The origins of people of the state (*awam-e-riyasat*) category of political belonging and governance in turn lay in agrarian land reforms carried out by the British colonial government in 1887. For a detailed historical excursus of this, see Robinson, *Body of Victim, Body of Warrior*, 34–36.

30. van Beek, 'Autonomy for Ladakh', 380.

31. Also see Aggarwal, *Beyond Lines of Control*, 38, for more on the preferences of Ladakhi Buddhists who clearly indicated a desire to be separated from the Kashmir Valley.

32. Lamb, *Incomplete Partition*, 96–97.

33. Hussain and Mehdi, 'Contours of Shia Political Discourse', 52–53.

34. Anam Zakaria also notes memories of 'trust and friendship' and 'inter-communal bonds' among the older generations in her research on Azad Kashmir. Zakaria, *Beyond the Great Divide*, 40.

35. I draw on Massey, 'Questions of Locality', 145–46. Massey makes a distinction between analysed histories of place and 'sense of place', which refers to 'the feelings that people carry around with them'. A dominant sense of place can be 'constructed out of the consciousness of the locality's place in the world'.

36. This created a sub-politics of recognition within the Kargil district as the Buddhists of Zangskar alleged discrimination by the Shi'i majority. See Gutschow, 'Politics of Being Buddhist'.

37. Agha Haider was a powerful religious leader in Suru-kartse and is famed for having allegedly made controversial millenarian proclamations on the imminent arrival of the Twelfth Imam in the 1950s. Another group of rival aghas in the Suru Valley, led by Agha Sayed Raza, contested this claim and took Agha Haidar to court. Munshi Habibullah is said to have helped Agha Haidar by getting the court case removed.

38. Wani, 'From the Sheikh's Days'.

39. See the edited volume by Zia and Bhat, *Desolation Called Peace*, to understand the development of Kashmiri political aspirations for *azadi* (independence) between 1947 and 1989 from the perspective of Kashmiris. Zia and Bhat challenge the depiction of this period as being peaceful and 1989 marking a rupture.

40. See Jamwal, 'Calm and Early Signs', 107.
41. Schofield, *Kashmir in the Crossfire*, 231.
42. See van Beek, 'The Art of Representation'; 'Public Secrets'.
43. Pinault, *Horse of Karbala*, 153.
44. In 2017 communal tensions flared up in Ladakh over a Buddhist girl's decision to marry a Muslim man from Kargil. Terming this the theft of a girl, the LBA threatened the entire Muslim community, asking them to either return the girl or leave the region. This case received widespread coverage, including in the international media. It reflected a growing intolerance of Hindu–Muslim marriages in the country, expressed in the Hindu right-wing campaign called 'love jihad' that targets Muslim men marrying Hindu women in India. See Saldon, 'I Am'.
45. Aggarwal, *Beyond Lines of Control*, 52.
46. It was only in 2015, after years of incessant requests by Kargili politicians, that the construction of the Zoji-la tunnel was finally approved.
47. On the denial of the basic humanity of Kashmiris by India, see Misri, 'Showing Humanity'.
48. Grist, 'Local Politics', 46.
49. See Haeri, *Law of Desire*; Al-Hadi, *The Truth as It Is*, on Shi'i temporary marriage. For an account of debates on lawfulness of *mut'a* between Shi'a and Sunni scholars, see Cilardo, 'A Dispute'.
50. Pinault, *Horse of Karbala*, 154.
51. Deshpande, *Contemporary India*.
52. Jeffery, 'Hearts, Minds, and Pockets', 35.
53. Religious poetry praising the Prophet and Imams recited on joyous and auspicious occasions.
54. van Beek, 'Imaginaries of Ladakhi Modernity', 168.

2

Reforming Self and Society

As the month of Ramadan approached in 2008, some of my reformist-minded interlocutors were looking forward to attending the *majalis* (religious congregations) of Shaykh Anwar. He was a popular cleric, allied with the IKMT, who came to Kargil from Iran every year. One late afternoon in mid-September, I managed to get an appointment with the shaykh. He was seated in front of a laptop next to a gas heater as the autumnal chill had crept in. After finishing his work, the shaykh turned his attention to me. As I introduced myself, he recalled being interviewed by two scholars from America a decade ago, and said, 'I never came to know what became of their work' – a salutary warning against extractive research. Then he narrated the story of his life.

Shaykh Anwar was born in Iraq. Hailing from a family of *zildar*s in the Suru Valley, his father had studied in Najaf and later moved to Iran, when the shaykh was around nine years old. After acquiring 'worldly education' (*duniya-i 'ilm*), Shaykh Anwar shifted to Islamic education at the age of eighteen. He recalled his very first visit to Kargil in the late 1980s: 'When I saw the pathetic conditions in Kargil, I thought they are such helpless people.... I felt great pity in my heart. I felt hatred for some old persons, who for their personal gain, were taking common people in the wrong direction.' This led him to return to Kargil every year for *tabligh* (preaching). Explaining his motivation, he said, 'I could easily have gone to Arab countries if I wanted to make money. But I wanted to work for my *qaum* [community].' After attending several of his *majalis*, in another meeting at the end of Ramadan, I asked him how he selected the topics for his lectures.

'I take into consideration the difficulties people are facing and the weaknesses present in a society,' he replied, adding that he kept in touch with friends and relatives in Kargil while in Iran to keep abreast of issues. Bemoaning that Kargil was a society seeped in ignorance (*jahiliyat*), he deployed the metaphor of a doctor dispensing cure through his *majalis* to an 'ill community' (*bimar qaum*).

Jahiliyat is a broad civilisational metaphor that holds material, symbolic and moral significance in Muslim societies.[1] It was not only Shaykh Anwar who characterised Kargili Shi'as as a *jahil qaum*. Although Kargil's perceived backwardness was blamed on political and economic marginalisation vis-à-vis its neighbours, the Kashmir Valley and Buddhist Leh, it was also attributed by many people in Kargil to ignorance within. An inferiority complex linked to historical stigmas attached to Ladakhi Shi'as became a fertile ground for the propagation of modernist reformist discourses by clerics such as Shaykh Anwar.

This chapter examines discourses of piety propagated by modernist reformists after the Iranian Revolution and their reception by ordinary believers, especially women and the youth. The question of reception has not received sufficient anthropological attention and yet is as important as the discourse and medium of dissemination.[2] Contrary to global perceptions of the Iranian Revolution (1979) representing the apotheosis of 'fundamentalist' Islam, I argue it offered discursive resources to Kargili Shi'as to inhabit a more confident sense of self and negotiate their belonging to India. For many, it spoke to trenchant desires of self- and place-making that would put Kargil and its youth on an equal footing with the Buddhists of Ladakh and the Muslims of the Valley. The crafting of Kargil's children into humane, educated and responsible individuals would not only be a measure of the reawakening of Islam in a society starved of its light in the eyes of reformists but also make the nation proud of the people of this region. Ushering in modernist reform, the IKMT instigated social change in Kargil through the repetition of key themes that structured the export of the revolution but contextualized these in relation to Kargil's history and location within India.[3]

Travelling Ideologues

Contrary to perceptions that the impact of the Iranian Revolution in the Muslim world as a whole may be 'inherently unmeasurable'[4] or is an 'optical illusion',[5] it could easily be discerned in Kargil. Too often overshadowed by its Islamic context, one of its more defining features has been lost in popular understanding: It was as much a 'social revolution' as an 'Islamic revolution'. Suroosh Irfani writes, 'The common denominator for all the forces that joined together [to bring about the revolution in Iran] ... was freedom – freedom for individual expression and thought, freedom from despotism, exploitation, and imperialism.'[6] The search for freedom from oppression resonated with people in Kargil on multiple levels: from the oppression of regional elites empowered during the Dogra regime, to discrimination by Buddhists and Sunnis, to a quest for freedom of individual expression. When I asked people about the impact of the revolution in Kargil, the two most common responses were: 'Its biggest message was that we must fight injustice and oppression (*zulm*)' and 'It has changed politics and education in Kargil'.

As the Islamic Republic of Iran came to life, its message spread to different corners of the Shi'i world.[7] With a view to establishing the leadership of the Iran over Twelver Shi'a across the world, Khomeini actively sought to export the ideology of the revolution through a variety of mediums. These included the setting up of new state institutions to sponsor students to go to their home countries for preaching (*tablighat*), media and publishing houses, and using the Hajj as an occasion for dissemination.[8] The Hujjatiyeh seminary in Qum was converted into an international religious school towards this end.[9] Jamiat al-Mustafa, or Al-Mustafa International University, became an umbrella institution for foreign students studying in Iranian seminaries.[10] The travel expenses of students returning home for preaching during Ramadan and Muharram were met by their seminaries and individual support from offices of *mujtahid*s (authority in jurisprudence). Besides short-term *tabligh*, students could also apply for longer terms, typically three years. They were often sent to regions in need of Shi'i teachers. Many clerics from Kargil had therefore spent considerable periods of time in Mumbai, Uttar Pradesh and the Kashmir Valley. Upon completion of their education in Iran, scholars could apply for long-term salaried positions through the Iran Cultural House in Delhi to which they remained accountable during the course of their employment.[11] Some of these scholars became champions of Khomeini's revolutionary ideologies in Kargil and supported the establishment of the IKMT by a group of young men, who increasingly had become critical of older clerics in the Islamia School.

Besides Khomeini, the revolution also owed its impact to a diverse set of individuals like Ali Shariati (Figure 2.1) and Murtaza Mutahhari who had shaped its intellectual content.[12] Their ideas filtered into Kargil via clerics and literature in the form of books, pamphlets, cassettes and CDs, published and distributed prolifically after the revolution.[13] This new media performed the work of 'emotional coordination through which a community is created at a translocal level'.[14]

Figure 2.1   A poster of Ali Shariati in the Kargil town bazaar, 2015, saying 'The Impact of the Revolution in Kargil Ladakh'

Source: Photograph by the author.

A young Kargili man, who had grown up in Mumbai where his father was a cleric, opened a shop called 'Islamic Media Centre' in Kargil town for a few years. It stocked *risala*s (manuals of conduct) by *mujtahid*s, CDs for children containing stories of the Prophet and his family, multimedia Qur'an, documentary films on the Iranian Revolution and books for youth by Mutahhari. Many of these media had been produced by the World Islamic Network (WIN), a Shi'i media house in Mumbai.[15] Even in the late 2000s, the increased availability of these media was a novelty for Kargil as contact with ideas in the transnational Shi'i realm historically had been restricted to interface with preachers and pilgrims. The circulation of printed material from the nineteenth century onwards to counter the influence of Christian missionaries and a rising Hindu consciousness in public space in the heartlands of India had not reached Kargil.[16] Geographical remoteness, difference in language and the late arrival of literacy hampered this connection. These factors were less of a barrier by the time literature from the revolution began to be distributed. Consequently, people could access religious and political thought at their own initiative and on an individual level. They did not have to depend on clerics. This triggered a gradual process of critical thinking, particularly among the younger generation.

Kargili students, especially men, who had travelled for work or studied in universities in Kashmir and beyond had been exposed to a rapidly modernising country. Even for those who had not travelled, television beamed images of modernity into homes, fostering new aspirations. The gap between Leh and Kargil expressed by Kargili Shi'as as backwardness in 'development' and 'modernisation' enhanced feelings of deprivation and exacerbated the lack of self-confidence. An important index of the Leh-pa (people of Leh) being modern was education, measured by their command of English. Almost everyone in Kargil, regardless of affiliation with the IKMT or Islamia School, attributed their backwardness in education to the older generation of clerics. Historically, learning English was deemed a sin (haram) in Kargil. I was often told that when anyone expressed an interest in 'modern education' (a euphemism for an education in English) in the past, religious leaders would chastise them, asking, 'Are you going to read A, B, C, D at your father's grave?'[17] This perception was attributed by many to older clerics in the Islamia School who had studied in Najaf at a time when English was shunned for being the language of the coloniser.[18] But this disapproval of English was not only a hangover from colonial times; it was also borne from vague perceptions of the threat of being afflicted with the ills of Western modernity that was part of the propaganda against the Shah of Iran. After the revolution, Iran came to be seen as an exemplar of Islamic modernity, appearing to offer the possibility of reconciling the embrace of worldly education with striving to be a pious Muslim. As one young man remarked, 'Earlier they used to say that playing chess is haram, but Khomeini said that it sharpens your brain.' Several others reiterated that Khomeini said it is alright even to go to China – associated with communism – to acquire knowledge. An Iran-returned cleric gushed that in Iran there were even schools for elderly people for 'Ayatollah Khomeini said no person should remain illiterate'.

The aspiration for an education in English began posing a challenge to the authority of older clerics. They were criticised for holding back the progress of the region in the interest of maintaining their power over an illiterate population. This aspiration contributed to opening up a space for the IKMT to propagate its version of Shi'i modernist reform that linked the necessity for access to modern education for all to addressing the subjugation experienced by the people of Kargil on multiple levels. Drawing upon the activist ideology of the Iranian Revolution that instigated a shift away from passively awaiting the arrival of the Twelfth Imam to relieve the world of oppression and suffering, modernist reformists propagated taking the reins of change in one's own hands by reforming both self and society.

At the most immediate level, the fight against 'injustice' was targeted at the alleged unjust functioning of the Islamia School, an issue that became the precursor to the establishment of the IKMT. The Islamia School had been founded in the 1950s by a group of clerics trained in Najaf with the support of rich business families in the region to fill the void created by the partition. In the past, students had trained under renowned teachers in Baltistan, whom they could no longer access after 1949. Over time, the Islamia School became the locus of Shi'i religious authority in the Kargil district. Besides running a seminary and offering moral guidance, it became involved in everyday dispute resolution and backstage political lobbying for parties and candidates. Its imposing three-storey building in the Kargil bazaar was constructed between 1952 and 1958 with the help of donations from people from all walks of life across the region; it thus held the emotional investment of the vast majority. Ayatollah Khoi, the supreme leader in Iraq at the time, is also said to have lent it financial support. Structurally, the Islamia School is headed by a president and supported by a secretary and a treasurer. Together with the Imam-e-Jumma (cleric who delivers the Friday sermon), these positions were all occupied by elderly shaykhs even in the late 2000s. Shaykh Ahmad Mohammadi (d. 2012) had for long held the position of president. He was considered to be one of the most learned ('*alim*) in the region and commanded widespread respect. Shaykh Mohammadi had studied in Najaf under Ayatollah Sayyid Muhsin al-Hakim, a *mujtahid* famous for his work on jurisprudence (*fiqh*).

Leading those demanding greater transparency in the Islamia School was another elderly cleric, Shaykh Hussain Zakiri (d. 2016). He was seen by many IKMT supporters as a cleric willing to respond to changing times.[19] According to Shaykh Zakiri, he had voiced an unspoken grievance that the School was being run like a 'dictatorship': Elections for the post of president had not been held; the use of funds was not transparent; decisions were taken without widespread consultation; younger scholars were seldom given space to speak. Shaykh Zakiri was allegedly expelled from the Islamia School when he started raising some of these issues, and some years later, a group of youth supported him in setting up the IKMT. Its reformist agenda targeted three spheres to bring what they deemed progressive change within Kargili society: modern education, Islamic banking and women's empowerment. Of these, modern education and women's empowerment were linked to broader discourses of selfhood to foster good citizens. Each of these spheres targeted specific sources of perceived injustice or inequality within Kargil that were blamed for hindering the progress of the *qaum* (community). The contestations between 'traditionalist' and 'modernist' thought – represented by the Islamia School and the IKMT – were neither unique to Kargil nor to Shi'i modernist reform.[20] With the founding of the IKMT, Kargili society became deeply split between the politico-religious factions. Even though the majority of people continued to follow the Islamia School, those aligned with the IKMT often articulated their allegiance as a matter of *'aqida* (creed).

'To Teach and Learn Is Worship'

The IKMT lost many supporters after a brief failed experiment with Islamic banking, when a lot of money was allegedly embezzled amid the turmoil of the Kargil War. Nonetheless, its youth base continued to grow over the years for it articulated and acted to address long-held frustrations and the feeling of being 'left behind'. This emotion was not merely one of seeking advancement within modernisation's development teleology. It also expressed a more intangible sentiment that demanded recognition as a community and place in its own right. It is in this context that the IKMT's emphasis on modern education became a lynchpin of its early survival as it emerged as a competitor to the Islamia School.

Acquiring an education in English became increasingly urgent in Kargil, echoing a trend across India. Modern education was seen as affording the possibility of employment in the civil administration. It was also, as I discussed in Chapter 1, driven by the desire to catch up with Leh. As in other parts of India, private schools were seen as offering better-quality education compared to government-run schools. As part of this trend, Shaykh Zakiri and a few others took the credit for founding a private school for modern education in 1984, even prior to the IKMT's establishment. Named the Mutahhari Public School, it claimed to adopt the vision of Shahid Mutahhari (Figure 2.2), a student of Khomeini. With a background in both seminary and university education, his intellectual influence on the Iranian Revolution was as significant as that of Ali Shariati, and he continues to be revered within Iranian seminaries. Much before the revolution, Mutahhari had commented critically on the redundancy of the clerical establishment to the ideological needs of modernity. He wrote, 'The Iranian Muslim intellectuals have become disillusioned with their own *'ulama* because, in the present situation, they do not produce anything but manuals of conduct (*risala-yi 'amaliya*) useful only to the general populace.'[21] Shaykh Zakiri claimed inspiration from Mutahhari's call for *'ulama* to respond to the demands of changing times lest they become redundant.

In the early 1980s common Shi'as had been reluctant to send their children to schools for modern education. In Kargil town, the first private school for modern education – the Suru Valley Public School – was set up in 1982 by Reverend Gergan from the Moravian Mission in Leh. Echoing the comment made by Shaykh Anwar, who spoke of Kargil as a place starved of light, Reverend Gergan said his

Figure 2.2   Main Bazaar, Kargil town, 2009

Source: Photograph by the author.

pastor had described Kargil as a 'wretched place' where 'people had nothing', where there was much work to be done. This left an impression on him. After completing his seminary training in Korea, he decided to work in Kargil.

> On May 27, 1982, we announced admissions to the Suru Valley Public School. The Sunnis and some open-minded Shi'as took the lead in getting their children admitted. At first people only brought boys for admission. But the teachers refused to make it into a boy's school. I never made Suru Valley a Christian School. It was a secular school. You cannot bring in religion as an obstacle to learning a, b, c, d. I never said you have to become a Christian to learn a, b, c, d. My involvement was like the salt in Khamiri roti [Kashmiri bread].... Then more private schools started opening, like the Mutahhari Public School; in one way as a competition, that we will also teach a, b, c, d.

The foundation of Mutahhari Public School by a religious organisation lent studying in English unqualified legitimacy in the years to come, sparking off a veritable flood of English-medium schools across the region. The *ulama* of the IKMT ran the affairs of Mutahhari Public School indirectly, leaving the curriculum and teaching to those trained in the secular education system. On the face of it, religious influence was only discernible in the green school uniforms that they claimed were designed with inspiration from Iran, the singing of religious hymns at morning assembly and the closure of the school on Shi'i ritual occasions in addition to government-mandated holidays. While the main focus was on worldly education, the IKMT produced special books published in Delhi with the help of the Iran Cultural Centre to teach children 'good values' and 'correct ritual practice'. [22] Children from Mutahhari School also participated in various events organised by the IKMT, which were key sites for ideological inculcation. As in other government schools for secular education across erstwhile J&K, a shaykh was deputed to teach Persian and Arabic. Over the years, several branches of Mutahhari Public School came up across the district.

Some years later, the Islamia School opened the Jaffaria Academy for Modern Education, named after the sixth Imam, Jaffar Sadiq, who is revered by Shi'as as a great scholar. For about a decade or more, as factional politics between the IKMT and Islamia School reached a peak, the majority of IKMT supporters enrolled their children in Mutahhari Public School, while those aligned with Islamia School tended to favour the Jaffaria Academy. Modern education as a locus of intra-sectarian competition reflected trends in other parts of India. [23] In Kargil, however, Shi'as claimed inspiration from West Asia. Over time, this divide between the IKMT and the Islamia School supporters melted away as everyone just wanted the best education for their children.

The thrust on modern education was not reserved for men. It aligned with another sphere of the IKMT's social reform agenda that was presented as 'women's empowerment'. Drawing upon the Islamic Republic's discourses on women, the IKMT started emphasising the integral part played by women in a society's progress. It asserted that women, too, could participate in various professions in the public realm alongside fulfilling their primary role of nurturing children and the household. Thus, women ought to be entitled to modern education. This again challenged a traditionalist stance in Kargil that had discouraged women's education in the past. In her seventies, with a faltering memory, Ustani Khadija from the elite Munshi family was the rare educated woman of her generation. She became one of the first women teachers in the district. She recalled the state of women's education in Kargil when she was growing up:

I was the first woman to study. When I used to study, the aghas hated us. Girls did not talk to us. Their parents did not allow them to play with us. There was no school for girls in Kargil in those days. When I was in class five [about ten–twelve years old], the government opened a school for girls but people were against this.

No one sent their girls to school except for some Hindu and Sikh shopkeepers.
I went to the school along with my three sisters.

This taboo on women's education in the past became evident from the fact that
many women who were in their forties and fifties in the late 2000s could not
speak or understand Urdu. This was a marker of literacy as Urdu was introduced
in government schools in J&K after 1947.[24] The IKMT's appropriation of
the Islamic Republic's discourse on women found an immediate niche in such
a context, offering women the possibility of the freedom to study. The classics
of Indian reformist discourses for women dating to the colonial period such as
Bihisthi Zewar,[25] a monumental didactic work on the benefits of female education,
were seldom referenced. It was the perceived status and lives of pious women in
Iran after the revolution that were upheld as inspiration. Discourses for 'women's
empowerment' were an important strand of travelling theory. Gendered ideologies
experienced by many as stifling in the Islamic Republic of Iran were seen as offering
degrees of freedom in Kargil at a particular historical juncture.[26]

Gendering Reform

A marked difference between Islamic reform in the colonial period in India and
modernist Shi'i reformist discourse was the emphasis placed on women's access
to and presence in public space. During the colonial era, women were relegated
to the private sphere, which came to be seen as a sort of 'fortress of Islam in a
sea of hostility'.[27] In contrast to this, modernist reformist discourses in Kargil
reflected the Islamic Republic's politics of gender segregation, where a shift from
prohibition to provision and protection characterised the reshaping of public space.
The production of new subjects drew on modern authoritative concepts and
discourses such as urban justice, women's rights and public health. New spaces
in Iran in the 1990s, such as women-only public parks to enable outdoor exercise,
illustrated that women were recognised as both mothers of the nation (with needs)
and citizens (with rights).[28] The IKMT's discourse of 'women's empowerment'
opened up public space to women in Kargil in forms that not only mimicked Iran
but also were distinct from it.

In the past, women's public presence in Kargil – of which the bazaar is a widely
used metaphor – was looked askance. The older generation recalled how women
were seldom seen in the bazaar in the past. They largely were confined to the
home, worked in the fields or tended to livestock. Since the late 1980s, women
in Kargil began to acquire modern education, enabling them to seek professional
jobs. Occupations such as teaching and nursing became popular; in later years,

Figure 2.3 A woman shopkeeper at a kitchenware shop in Apo Bazaar, Kargil town, 2015

Source: Photograph by the author.

women also became doctors and engineers. Women began to travel to work, taking public transport. Sharing a seat with an unknown man on the bus did not raise any eyebrows. Several Muslim women also ran shops in the bazaar in Kargil town (Figure 2.3). In the past, most women shopkeepers were usually Buddhist or from the small community of Tibetan exiles.

Women also began to slowly venture into restaurants and teashops in the bazaar to share in the luxury of eating out. This growing presence of women in public space was to a significant extent an outcome of a gradual process and not attributable only to modernist reform. Still, as a boy in his late teens observed in 2009: 'Unlike the Buddhist women who roam freely in the bazaar, Muslim girls do not linger after finishing their snack or tea.' It was also rare to see women in the bazaar after the *azan* (call to prayer) at dusk. Thus, a sense of tentativeness marked women's movements in public spaces in the 1990s and 2000s. As their hesitation gradually diminished, some men responded with mockery and sarcasm. When women from Hardas village marched to Kargil town to protest the Hill Council and the district administration's neglect of the acute water problem in their village, a man standing outside the Islamia School remarked, 'These women only want to do propaganda.' Another young shopkeeper laughed and made fun of them: 'These women just use the excuse of water to come to the bazaar to eat *momo*s and *thukpa* [Tibetan dumplings and noodle soup].' It was this prevailing *attitude* to women's presence in public spaces that was challenged by the IKMT's reformist agenda.

Women's presence in public space was propagated by the IKMT with reference to the Islamic Republic's moral discourse that preached strict adherence to the hijab (headscarf). The IKMT exhorted women to wear the hijab in a 'proper' way, chastising the casual manner in which they draped their colourful *dupatta*s. Many women aligned to the IKMT could be recognised by the way they wrapped their headscarves tightly around their faces, covering a greater part of the forehead in Iranian-style hijab. Shi'i modernists in Kargil were, however, extremely critical of the *niqab* (face veil), associating it with Wahhabi or 'fundamentalist' (*kattar*) Islam. One day a student asked her teacher at an IKMT Qur'an school whether women should cover their faces as many Muslim women in other parts of India did. Evidently irritated by the question, she replied, 'If we did that, we would not be able to do any work.' The teacher reiterated that while veiling is essential to a woman's morality, a full burqa would prevent her from entering several professions. This question reflected how young people in Kargil were increasingly influenced by images of Islamic propriety from other parts of India. Rather than being blindly received, reformist discourses from Iran were often judged with reference to practices in other Muslim communities in India.

Mimicking Iran, the IKMT also started organising special events for women. The birthday of Zainab, Imam Husayn's sister, was celebrated as 'Nurse Day' for she is believed to have nursed Islam back to life after the Battle of Karbala. In 2020, this day was dedicated to frontline health professionals to honour their service during the COVID-19 pandemic. One of the most popular events was the annual celebration of the birthday of Fatima Zahra, the Prophet's daughter, as 'International Women's Day' (*yaum-e-khawatin*), a designation given to this ritual occasion by the Islamic Republic.[29] The IKMT's women's cell, the Zainabia Women Welfare Society, was put in charge of organising this event. A few days prior to the event in 2008, the head of the Zainabia showed me letters printed on the IKMT's letterhead that were being dispatched to various departments of the district administration to request a generator, a water tanker, a tent and other infrastructure necessary for the gathering. This clearly indicated cooperation between the state and religious institutions as part of the negligible freedoms allowed on this Shi'i frontier. In the days leading up to *yaum-e-khawatin*, posters of women in Iran were displayed in strategic places in the bazaar.

One poster showed photos of Iranian women in hijab in different roles – from being in the army to TV show anchors, with a quote by Imam Jaffar Sadiq: 'Modesty is the symbol of faith and whosoever has no modesty (hijab), has no religion.' Regardless of their factional affiliation, large numbers of women, especially from Kargil town, enthusiastically participated in this all-women's event. Celebrated as *choti* Eid (minor Eid), they came dressed in their best clothes and fingernails freshly coloured with henna. It was as much an occasion for them to socialise as to listen to lectures on Shi'i role models for women, or to share in the excitement of maybe winning a prize in the Qur'an quiz. At the end of the *majlis*, they surged towards the van parked outside the tent from which the *tabarruk* (blessing) of yellow rice was being distributed. Men could not deny their wives and daughters permission to participate in the Eid of Fatima Zahra.

The Zainabia Women Welfare Society also instituted daily classes for women during the month of Ramadan. Focusing on Qur'anic exegesis and question-and-answer sessions relating to correct religious practice, these classes were also a space for women to perform the noon prayer collectively. For many women, performing *namaz* together was perhaps the most valuable aspect of the *majlis*. They would often come with their toddlers, whose little figures bobbed out among the sea of prostrating women, as a shaykh from the IKMT led the prayer. During these lectures, those who chatted were told to keep quiet. They were exhorted to learn and not just focus on *matam* and prayer, important as these may be. 'You talk to *khuda* [god], but you don't know why?', 'You pray morning and evening, but why?' asked Shaykh Rajai in one such *majlis*. Most of the lectures were devoted to explaining the finer details of correct Islamic practice (*ahkam*) and the logic behind belief.

In a Ramadan *majlis* in 2011, a special speaker had been invited from the district medical department to talk to the women on vaccinations and issues of health and hygiene. A question that women frequently asked was whether it is permissible to postpone a menstrual cycle by taking medicine while on Hajj or *ziyarat* (Shi'i pilgrimage). Norms of purity and pollution prohibit women from reading prayers while menstruating. Consequently, they lose the opportunity to gain the additional merit that accrues from praying in particularly sacred spaces such as the shrines of the Imams. Clerics explained that some *mujtahid*s permit women to take medicines to prevent menstruation while on pilgrimage. Such spaces thus reframed ideas of proper religious practice.

Women were told to conduct themselves in public space with modesty, confidence and discipline through embodied practices like talking softly but confidently, to not make eye contact with strange men in the bazaar, but also to claim public space through participation in educational forums, including protest marches. Over the years, they began to be mobilised to join protest marches behind men on important ritual occasions such as the Day of Quds.[30] A separate seminary for women was opened in 2008. Called Jami'at al-Zahra, it was named after one of the two seminaries for women in Qum and advertised as the first 'Islamic Institute' for women in the region. Jami'at al-Zahra expanded over the years and started following the curriculum set by Al-Mustafa International University in Qum. By 2018, women in Kargil were also gathering alongside men for the Eid ul-Fitr prayer in public space; they were no longer confined to the home for this special occasion.

At the helm of these all-women's spaces was a newly trained cadre of women preachers, popularly referred to as *hajji mo*.[31] A small but growing number of women trained in Iranian seminaries acted as the emblems of and spokespersons for reformist discourses on empowerment of women. The *hajji mos* had typically studied for a few years in Jami'at al-Zahra[32] or Bint al-Huda in Qum.[33] They were easily recognised by the Iranian *chador* they adorned; the *chador* seemed to be the female equivalent of the cleric's turban and cloak in Kargil's context.

I would frequent a Qur'an school for girls in Kargil town run by the IKMT. Regular interactions with Hajji Amina, the teacher, and students there gave me further insight into the gendering of reformist discourse and the affective attachment to Iran.

Hajji Amina: Preacher, Wife, Mother and Her Self

Carefully wrapped in her *chador*, Hajji Amina walked a few miles every afternoon to the Kargil bazaar to hold classes at a *maktab* (Qur'an school) for girls. Once inside, she would shed the *chador* to reveal a long Kashmiri-style abaya. As the class progressed, her carefully cultivated solemn demeanour would transform to reveal a jovial young woman who shared a light-hearted camaraderie with her students. One Friday, before the other students arrived, huddling into her abaya, Hajji Amina remarked she was cold, having just bathed and washed her hair since it was *jum'a* (Friday). She candidly pulled out her still wet tresses from under her hijab and recalled wistfully, 'My hair is so long now. When I was in Iran, I used to keep it short. Now my husband likes it long.' In the first few years after returning from Iran, it appeared that she would also thread her eyebrows, the mark of a married woman in Iran.

Upon getting married at the age of eighteen, Hajji Amina joined her husband in Iran, who was studying there at the time. Looking a little worn out one day, she told me how she got very tired every day as she woke with the *azan* (call to prayer) at dawn and after praying started making *roti*s (leavened bread) for breakfast. Suddenly in mid-sentence her eyes lit up and she recalled:

> When I first went to Iran, I did not know how to cook anything except rice as my mother used to make the *roti*s at home. My husband used to cook in those days. In fact, in Iran, we always bought fresh *roti*s from the bazaar every morning. We would also often go out to restaurants to eat, and to parks and cinemas.

Then she added with a sigh: 'Now my life in Kargil is so different'. The idea of romance excited Hajji Amina. Knowing I was unmarried, she looked at me with a glint of mischief in her eyes one day and teased, 'But surely you must have an *ashiq* (lover)? Come on, everyone in this world has an *ashiq*, even here in Kargil.' I expressed surprise, wondering aloud where young boys and girls in Kargil courted. 'Of course they don't meet in the bazaar for that instantly leads to gossip. They go and meet in faraway and lonely places. Earlier lovers would send letters to each other through friends. It used to be great fun. Now romance develops over the mobile phone,' she replied, giggling.

Hajji Amina had studied at the Jami'at al-Zahra seminary in Qum for five years. Praising the education system in Iran, she remarked:

> In Iran the system is so good that there are schools even for older, uneducated women. Children there don't go for tuition as the mothers themselves are educated and can teach them at home. My daughter's school in Iran held regular meetings to explain to parents how to help children with their studies.... There is nothing like this in Kargil.

Recalling her daily routine in Iran, she said, 'When we lived in Iran, all of us studied – every morning, the agha [referring to her husband] went to his college, I went to mine, and my daughter to her school.' Hajji Amina constantly reiterated to her students the importance of the hijab for it allowed a woman 'to do many things', always with reference to women's lives in Iran. She described Jami'at al-Zahra in Qum as a place that offered every facility to girls – they could even go swimming there. In 2009, when the Green Movement protests were raging in Iran, I mentioned the political turmoil to her. With a grave look on her face, she said, 'We were all very tense earlier as Iran is the only *markaz* [centre]. In reality, however, the protests were confined to only a few areas of Tehran, and also the situation improved after last Friday's *khutba* [sermon] delivered by the *rahbar* [Ayatollah Khamenei].'

Hajji Amina's reminiscences of Iran juxtaposed with her life in Kargil lend insight into the appeal of Islamic Republic-style women's emancipation and the consequent romanticisation of the lifestyle of women in Iran by the *hajji mo*s. Although Jami'at al-Zahra may have 'lost its modernism' and become a 'bastion of the school of traditional jurisprudence',[34] in Kargil's context, Iranian seminaries were perceived as 'modern' as much for the facilities they offered as for the prospect of higher religious education. Nostalgia for life in Iran was not expressed solely in terms of an Islamic moral discourse. Kargili women in Iran could experience public space in ways that were alien to Kargil. Small pleasures of social life such as visiting the cinema or buying bread from the bazaar were perceived as luxuries in the context of life in Kargil. Going for a picnic with family in a public garden or visiting the shrine of Fatemeh Masume on Thursday evenings was an outing they cherished. Thus, contrary to their public appearance, the subjectivity of women like Hajji Amina was shaped by the intersection of emotional and intellectual attachments and Shi'i piety. Iranian modernity was a model for emulation for a host of factors that lay beyond seminary walls.

Women's Selfhood

The Qur'an school where Hajji Amina taught was housed in two modest rented rooms in a newly constructed building looking out onto the River Suru, running through Kargil town. A photograph of the then Iranian president Ahmadinejad hung on a wall leading into a corridor. Outside the last curtained door, shoes of various sizes lay piled in an untidy heap. Inside, a group of girls between the ages of five or six and late teens sat on the floor in small groups reciting the Qur'an. Most of them wore colourful *salwar-kameez* with *dupatta*s draped around as headscarves while a few girls had pinned theirs more tightly around their foreheads with paperclips. When I walked in, they would all shake hands with me in turn. On most days, a smaller group of girls in their late teens would come to learn Farsi, *akhlaq* (morality and ethics) and *ahkam* in the early afternoon. Most of the girls in this group had either passed their matriculation or dropped out of school. Many of the older girls saw the Qur'an school as an avenue for pursuing some sort of knowledge even after leaving school. It was also a respite from the daily domestic routine for a couple of hours. Then around 4 p.m., younger girls, many still in their school uniforms, came to recite the Qur'an. On Fridays, the routine changed to include reading the *Du'a-e-Kumail* after their lessons.

One Friday in 2009, Hajji Amina told the girls that they would also start preparations for the special programme that was being organised for the upcoming Shab-e-Barat (birthday of the Twelfth Imam) celebration. That year the girls would not only sing some religious songs (*nath-i sharif*) but also perform a short play. The rehearsals started with the *hajji mo* playing a *nath-i sharif* in Farsi from her mobile phone for the girls to imitate the correct accent and words. A couple of girls practised comparing the programme in Urdu, Farsi and English. A little while later, a young man arrived to train the girls in the art of theatre.

It was an adaptation of a play that Hajji Amina explained she had seen in Iran. The play presented a critique of traditional practices of healing – such as going to a *lama* or *lhamo* (Buddhist oracles) or *akhun* (Muslim amulet givers). The girls were told to sit in a circle. Hajji Mo had ordered some *samosas* (a deep fried snack consisting of a triangle of thin pastry filled with meat or vegetables) as they would all be staying longer than usual. As the male teacher allotted roles and enacted them to show the girls what they need to do, they repeated a few dialogues with hesitation. Preparing a play was a new and exciting experience. It entailed shedding shyness and getting into the skin of a character. In the play a young girl who repeatedly falls ill is taken by her father to different types of healers in search of a cure. The young man enacted the scene when the girl is taken to a Buddhist *lama*, chanting a mantra while rotating his prayer wheel to cure her. Her next visit is to the *akhun*, who reads a *du'a* and blows air on her face. The girls periodically burst into shy giggles, thoroughly amused by these enactments. Everyone, including Hajji Amina, appeared to be having fun. She explained the message the play was meant to impart to its audience: 'These are all "unscientific" and "irrational" practices. If people feel better after visiting faith healers, it is because of their belief and not the efficacy of the practice itself. Ill people should be taken to a trained medical doctor.' The significance of the play lay beyond its message of the importance of rational practice. Its performance was a pedagogical tool to impart confidence to the girls, to craft young women who could hold their own in public forums.

Such spaces became important sites for the IKMT to propagate the Islamic Republic's moral discourse on women. Unlike Iran, however, these new spaces for women in Kargil were largely confined to the religious realm. Though modernist reformist discourse encouraged women's participation in public, professional life, it emphasised the moral primacy accorded to their roles as mothers and wives. What was the impact of these discourses on women's subjectivity? How did they respond to the reiteration of normative roles?

As the rights of women to study modern education, to exercise, to become professionals gained greater traction, many younger women did not privilege attending *majalis* if these clashed with going to school and college. Even for those who proclaimed allegiance to the IKMT, there was still a long way to go before Kargil could achieve the level of what they perceived as women's emancipation in Iran. A friend quipped that men in Iran did not have as much power over their wives! Another young woman, who had returned to Kargil in 2020 after finishing an MA in geology from Kashmir University, confided, 'Women might get educated, but then they have to marry and can't do a job sometimes.... But anyway, education is an end in itself, for becoming a good human.'

Her pithy remark signified the conflicting binds that Kargili women continued to deal with. But subtle reconfigurations of gender roles created some room for manoeuvre.

The repeated glorification of the role of the mother was couched in the responsibility she holds to raise enlightened children. A *hajji mo* stated in a speech on *yaum-e-khawatin*:

> It is only an educated woman who can give her children, the future of society, a proper Islamic upbringing. If we want to improve our social environment, the first thing to do is to 'make' our family. Society is a sum total of households. A *du'a* is not enough to enlighten a child; the mother must be educated. Her thinking has a direct impact on children.

This marked a shift in the meaning attached to the role of the woman from being just the 'bearer of the womb' to being a nurturer and educator, a role traditionally played by men.[35] The prime responsibility for bringing up a rational and moral next generation that would work for the progress of the community and nation was placed on the mother. Echoing Iran, this discourse was tied to the larger project of both men and women being important to the making of the nation (*millat*),[36] extending the progress of the *qaum* from community to region and nation. Linking this reconfigured definition of the mother to a wider project of 'nation formation' was neither unique to Shi'i reformism nor Kargil, but it was again attributed to the Islamic Republic.[37]

While reformist discourses were authorised with reference to Iran, they were distilled through the Indian context to make sense of them. This became evident in the time devoted to the question-and-answer part in Ramadan *majalis*. This not only reflected ongoing calibrations between revolutionary ideologies with negotiating belonging to India, but also signalled critical reflection, especially among younger women.

Reception of Reformist Discourse

A popular story in women's *majalis* related their status in society before the advent of Islam, in the time of *jahiliyat* in Arabia: It was a time when baby girls were buried alive while goats were sacrificed in celebration of a boy's birth. It was only when the Prophet accorded special status to his daughter, Fatima Zahra, that people realised that the birth of a girl is a gift that must be treasured. When relating this story in some *majalis*, Kargili preachers compared the time of *jahiliyat* in Arabia with the custom of *sati*[38] in Hindustan. They emphasised how this practice came to be disparaged by Hindu reformist discourse several centuries after Islam elevated the status of women in Arabia. This comparison challenged the widely held perception of women's subordination and Islam being synonymous with each other. The story flowed into explaining the importance of hijab: 'If women are akin to precious jewels, they must be safeguarded by being covered.' The hijab became the marker of an Islamic society distinct from its barbaric predecessors or indeed even its contemporary counterparts. Thus, the polemic: 'It is because women in the West roam around naked with their heads uncovered that there is a greater incidence of rape in their societies.' From this perspective the absence of veiling was made an index of the *jahiliyat* of a society.

This narrative clearly held appeal for women in Kargil. Many of them would not only vigorously nod their heads in agreement during *majalis* but also repeat it in the context of our own cross-cultural conversations on the status of women in society. Their reception of this moral discourse was sieved through Hindi soap operas on television that depicted the lives of Hindu households in mainland India.[39] It had the effect of stripping this moral discourse of the virulence lent by its anti-Western rhetoric. I was told countless times, 'You need not cover your head as your religion does not tell you to.' I also was often asked how many siblings I had. My response, 'one sister', would provoke sympathy: 'Too bad you don't have a brother'. So, when I teased them with the observation that the 'precious' status of women in Islam in this narrative did not seem to influence the sense of misfortune that Kargili women continued to attach to not having a son, they countered, 'Yes, but we would never abort a female foetus as happens in so many places in Hindustan.'

Marriage was a favourite topic of discussion, inside and outside *majalis*. Conversations on marriage were often provoked by a rising trend of 'run-away' marriages – a euphemism for love marriages and elopement – that the region was witnessing. With the increased presence of women in public spaces, co-educational schools and colleges, as well as ideas of romance received through television and social media, more and more young people in Kargil were marrying for love. While courtship in public was a rare sight, certain spaces like the bus station, a public garden in Kargil town or Muharram *majalis* provided young men and women opportunities to 'check each other out'. Unlike the past, when attractions were fleeting moments of silent communication, the mobile phone ushered in a new era of romance. Its privacy enabled fleeting attractions to transform into enduring courtship. People joked, 'The mobile has become the new *halpa* [traditional matchmaker] in our society.' Everyone secretly enjoyed the prospect of a romantic rendezvous, but many people also disapproved of love marriages. This related to the perceived moral decline of society in 'modern' times, portrayed as a sign of sexual licentiousness in society by reformist discourse.

'Do you want *Hukumat-e-Islami* or *Hukumat-e-sexy* in Kargil?' a cleric admonished the youth in a Muharram *majlis*, referring to young women who wore make-up. The legitimacy of love marriage was also linked to the injunction to ask for the father's permission to marry. Young women asked, 'If the mother is so important, why is the permission of a father so essential at the time of marriage?'[40] Despite the idealisation of arranged marriage, run-away marriages continue in Kargil and were often even pre-arranged in order to cut down wedding expenses. Lavish weddings where Kashmiri *wazwan* was served and *jahez* (dowry in the form of household furniture and electronic consumer goods) was given were becoming a norm among the wealthy. This placed pressure on those who could not afford these and became a source of consternation for others concerned with the negative influence of social customs in the Valley and beyond reaching Kargil.

The Islamic Republic's moral discourse on marriage found an ironically appropriate home in this context. Even as preachers reiterated the necessity of marriage in Islam, they urged young people to wait until they had educated themselves and were 'mature' enough to handle the responsibilities of marriage. They stressed the importance of looking for enduring qualities of belief and sincerity in a prospective partner, instead of getting carried away by outward characteristics like fashion and romantic love, considered superficial and ephemeral. Parents were told not to force their children to marry a person of their choice and that prospective partners must be allowed time to get acquainted with each other. The ideal relationship between spouses was presented as one of 'friendship', echoing liberal ideas of companionate marriage, even though emphasis was placed on each partner fulfilling the specific roles assigned to them to nurture a happy household. Although the immediate goal of this discourse was to curb the perceived moral decline of Kargili society, it created some space for women (and men) to choose a life partner. Using the logic of this discourse to reject their parents' choice, it became a means of exercising individual agency. Furthermore, the role of the woman as wife was reconfigured as the man's companion in life rather than a mere fulfiller of biological roles.[41] In Kargil, women filtered this discourse through ideas echoing liberal feminism. This was reflected in questions asked at *majalis*: 'So if a woman is indeed the equal of a man, why can't she become an Imam-e-Jumma or a *mujtahid*?' Answers to such questions emphasised the idea of 'equality with difference' (*masavat*), which asserted that God created biological differences between men and women to fulfil different roles in society. The work of nurturing the husband (*shauhardari*) and household (*khanedari*) was presented as the woman's *jihad*; she did not need to step into the battlefield to attain paradise.

Gendered reformist ideas and ideologies propagated through sermons and lectures, and experimental ways such as role-playing, propagated a 'new model of ideal moral womanhood'.[42] Similar to piety movements in other parts of the world, women in Kargil were attracted to reformist spaces, not towards any political end but primarily to learn about correct religious practice (*ahkam*) and to earn merit (*sawab*). I suggest, however, that the effects of moral discourses exceeded the objective of moral womanhood as an outcome of the way the discourse was *received* by women.

In focusing on the reception of reformist discourses, I consider the issue of 'agency' and 'freedom' somewhat differently from Saba Mahmood whose seminal work on the mosque movement in Cairo[43] has shaped the anthropological debate on gender and Islam since its publication in 2005. Although Kargili women participated in these spaces to cultivate 'ideal virtuous selves', resonating with Mahmood's analysis, agency was not derived primarily through the habitation of norms to which they subscribed, such that embodied submission to religious authority became instinctive. I found that Shi'i women themselves held dear certain ideas of freedom and agency that did not align neatly with either Western liberal ideas of freedom that Mahmood critiques or with the denial of freedom that critics of reformist discourses allege. I suggest that perceptions and experiences of agency and freedom are deeply contextual and shaped by individual biography such that the 'narrative arc of life'[44] of individual women becomes ethnographically important. Even if reformist discourses were framed in opposition to Western liberal feminism, their reception by Muslim women negated the sharp contrast that is set up between 'liberal' and 'orthodox' through which ideas of agency and freedom are imputed meaning.

As the biography of Hajji Amina has illustrated, modernist Shi'i ideas, as they travelled across contexts, found different interpretations, offering differing degrees of freedom. Various symbolic codes, of which the hijab is an example par excellence, which are seen as being imposed 'from above' are not 'simply imposed'. Fariba Adelkhah argues that these are 'the product of multiple popular practices, *multiple arts de faire* or practices of everyday life that contribute to the invention of Islamic modernity'.[45] Following Adelkhah, I suggest that from the perspective of individual room to manoeuvre, freedom becomes a relative concept. This is not to reproduce some prescriptive notion of freedom that insidiously works its way back to the norms of liberal discourse. But neither does this mean that women do not hold notions of becoming freer: freedom defined from their own perspective and context. Women in Kargil would often articulate being allowed modern education in terms of greater *azadi*. However, when a trainer from Delhi held a workshop at a local non-governmental organization (NGO) and tried to question the hijab, it annoyed them. They did not want to be rescued from Islam by outsiders.[46] Thus, rather than imposing prescriptive notions of freedom, their relationship to reformist discourse is perhaps better interpreted as a 'practice of freedom'.[47]

It was at the level of individual thought that the affective charge of modernist Shi'i reform was perhaps most intense for it touched upon core Islamic precepts underlying the formation of a pious Shi'i subjectivity.

Passion for Reason

Even prior to the availability of new media, the appreciation for 'critical debate', which was influenced by revolutionary ideology,[48] was simmering among a few individuals. One of them was Haider *sahib*. Many years ago, he had challenged a respected cleric of the Islamia School on the inclusion of a particular word in a hadith. Unconvinced by the shaykh's answer to his doubt, he had continued to question him. This was not something the cleric could countenance. Eventually, Haider left the Islamia School as his frustration with the *ulama* grew and became a staunch supporter of the IKMT.

Haider *sahib* was well known in Kargil town for his independent thinking and religious knowledge despite a lack of formal training. In the early years of my fieldwork, he was employed in the police and was posted in the Valley. He would return to Kargil every few weeks to meet his family. Often dressed in a polo-neck cardigan and a tweed jacket over trousers, he had a determined and distinguished bearing and evoked for me the archetypical cinematic image of a philosophy professor. The first time I met him was among a group of his friends, in their early to late thirties, from different backgrounds and professions – politician, veterinary doctor and NGO worker – I was acquainted with. All of them were educated people with a terrific sense of humour. They would generously offer suggestions for my research and immediately endorsed my interest in wanting to speak with Haider *sahib*.

Quite openly sceptical of clerics, this group of friends wistfully reminisced about the classes that Haider *sahib* held in 1987 for a closed circle of like-minded people, where he delivered lectures to provoke critical engagement on religious topics. In that first meeting, as these men praised Haider for liberating their minds, he sat smiling, quietly appraising me from the other end of the room. When I was leaving, perhaps visibly disappointed by his silence, he invited me to join the group on a work outing to Drass the following day. The next day, the others insisted that I sit in the front seat of the jeep, a customary way of according respect to guests. When Haider *sahib* teased them for 'small' thinking, they quickly relented, and I found myself in the back easily absorbed into the bonhomie of this group of friends, clearly delighted to be spending a day out in the countryside in each other's company. The banter of the journey soon gave way to serious discussion as Haider *sahib* asked me what I understood by the term *din*. To me it simply meant religion, the common meaning of the word. I had a sense I was being tested. He shook his head and said, 'Unless you understand the difference between *mazhab* and *din*, you will not understand anything.' Puzzled, I could only say, 'Yes, but both mean religion...?' The others laughed telling me, 'Ah! Now you will get a taste of what Haider is all about.' And indeed, I did get a flavour of his thinking, as he explained to me:

> *Mazhab* is needed in order to reach and understand *din*. It is like a pathway. Try and understand this difference through the *kalimat tauhid*, the opening lines of the Qur'an: 'Lā 'ilāha 'illa Allāh Muhammad-ur Rasūlullāh' [There is no god but God, and Muhammad is the messenger of God]. In the two words *'la 'ilaha*, *'la* is the negation of any other and *'ilaha* is the validation of only One. This is the essence of Islam. Islam is equal to *din*, the one and only Muhammad Rasūlullāh', while *mazhab* encompasses 124,000 *pigambar*s [messengers of God] starting from Adam. Most people take *mazhab* to be the ultimate destination. But *mazhab* only provides the *qanun*, the rules and rituals by which to lead life, while *din* constitutes the *a'in*, or fundamental principle of belief. It is *mazhab* that distinguishes one religion from another, whereas *din*, as submission before God, is common to all religions. It is the first principle or basic truth, which all religions accept, and leads further to an examination of other truths, such as compassion and honesty, which no religion negates.

Haidar *sahib*'s commentary made sense to me only later, after much pondering. I began to see why his thinking on a higher philosophical plane would not be easily acceptable to standard clerical discourse. For although he reaffirmed Islam and the fundamental tenet of the faith, by distinguishing *din* from *mazhab*, he seemed to suggest a space for a non-dogmatic interpretation that spoke to a more universal human condition.[49]

Later in Drass, as the chilly spring morning gave way to strong mountain sunshine, while the others inspected a potential site for a hydraulic project, Haidar *sahib* told me about the hardships he had faced in life:

> My family was very poor. When I was in the government middle school, I needed 50 rupees to register for the class ten [matriculation] exams. But I didn't have money even for this. So I went to the turbaned people [clerics] as they gave money to the poor. But they refused, saying I was studying the other type of education. They would only give me money for religious education. Failing to get money for the exam, I went to Leh to do labour work. Since my handwriting in Urdu and Hindi

was very good, I managed to get a job as a *munshi* (scribe) at a construction site where I had to enter the names of labourers in a register. I used to read a lot of novels at the time. Authors like Ibn Habib, Iqbal.... I would relate stories from the books I read to people and soon became very popular among them. I loved reading. Many years later I decided to study the Qur'an on my own. First it went three feet over my head. But then I slowly started analysing every word. I was also deeply influenced by the works of Ali Shariati.

Ideologues like Ali Shariati, influenced by thinkers like Frantz Fanon and Jean-Paul Sartre, for instance, argued that Islam already contained within it all progressive Western thought.[50] But people needed to access this 'authentic' Islam through their own readings of it rather than through the clergy.

Over the years, every time I visited Kargil and met Haidar *sahib*, he would test my capacity to reflect upon the question of God through the lens of whatever philosopher he was reading at the time – ranging from Muhammad Iqbal to Sartre and Friedrich Nietzsche – in Urdu translation. In 2015, as we sat around sipping tea in one of the newer restaurants in the Kargil bazaar, a friend of his teased him for being a 'communist atheist' when he started discussing Nietzsche – who had famously proclaimed 'God is dead' – with me. Although Haidar *sahib* was reformist-minded, he was not uncritical of Iran: 'Why don't they [Iran] send us *mujtahids* or people who are knowledgeable to give lectures on particular topics? Iran is foisting Farsi here.' A few days earlier Haidar *sahib* had gone for the Friday prayers to Minji village on the outskirts of Kargil town where the IKMT held *jum'a* on the premises of the Imam Khomeini Madrasa for boys. 'There a person was speaking in Farsi. A boy in front of me was crying. I asked him, "Why are you crying? You don't understand Farsi." He replied, "Because others are crying",' Haidar *sahib* related to elaborate his point about unthinking imitation.

I became further acquainted with Haidar *sahib*'s thinking through his sons. He had three sons and one daughter. The eldest son had studied in Chandigarh and, while teaching at the Degree College in Kargil, was also studying for the Kashmir Civil Services examination. I would often run into him at the local newspaper shop where he came to buy a copy of an English-language daily. The daughter was studying in the government school. His wife, like most women of her generation, mostly spoke in Purigi, although she understood a little bit of Urdu and was perhaps the most obviously pious person in the family. One day after attending a *majlis* (gathering) commemorating the death anniversary of Fatima Zahra (the Prophet's daughter), which included mourning (*matam*), I naively remarked to Haidar *sahib*'s younger son that many women's tears did not seem 'real'. Much to my surprise, instead of explaining the practice of *matam*, he said:

Most people in Kargil do not really understand what they are shedding tears for. When I go to these *majalis*, many times tears just don't come to my eyes for the *'ulama* repeat the same old *qisas* [stories] year after year without making any connection to modern times. This fails to move me. My father says there is no compulsion to do *matam* if it does not make sense to you. He himself does not like going for such *majalis*.

Haidar *sahib* had inculcated in his sons an attitude of questioning blind faith, of belief based on rationality and of placing any belief in the context of modern realities. On another occasion, his elder son explained the ritual of daily prayer to me as also being good from a 'scientific' point of view: 'It is just like yoga and meditation, an act of concentration and exercise, good for the body and mind.' Haidar *sahib* and his sons would often endearingly tease their mother for being blindly religious. Yet she clearly appreciated the discussions that raged between father and sons. During the Ramadan preaching season, she told me she liked a particular shaykh from Iran best as he explained Islam clearly, with humour and according to current times. Another day she proudly pointed to her husband's modest bookshelf.

Haidar's sons seemed to embody Ali Shariati's teachings, which had influenced their father's thinking. Seeking a 'protestant reformation' in Shi'ism, Shariati urged the educated youth in Iran in the 1970s to read original texts for themselves and to purge religion of superstitious beliefs. Shariati offered a modernist re-interpretation of Shi'ism, attacking traditionalist clergy for corrupt manipulation of religious belief. He placed the 'rational' and 'responsible individual' at the centre of his thinking.[51] In a will that he drew up in 1969, Shariati hoped that his sons would grow up to be independent-minded and travel the world rejecting *tikrar* (repetition), *tarjuman* (translations) and *taqlid* (imitation)[52] – dreams that Haidar *sahib* harboured for his own sons.

Haidar *sahib* encouraged his sons not to follow clerics blindly. The scepticism of his son, Sajjad, towards weeping in *majalis*, though a somewhat extreme sentiment, which most people did not subscribe to during Muharram, reflected a broader discourse propounded by Twelver Shi'i modernist reformists. This was the emphasis placed on the use of *'aql* (rational faculty). Like his father, Sajjad was also aligned with the IKMT and did not practice *zanjirzani* (shedding blood) during Muharram. The IKMT strictly adhered to Ayatollah Khamenei's fatwa banning bloody flagellation. In the Shi'i world while the injunctions of some *mujtahids* followed suit, others left this to the choice of the believer.[53] Those aligned with the Islamia School continued the practice of *zanjirzani* as is the case in Iraq and several other parts of the Shi'i world. IKMT followers explained this ban on flagellation as a move to rectify the image of Shi'as as barbaric in the Western imagination, especially following the fundamentalist portrayal of the Iranian Revolution. Other young men also explained the ban in terms of the everyday exercise of *'aql*.

One summer day, I visited the border village of Badgam that was aligned with the Islamia School, with a staunch IKMT friend, Nasir, who had some relatives there. Criticising the practice of *zanjirzani*, Nasir had once remarked, 'If people really want to shed blood, rather than flagellating themselves and spilling it all over the place, especially in this age of AIDS, they should donate it to a blood bank instead.' Nasir was studying for a master's degree in human rights at a well-known university in Delhi and was actively involved in student politics and debates. Ever agile and inquisitive, he was eager to open the world to his less-exposed friends and relatives in Kargil over his summer holiday visit. He would constantly complain about Kargili youth being 'kept in darkness' by clerics. In his mission to try and enlighten his cousins and to ensure that our sojourn would be 'data rich' for my research, grinning, he purposely provoked his cousins and elderly uncle in Badgam into a discussion on *zanjirzani*.

> Nasir (in a slightly mocking tone): Why do you still take out blood during Muharram?
>
> Uncle (quietly): Out of sadness and *ishq* [love] for Husayn.
>
> Nasir: But why take out blood?
>
> Uncle: Because Husayn's blood flowed....
>
> Nasir: But which *mujtahid* has given permission for *kammazani*?
>
> Uncle: No one has given *hukum* [command]; it is an old custom.
>
> Cousin: They do it in Karbala. Where is the *markaz* [centre] of Islam? The Qur'an tells us.... (Nasir cuts him short).
>
> Nasir (in an impatient, exasperated tone): Which *ayat* of the Qur'an? Give me proof....

This exchange showed that while young men like Nasir had little patience for what they considered 'irrational' thinking, for many Kargilis shedding blood for Imam Husayn was the ultimate act of piety. A friend whose twelve-year-old son had flagellated himself at Muharram asserted with great emotion that 'the fact that people who shed blood do not fall ill or die is proof of the blessing of Imam Husayn bestowed upon that person. It is proof of the sacredness of the act'. The practice of flagellation embodied the tension between the head (*dimag*) and the heart (*dil*).

Touching on the core of people's devotion, it became the most unambiguous marker of factional affiliation.[54]

Every Muharram, the IKMT procession was marked by an absence of bloody flagellation, while the Islamia School continued to endorse the practice. But by Muharram in 2021, I found both institutions had set up blood-donation camps even while Islamia School supporters practised *zanjirzani*. A journalist friend showed me a picture of two army men donating blood at the School's camp. In stark contrast to the Valley, Kargili Shi'as cling to negligible freedoms and highlight any positive interaction with the military. Beneath the freedom to practise their religion publicly was, however, a deeper process of self- and place-making. This was underlined by shifts in conceptions of piety that entwined individual merit with the social and material progress of society.

From 'How' to 'Why'

Modernist reformist discourse placed renewed emphasis on the use of *'aql* – the rational faculty with which every human being is endowed. It is the faculty that governs all other faculties and orders them in harmony with each other.[55] As the foundation of piety, expressed in the concept of *taqwa* (virtuous fear of God), the exercise of *'aql* acquired an enhanced status in the mid-eighteenth century when the Usuli school of Shi'i jurisprudence gained ascendance in Iran. As a reformist Kargili cleric explained to me, *taqwa* is cultivated through the privileging of *'aql* over the base self (*nafs*) by an individual. Ideally, *taqwa* must be integral to any action undertaken by a human being rather than just being a spur to action.[56]

In modernist reformist discourses, subtle shifts in the application of *'aql* became discernible: from the *how* of an action (*ahkam*) to the *why* of an action, to conscious reflection on appropriate *conditions* for action and application of reasoning to make ethical choices. These shifts were again reflected in the questions posed by young men to clerics during the IKMT's Ramadan and Muharram *majalis*. A question that frequently came up related to the appropriate conditions for undertaking the Hajj pilgrimage. Criticising rich people going on pilgrimage several times in their life, a young man sardonically commented, 'The *ka'ba* has become like a car-wash. People feel they can go there again and again to wash off their sins.' Clerics would explain that it was not legitimate to go on Hajj more than once if it was at the expense of children's education or family needs. One shaykh exhorted his audience to understand when an action may or may not be *wajib* (compulsory): 'The Hajj is *wajib* if a person is wealthy. Similarly, *roza* (fasting) is *wajib* only if a person is healthy.' Changes in the structure of Muharram *majalis* reflected the emphasis on using *'aql* in a reflective manner.

The IKMT *majalis* devoted as much time to lectures to educate people about Islam and how it relates to contemporary life as to ritual lamentation. The audience was periodically reminded that the *majlis* is a forum for learning; the motive for attending should not be limited to earning merit by crying.[57] Yet a Kargili student studying in Qum also asserted that weeping in *majalis* is also a symbol of protest, for it is a proclamation that 'we are the party of Imam Husayn'.

In everyday life, young men like Nasir interpreted *'aql* as simply using one's intelligence and 'common sense'. Shaykh Anwar explained this changing disposition among some of the more educated youth in Kargil as the ability to ask questions of *falsafa*, the tradition of philosophical reflection, which saw a renewal in seminaries in Iran after the revolution.[58] 'Many of these questions arose from their knowledge of and discussions with peers from other religions. So they asked why something that is *ja'iz* (permissible) in another religion is considered haram in Islam or vice versa.' 'This kind of questioning,' he added, 'shows that there is progress in their *fikr* [thought] and also compels the *'ulama* themselves to study other religions.' Although the majority of students in Iranian seminaries, including Kargili scholars, still preferred to study *fiqh*, those who chose *falsafa* had begun to be accorded greater respect. This was reflected in the admiration for Shaykh Anwar, who had studied *falsafa* in Qum; many IKMT-aligned youth referred to him as *doktor*. Praising him, a teenaged boy explained to me that the extent of his knowledge was equivalent to someone with a PhD in secular education.[59]

Religious practices are reworked in relation to changing times and spaces. Concerns relating to correct practice or *ahkam* in Kargil emanated from issues related to 'modern' times and the conundrums posed by living in a country where Muslims are in a minority and the overall ethos is not Islamic. For example, a girl studying in high school asked a preacher whether it was permissible for women to enter professions such as the police in non-Muslim societies where the uniform is not Islamic. Another example of the moral dilemmas people grappled with related to the practice of *chattu* – the custom of not accepting food cooked by a non-Muslim – that I discussed in the previous chapter. A young man who did not practise *chattu* claimed to be following the injunctions of his *mujtahid*, Ayatollah Makarim Shirazi, that Shi'as living in countries with large non-Muslim populations should accept food from them to 'maintain good relations'. He added that he had taken up *taqlid* (emulation) of Makarim Shirazi because it appealed to his *'aql*. Another teenager who did not practice *chattu* described himself as having a 'secular' outlook. Such young men often derided those who practised *chattu* for being narrow-minded and not *roshan-fikr* (enlightened). They conjectured that such practices might be a deterrent to getting selected in the Ladakh Scouts regiment of the Indian army that had historically been disproportionately composed of Ladakhi Buddhists, especially before the Kargil War when the state did not trust the Muslims of Ladakh.

We see here how the practice of *chattu* took on ethical significance at the level of individual disposition intimately entwined with negotiations of belonging to Hindustan. It is important to note, however, that it is not as if those who practised *chattu* did not value amicable relations with other communities. Rather, this particular narrative reflected 'morality as a dimension of everyday life', which, as Veena Das argues, may or may not relate to an Islamic teleology.[60] Based on her work in mixed Muslim–Hindu neighbourhoods in Delhi, Das makes an important case for considering relational life itself as a 'form of moral perfectionism', which often privileges the emotions of relating to others even if this entails disregarding proscriptions in authoritative Islamic discourses. Thus, the expression of having a 'secular' attitude – as a practice of secularity – could be understood as a form of moral striving. However, in contrast to Das, I suggest that here the ethics of relating to the 'other' were understood and authenticated from within the Shi'i discursive tradition and did not necessarily entail the disregard of authoritative Islamic discourses. Eschewing the dichotomy of disregard of norms or total submission to them, the contextual and contingent interpretations of Shi'i norms by individuals were illustrations of the conceptualisation of Islamic discursive traditions as offering 'signposts' to followers to guide conduct. This left open room for interpretation, debate, innovation and reformulation that 'unfold through the practices of ordinary people'.[61]

The mark of a modern Shi'a was the ability to discern using *'aql* as to which *mujtahid*'s injunctions best suit the context. This was necessitated as much by the desire to live an ethical life as an individual as by the predicaments of belonging faced by a double minority. Kargili Shi'as distinguished themselves from Muslims in the Valley and other parts of India to project a self-conscious sectarian identity alongside reiterating the necessity of Islamic unity. The effect of invoking the Islamic Republic's conceptions of modernity exceeded the crafting of pious subjects. It was also a call to action.

Call to Action

The emphasis on *'aql* and the affective dispositions it fostered were not confined to the realm of pious self-cultivation or philosophical ponderings. It was translated into a call for action that not only related to the agenda for social reform at the local level but also extended to the predicaments of belonging in Hindustan. A stanza from a poem by Allama Iqbal, one of the most important thinker-philosophers of modern Islam, often quoted by young men aligned with the IKMT, expressed this disposition:

Nikal kar khanaqahon se
adaa kar rasme shabbiri
Ki fakr wah khanaqah hai
Fakat anduh vahdilgiri

(Get out of the *khanaqah*s and perform the ritual of Shabbir [Husayn]
For the poverty of the *khanaqah*s is naught but anxiety and affliction.)[62]

Nasir and his friend Ali had recited these lines to me one day while making our way up a steep slope to the *khanaqah* in Baroo village, a mile away from the Kargil bazaar.[63] The Baroo *khanaqah* is an important site in the sacred geography of the region. People from far and wide travel to the *khanaqah* to pray for divine intervention in life problems, tying threads to mark their devotion just as they do at Sufi shrines. Such is the belief in the miraculous powers of this *khanaqah* that according to local legend its walls constructed themselves. When I expressed an interest in visiting the *khanaqah*, Nasir and Ali had laughed, scoffing that surely an educated person like me did not believe in 'such places'. Then, reciting the lines by Iqbal, Nasir explained that the poet calls out to young people to leave the darkness of *khanaqah*s and fulfil their duty in society. Ali added, '*Khanaqah*s are symbols of blind faith; people who do not use their *'aql* visit *khanaqah*s'. Although an example of the purificatory impulses of reformist Islam,[64] this criticism of faith in *khanaqah*s reflected an important change in conceptions of religiosity in Kargil.

Interpreting the lines of the poem here, Akbar Hyder writes:

> Had Husayn simply valued poverty, then he would have withdrawn into a *khanaqah* and forsaken political activism. But Husayn rose above the epidemic dichotomies of wealth and poverty, asceticism and indulgence, to evoke *khudi*, that higher self which is predicated essentially on love, knowledge, and action.[65]

Iqbal's concept of the higher self (*khudi*) represents the triumph of *'aql* over the base self of the individual. In modernist discourse, the exercise of *'aql* was not restricted to using the 'faculty of moral discrimination'[66] to prevent individual sin. It also must be fostered by and validated through social and political action. The call for action was integral to Iqbal's agenda of socio-religious reform. In this verse, he transforms the meaning of Karbala and Husayn's martyrdom into a political project.[67] Iqbal had called out to Muslims in the Kashmir Valley to awaken their *khudi* to fight Dogra oppression and was critical of Kashmiri Muslim dependence on Sufi practice, for religious tutelage was seen as limiting human action.[68]

The realisation of the higher self must be achieved through both personal faith and 'public piety' wherein 'action in this world is inseparably linked to the world hereafter', laying the foundation for both the spiritual *and* material progress of society.[69] Personal salvation was, then, entwined with activities undertaken in the here and now.[70] Resonant of initiatives among the Shi'as of south Beirut that Lara Deeb writes about, public piety in Kargil found expression in youth voluntary initiatives for the betterment of society at the local level. These meshed with negotiations of belonging. Reformist discourses contributed to the 'freedom' to think critically and act within captivity.

Youth Voluntarism

An ethic of reciprocity and mutual cooperation historically has been the bedrock of Ladakhi society among Buddhists and Muslims. Youth voluntary initiatives were thus nothing new to Kargil but a reflection of this regional ethic. The influence of modernist reform, however, and its call for action in this world provoked new kinds of initiatives that sought to address both the spiritual and material progress of society. While young people in Kargil continued to be involved in serving the community on ritual occasions, from the organisation of weddings to *majalis*, they also started engaging in new activities geared towards social reform. These ranged from forming village education committees that made inspection visits to schools to ensure teachers were showing up for 'duty' to running English coaching classes during winter school holidays.[71]

Another important activity of youth volunteers was to open libraries that would give access to Islamic literature and other resources. With the aim to 'promote religion along with university education', these libraries tapped into Shi'i internationalism's efforts to raise awareness about Islam in the modern world. In 2009, some 'Hussaini youth' set up a library in Kargil, which they proudly called 'The Islamic Cultural Centre'.[72] Housed in two small rooms, it held a diverse collection of books in Urdu, English and Farsi donated by the Iran Cultural Centre in Delhi. Titles ranging from *The Constitution of the Islamic Republic of Iran*, *Anecdotes of Pious Men* by Murtaza Mutahhari, *The World of Fatwas* by Indian journalist Arun Shourie, a critique in Farsi of the *Satanic Verses*, English copies of *Nahj al-Balagha*, to books on computers and English grammar and composition lined the shelves. Separate reading hours were allocated for girls and boys. Although access to an entire virtual world of Shi'i knowledge meant these volumes were seldom read, the library nonetheless afforded a space of refuge.[73]

One autumn afternoon, I found my friend, Zaynab, immersed in a volume in the library. She was a feisty thirty-year-old woman, married, with one son.

Zaynab was studying for an undergraduate degree in Arabic through a correspondence course at Kashmir University, while simultaneously teaching at the Mutahhari Primary School when I first met her with a group of IKMT-aligned women. Ever enthusiastic to have a chat, she started explaining the library's *raison d'être* to me – that it is important for people to come and read for themselves and get acquainted with the true meaning of Islam. Zaynab hoped that the library would eventually become a place for people to get acquainted with each other and have discussions on different topics. Clearly pleased to have company that afternoon, she asked me why I thought God had created this world and human beings. As I struggled to come up with a suitable answer, she cast aside the question and issued forth on how the teachings of all religions are essentially the same: 'Ashoka, who was a Buddhist, preached not to kill any creature, and Wordsworth, the English poet, wrote of how life exists in trees and nature and should not be harmed.' On another day, she showed me samples of artwork that her students had produced at the Mutahhari School, explaining that intelligence could be expressed in so many different ways and must be nurtured as such. Zaynab struck me as a woman whose intellectual capacity exceeded the confines of her life in Kargil. She regretted that she had got married too early and wanted to study and explore the world. As I got to know her better, she would also mock the *hajji mo*s for creating a cult of the self and blindly following reformist injunctions.

At the time, few women frequented this library. A decade later, a group of young men opened another library, the Khwaja Ghulam Us-Saiydain Library, named after a prominent Indian educationist. Sponsored by his wife, the library's larger and more formal space was provided by the IKMT in its newly constructed towers in Kargil town. When I visited in August 2021, several young men and women were studying in its quiet space. On one shelf, I came across copies of a journal *Karwaan-e-Umeed* (Caravan of Hope), an annual magazine produced by the Kargil Students Association in Delhi. As more young people studied in universities in Jammu, Punjab and Delhi, youth voluntary associations became a community of support. The submersion of factional differences outside Kargil by the Hussaini Youth Federation reflected wariness of the divisiveness of the IKMT–Islamia School factional politics. It also pointed to the vulnerability that Kargili students experienced outside Kargil. One day Nasir related to me the story of becoming acutely aware of his Shi'i identity:

> When I went for admission to Amar Singh College in Srinagar, a clerk recognised from my name that I was a Shi'a. He made fun of me saying, 'You Shi'a, nothing will become of you.' I felt very hurt and angry, and for the first time became conscious of my Shi'i identity. So I went in search of a Shi'i professor in the university and told

him about this incident. It is then that I decided to seriously start studying religious books. I bought books worth 3000 rupees and started reading about Shi'ism and Islam. Then I started activism in the university and told other Shi'i students that they should also read *namaz* in the university mosque. It doesn't belong only to Sunnis and is for all students.

Nasir's narrative reiterated the role played by public piety initiatives taken by youth associations in raising awareness about Shi'ism. These contributed to the affective well-being of the community through the cultivation of an intangible sense of confidence in identity. 'Education is as an end in itself rather than being merely a means to material progress,' Fida, a friend of Nasir, passionately explained to me. Fida was working as a resource person for the Indian government's 'Sarva Shiksha Abhiyan' (Education for All) programme at the time. He ardently proclaimed, 'The identity of a person finishes when they become *gulam* [subservient]. Superiority and inferiority are a product of knowledge, and education and is not about being born somewhere.' He was to be married a month later to the daughter of a learned Shi'a cleric in the Valley.

Freedom from subservience is one of the key expressions of sectarian consciousness. In the 2019 Ashura procession in Delhi, the All Kargil Students Association carried a large banner with pictures of Khomeini, Khamenei and Sistani with the message 'Be a Free Man: The Procession is in Solidarity with All the Oppressed and against All the Oppressors of the World'. Multiple significations of freedom were held here: freedom from the petty politicking of clerics; freedom from discrimination in the Valley, Leh and beyond; freedom from Western imperialism.

Even as connections with Shi'i youth across India were strengthened under the umbrella of 'Hussaini youth', influences from West Asia also inspired voluntarism in Kargil. The IKMT's Youth Wing, called Basij-e-Imam, drew upon ideas of social service from the Islamic Republic. It mobilised volunteers to provide labour and aid in times of need and disaster. During the 2014 floods in the Kashmir Valley, for instance, every night several trucks, including those of the Basij-e-Imam and the Islamia School Youth Wing, left for Srinagar carrying aid. Volunteers went to Srinagar to do relief work, especially for rescuing stranded Kargilis. Stories about Kargili Shi'as being excluded from rescue efforts and even being thrown off dinghies circulated, reinforcing the historical feeling of sectarian discrimination in the Valley. Nevertheless Kargili volunteers emphasised that the aid they were carrying on behalf of the people of Kargil were a measure of their *insaniyat* and empathy for the suffering of everyone in the Valley regardless of sect. The Basij-e-Imam took their name from the Islamic Republic's infamous Basij paramilitary organisation that was created after the revolution, widely critiqued for its moral policing. While controversial and categorised in various ways in Iran – voluntary NGO, mass-administered organisation, political party, militia[74] – it was the voluntarism and disaster-relief aspects of its official definition that were invoked by the IKMT in Kargil's context.

Some young men also claimed inspiration from the Hizbollah. 'To reach *jannat* you need to do social work – *insaniyat ka kaam* [To reach heaven you need to do work for humanity],' explained one of these young men, Asgar. His interest in 'revolutionary ideas' was triggered in 2006 'when the Hizbollah fought a war ... the Hizbollah is doing a lot of good work like building schools, bridges, etc.,' Asgar stated. Symbolic constructions of the IKMT's identity had often included the display of the Hizbollah flag in its processions and events. But Asgar proclaimed that he was 'independent', not affiliated with the IKMT. Asgar combined butchering work with studying for a BSc degree through distance learning.

In his early twenties, Ashraf was another young man who was deeply inspired by Hasan Nasrallah and the Hizbollah. During Muharram of 2008, when Gaza was being bombarded by Israel, he mentioned that he was not attending *majalis* regularly that year. He spent more time watching Iranian television to follow the news on Gaza. Explaining that it was the duty of all Muslims to protest against such oppression, he said he was ready to go fight alongside Palestine if the *rahbar* (Khamenei) were to give such a call. But he also realised that patriotism to one's own nation (*watan*) comes first. Ashraf attributed the ethic of privileging loyalty to one's own nation to Khomeini, saying that he had discouraged foreign nationals studying in Iran to join the Iran–Iraq War. Kargili embedding within transnational Shi'i horizons was always calibrated with belonging to India. The embedding of self and place-making within these wider horizons sustained the desire for freedom in captivity, for these afforded inspiration to think critically and act ethically within existing constraints.

⊰⊱

Engagement with modernist reformist discourses in Kargil generated great zeal and passion among proponents and practitioners. Even for those who were critical of and not allied with the IKMT, the *inqilabi nazariya* generated by the Iranian Revolution was a source of inspiration. The impact of liberation theology integral to this *nazariya* offers ethnographic evidence for Behrooz Ghamari-Tabrizi's argument for considering the 'conceptual significance of the Iranian Revolution' and dislodging its historiography from the Enlightenment as 'the Universal Referent'.[75] The emphasis placed on rational thinking in Kargil became for many an element in their very structure of emotion. Self-conscious exercise of *'aql*, whether in the realms of ritual practice or everyday ethical action, was not a reflection of a process of secularisation. It was deeply rooted within the philosophical tradition of Islam. One of the major successes of Western Enlightenment philosophy was the dichotomy it entrenched between reason and faith, as being mutually exclusive. This has colonised discussions of agency and freedom and associated debates on religion and secularism. However, as historians of emotion in Muslim societies have pointed out, emotions are not a 'counter-concept to rationality and knowledge' but 'constitute a crucial element of actors' interpretations of the world they inhabit, and in many cases, provide the motivation to translate knowledge into action'.[76]

Furthermore, reason in this modernist Shi'i discursive tradition was neither interpreted nor exercised in the Kantian sense for its own sake: as an *absolute exercise of freedom* that entailed a release from all forms of 'self-inflicted tutelage' that might stifle the use of reason.[77] As in Enlightenment thought, of which Immanuel Kant was an influential proponent, in Shi'i modernist discourse, too, individual reasoning is tied to ideas of the public good. Yet the epistemological foundation is quite different. In the latter, it is only when the ability to reason is cultivated as a form of *moral striving* can it be exercised for the public good. This individual exercise of reasoning does not entail a retreat into an interior self but is a path to taking ethical action in the service of the *qaum*. Shi'i selfhood in Iranian Revolutionary discourse is ultimately relational. Both the IKMT and the Islamia School, despite their differences, agreed that the common good of Kargil could only be achieved by addressing historical forces of oppression that had occluded the region's political subjectivity and shackled selfhood.

> Those who are *mayus* [despondent] are not Shi'a and *musalman*. Keep your *'izzat* [respect] and *huquq* [rights] alive. Keep the *josh* [passion] to work for the progress of the *qaum* alive.... All across Hindustan people should know that the youth of Kargil are *zinda dil* [feisty].

This resounding call to action, to fight for one's rights, was part of a speech given by a charismatic leader, Asgar Ali Karbalai. He embodied the turn to an activist Shi'i politics under the banner of fighting for justice. This led to an acute politicisation of Kargili society, eventually leading to widespread cynicism with the participation of the IKMT and the Islamia School in politics.

Notes

1. In its original conception, during the time of Prophet Muhammad and his companions, *jahiliyat* referred to the tribal sense of honour marked by arrogance and a passionate temper. It was to be replaced with the reigning in of the soul from anger. However, *jahiliyat* is a dynamic concept, which is not restricted to the time before Islam. It connotes a spiritual state of being that can resurface at any time in an individual or society where the hold of Islam has become weak. Izutsu, *Structure of the Ethical Terms in the Koran*, 27. This is seen to happen, for instance, when modernity leads to the seeping in of problems such as sexual promiscuity, the breakdown of family values or consumerism, widely perceived as signs of the spiritual hollowness of Western society by the Islamic world. It is these that Muslim societies reject, not modernity per se. Deeb, *Enchanted Modern*, 25.

2. On reception of Qur'anic exegesis in Jamaat-e-Islami-affiliated reading circles in Dhaka, see Huq, 'Reading the Quran'.

3. See Fuchs, on these themes. *In a Pure Muslim Land*, 144–45.

4. Keddie, *Iran and the Muslim World*, 118.

5. Roy, *Failure of Political Islam*, 185.

6. Irfani, *Iran's Islamic Revolution*, 160–61.

7. The effects of the revolution manifested in varied ways. In Pakistan, its success encouraged greater sectarian assertion. See Abou Zahab, 'Regional Dimension of Sectarian Conflicts'; Zaman, 'Sectarianism in Pakistan'. In Afghanistan, graduates from Iranian seminaries played a major role in bringing about social change in the Hazarajat region in the 1980s. See Olszewska, 'Poetry and Its Social Context', 74.

8. Esposito, *The Iranian Revolution*, 3, 31; Fischer and Abedi, *Debating Muslims*, 156; Rajaee, 'Iranian Ideology and Worldview', 72; Ramazani, 'Iran's Export of the Revolution', 55–56. See Bajoghli, *Iran Reframed*, on the theocratic regime's cultural producers. According to a senior retired official from the Ministry of External Affairs in India, the Embassy of the Republic of Iran made a request to open a consulate in the Kashmir Valley in the 1980s. Although permission was not granted, it was likely associated with the export of the revolution.

9. Ramazani, 'Iran's Export of the Revolution', 74.

10. Al-Mustafa International University, 'About Us'.

11. The Ministry of Culture and Islamic Guidance in Iran, created in 1987, established cultural sections separate from the Iranian embassies in countries to foster cultural exchange. These centres became conduits for the 'cultural politics' of post-revolution Iran. Shaery-Eisenlohr, *Shi'ite Lebanon*, 161.

12. Esposito, *The Iranian Revolution*; Keddie, *Iran and the Muslim World*.

13. 'Small media' – pamphlets, booklets, posters and photocopied statements – played an important role in mass mobilisation during the Iranian Revolution. Recordings of Khomeini's sermons on cassette circulated even while he was still

in exile. Bakhash, *The Reign of the Ayatollahs*; Mohammadi and Mohammadi, *Small Media, Big Revolution*.

14. Pernau, 'Feeling Communities', 17.
15. R. Gupta, 'Seeking Knowledge'.
16. Robinson, *Islam and Muslim History*, 69.
17. R. Gupta, 'Experiments with Khomeini's Revolution'.
18. With the declaration of the British mandate in Iraq in 1920, senior Shiʻi *ʻulama* in the shrine cities declared any association with the British to be illicit. Cole, *Sacred Space*, 174. In general, the colonial or 'quasi-colonial' experience contributed to a resistance to change among *ʻulama*. Rahman, *Islam and Modernity*, 63.
19. By dealing with particular issues and problems in their societies, the role of clerics goes beyond the interpretation of the sharia. Zaman, *The Ulama*.
20. I build upon a body of anthropological scholarship that relates the rise of reform to wider historical and contemporary sociopolitical contexts. Hefner, *Civil Islam*; Marsden, *Living Islam*; Mayaram, *Resisting Regimes*; Osella and Osella, 'Islamism and Social Reform in Kerala'; Schielke, 'Being a Nonbeliever'. Deeb's discussion of the role Islamic reform played in becoming a 'pious modern' Shiʻa being tied up with the historically perceived 'reclaiming and reconstruction of a stigmatized identity' in Lebanon is especially resonant. Deeb, *Enchanted Modern*, 36.
21. Motahhari and Dabashi, 'The Fundamental Problem', 172.
22. This echoed modernist endeavours in the late nineteenth century. Examples include Sayyid Ahmad Khan of Aligarh in India and Namik Kemal of Turkey. Rahman, *Islam and Modernity*, 50–52.
23. The discouragement of modern education has been a 'defining trope of competition' among Sunni modernist and traditionalist factions in Kerala. Osella and Osella, 'Islamism and Social Reform in Kerala', 326–28.
24. The promotion of Urdu was not a pan-Indian phenomenon. After independence, Urdu was marginalised in India and state governments were made responsible for its promotion. Jeffery, 'Hearts, Minds, and Pockets', 25.
25. Metcalf, *Perfecting Women*.
26. Even in Iran for many middle-class and working women, access to education offered new opportunities that enabled them to challenge patriarchal restrictions. See Shams, 'Revolutionary Religiosity'.
27. Devji, 'Gender and the Politics of Space', 150.
28. Shahrokni, 'The Mother's Paradise'.
29. Adelkhah, 'Framing the Public Sphere', 233.
30. The Day of Quds is held on the last Friday of the month of Ramadan across the Muslim world to express solidarity with Palestine.
31. *Mo* is the particle that denotes the feminine in Purigi. *Hajji* refers to anyone who has been on the Hajj and *ziyarat*.

32. Officially opened to foreign students in 1986, Jami'at al-Zahra was the first women's seminary in Iran, set up in response to the lobbying of a small group of women in the 1960s.

33. Both these seminaries are run under the aegis of Al-Mustafa International University, an umbrella institution for international students. Unlike Kargil, large numbers of women from other parts of India, particularly Uttar Pradesh, study in Qum. According to a group of these girls at Bint al-Huda, they were selected through the admission drives that Al-Mustafa University conducts in India. Interviews, October 2009, Qum.

34. Mir-Hosseini, *Islam and Gender*, 17.

35. Najmabadi, 'Crafting an Educated Housewife', 91.

36. Najmabadi, *Women with Mustaches*.

37. Najmabadi, 'Crafting an Educated Housewife', 93, 102. This is not unique to Islamic discourse. See Mankekar, 'Women Oriented Narratives', on the centrality of women in the post-colonial Indian state's project of nationhood, reflected in soap operas typically portraying Hindu women.

38. *Sati* was a custom of a Hindu widow immolating herself in the funeral pyre of her deceased husband. It was declared illegal in India in 1987.

39. Das, 'Moral and Spiritual Striving in the Everyday', 235, too, notes how questions relating to religious obligations are framed with reference to Hindus in a Muslim neighbourhood in Delhi.

40. '*Jannat* [paradise] lies beneath the feet of a mother' was a well-known hadith (saying of the Prophet) that people often cited.

41. Najmabadi, 'Crafting an Educated Housewife', 94.

42. Deeb, *Enchanted Modern*, 116.

43. Mahmood, *Politics of Piety*.

44. Mattingly, 'Two Virtue Ethics', 170.

45. Adelkhah, 'Islamophobia and Malaise in Anthropology', 218. (original emphasis).

46. Abu-Lughod, 'Do Muslim Women Really Need Saving'.

47. Laidlaw, 'For an Anthropology of Ethics', 324.

48. See Fischer, *From Religious Dispute to Revolution*.

49. This commentary reflects the poet Ghalib's thinking. In one of his couplets, he asserted that if rituals did not separate communities, they would all believe in the unity of God. Only then would true faith be established. Jalal, *Self and Sovereignty*, 3.

50. Crooke, *Resistance*, 93–94.

51. Adelkhah, *Being Modern*, 5.

52. Fischer and Abedi, *Debating Muslims*, 218.

53. On the implications on modern subjectivity of the unsettled nature of debates on ritual and worship in post-revolution Iran, see Haeri, 'The Sincere Subject'.

54. For hundreds of years, Shi'as have mourned the martyrdom of Husayn by flagellating themselves using swords, knives and chains. The most commonly held image of Shi'ism, *zanjirzani* (chain slashing) or *kammazani* (sword slashing), has provoked a portrayal of the Shi'as as barbaric. The practice has been condemned through the ages by people of other faiths and often most harshly by the Sunnis.

55. Lapidus, 'Knowledge, Virtue, and Action', 44.

56. Asad, *Formations of the Secular*, 90.

57. See Deeb, *Enchanted Modern*, 143, on similar changes in *majalis* in Lebanon, and Hirschkind, 'The Ethics of Listening', 630, on the emphasis preachers place on crying being more than its emotional experience.

58. *Falsafa* is an intellectual tradition of philosophical reflection in Islam. It brings up questions on the place of reason and personal opinion that are similar to the ones raised by philosophers of the Enlightenment. Mernissi, *Islam and Democracy*, 21. The study of *falsafa* was relegated to a marginal position in Shi'ite seminaries over the course of history. *Fiqh* (science of Islamic jurisprudence) held a privileged position. Furthermore, in the context of nineteenth-century colonisation, Muslim nationalists in the Arab world reactivated a Muslim past that did not 'anchor modern identity in the rationalist tradition' but rather the past was a shelter, protected by culture. Mernissi, *Islam and Democracy*, 42.

59. Even within seminaries, increasing emphasis was placed on combining the Islamic curriculum with the study of subjects like sociology. Crooke, *Resistance*, 18, observes that 'Islamist political and philosophical thinking – at least in Tehran – parallels western critical theory in some aspects of its analysis, and perhaps it is no surprise that a leading German critical theorist, Jürgen Habermas, is so widely read in Tehran'.

60. Das, 'Moral and Spiritual Striving', 233.

61. Tayob, 'Islam as a Lived Tradition', 25–27.

62. I have taken this translation of the original poem in Urdu from Hyder, 'Iqbal and Karbala', 350.

63. A *khanaqah* is akin to a Sufi lodge. In local lore, *khanaqah*s were spaces where the first preachers in the region peacefully beckoned and gradually converted people to Islam.

64. Modernist reformers like Muhammad Rashid Rida in the early twentieth century argued that visitation to the shrines of the Imams must be limited to remembering and paying respect to the dead. Making wishes, votive offerings, recitation of poetry, and so on were deemed unlawful. Nakash, 'Visitation of the Shrines', 158. For examples from South Asia, see Gardener, 'Mullahs, Migrants, Miracles'; van der Veer, 'Playing or Praying'.

65. Hyder, 'Iqbal and Karbala', 350.

66. Metcalf, *Moral Conduct and Authority*, 10.

67. Perhaps Iqbal was an oft-quoted philosopher in Kargil because despite being a Sunni himself, he 'moved from the Muslim community to humanity itself, in that longing for the wider world that we have seen belongs so close to the heart of a minority'. Devji, *Muslim Zion*, 227. Iqbal's verses gave voice to sentiments that were not easily articulated.

68. Rashid, 'He Who Has Steel Has Everything'.

69. Deeb, *Enchanted Modern*, 195.

70. The shift to 'this-worldly' aspects of Islam in the subcontinent in the nineteenth century was evident in other movements such as the Faraizis, Deobandis and the Ahl-i Hadis. Robinson, *Islam and Muslim History*, 105. Underlined by similar ideas of Muslims taking on responsibility for creating a good and just society on earth, Shi'i modernist discourse also connected this to the material progress of society.

71. Osella and Osella, 'Islamism and Social Reform', 338, mention a similar trend in the rise of new forms of sociality that included involvement in NGOs and various public functions in Kerala.

72. Such libraries can be found across Shi'i India. They demonstrate a shift towards religious learning outside the *madrasa*.

73. The internet is an independent source of knowledge for young people and a space to express opinions and share news-clippings from other parts of India and Iran. See, for example, the blog Shahīd Mutahhari Students Organisation, Kargil, http://smso.blogfa.com (accessed on 15 June 2022). These blogs appear to be modelled on transnational Shi'i sites that carry news about Shi'i communities from different parts of the world (for example, Jafariya News, http://www. jafariyanews.com [accessed on 15 June 2022]). Kargili Shi'as also contribute news from Kargil.

74. Golkar, *Captive Society*. See Bajoghli, *Iran Reframed*, on the Basij's shift in focus from voluntarism on the warfront during the Iran–Iraq War to cultural warfare through media productions.

75. Ghamari-Tabrizi, *Foucault in Iran*, xiii.

76. Pernau, 'Feeling Communities', 17.

77. Foucault, 'What Is Enlightenment?'.

3

Fighting for Justice

Selective ideological and programmatic appropriations of transnational Shi'i discourses from West Asia were not restricted to reforming self and society. Experiments with Khomeini's revolution were also mobilised in the realm of politics through a more active engagement with electoral democracy. Legitimised by 'fighting for justice', both the IKMT and the Islamia School directly entered local politics. Until India revoked Article 370 against the wishes of Kashmiris and Kargilis, people in Kargil praised Indian democracy. They invested hope in representative democracy as an avenue for freedom from oppression. This chapter takes you on a journey into local politics and the crystallisation of political consciousness. It describes the acute politicisation of Kargili society and further analyses calibrations of Shi'i political theology with Indian nationalism.

A defining feature of the Iranian Revolution was a move away from the traditional Shi'i political stance that was dominated by a soteriological outlook that emphasised redemptive suffering to actively fighting for justice in this world. Historically, Twelver Shi'as have believed that the Twelfth Imam, Mahdi, the current spiritual and political head of the community, is in occultation and that no temporal ruler could legitimately fulfil his role. They see themselves as a community of suffering awaiting the return of the Mahdi to bring about justice in this world. This outlook manifested in Shi'as accepting the necessity of a passive political stance around the world.[1] Often minorities, and living under oppressive regimes, Shi'i communities in diverse contexts have historically accommodated themselves to different nation states.[2] In this classical Shi'i stance, the spiritual sphere is separate from the political, and the two could be united only upon the return of the Twelfth Imam. Thus, a political leader of *this world* could not be the spiritual head of the Twelver Shiʻa. Khomeini's revolutionary ideology urged a shift away from this passive position. He argued that religion and politics are inseparable, calling for the shedding of a passive attitude towards the experience of injustice. Fighting against injustice in this life was crucial to redemption in the afterlife.

Political action came to be redefined within the Karbala paradigm, which recounts Imam Husayn's battle against the unjust rule of the Umayyad regime in 680 CE. The resilience of Husayn's suffering and his subsequent martyrdom in the battle of Karbala were re-signified through the political ideology of the Iranian Revolution as an active struggle for justice and freedom from oppression. Thus, although considered 'traditionalist', the revolution brought about a radical transformation within Shiʻism.[3]

After the revolution, the braiding of religion and politics was put into practice in Iran through the institution of the *vilayat-i faqih* (guardianship of the jurist). The supreme jurist became the direct and legitimate inheritor of both the political and religious authority of the Prophet and the Imams.[4] The *vilayat-i faqih* began to play a direct role in politics and the day-to-day running of the Islamic Republic. Khomeini himself took up this position first and was succeeded by Ali Khamenei.[5]

Intra-sectarian Polemics

One hot afternoon in June 2008, I was returning to Kargil town from Wakha-Mulbekh, a village located along the Leh–Kargil stretch of National Highway 1. I was suddenly shaken out of stupor induced by road rhythm by the sight of a long cavalcade of cars and motorcycles packed with men and pasted with posters of Ayatollahs Khomeini and Khamenei. They approached Wakha-Mulbekh waving green and red flags printed with the IKMT logo. They were going to welcome a delegation of Iranian representatives who were travelling to Kargil for the annual commemoration of Khomeini's death anniversary (*barsi*). Organised by the IKMT, this event was a replica of the much larger one in Iran in which thousands of people participate every year.[6]

A massive tent had been erected by the IKMT outside its offices in the Kargil Bazaar for the *majlis* to be held the next morning. Separate entrances led to spaces for men and women. Huge portraits of Khomeini and Khamenei looked upon the audience from behind the stage, and banners printed with didactic injunctions adorned the tent. One banner read 'Even today we have to follow the path and guidance of Khomeini', while another extolled him as 'the one whose sun will never set', unwittingly alluding to his quest for a kind of imperial immortality. The tent filled up rapidly as men and women, old and young, streamed in with children. The proceedings began with an IKMT cleric explaining the significance of the day in Purigi. He bestowed merit upon the audience for their participation. This was followed by a lecture on the purpose of the Iranian Revolution and the scores of people martyred to establish an Islamic government. Reiterating solidarity with Khomeini's cause, the cleric fervently declared:

> Till we have life, our yearning for Khomeini will remain intact.... It is our wish to follow the path of the *rahbar* [literally 'one who shows the way'], the *vilayat-i faqih* ... we must give up our lives to follow in their path. Youth and women should come forward to commemorate this day.

A young boy, no older than ten years, from the Mutahhari Primary School then sang a *tarana* (Islamic song) in Urdu in a powerful, haunting voice, casting a magical hush over the audience. They repeated the chorus calling out the name of the *rahbar*, Ali Khamenei. The lyrics of the song proclaimed that till the return of the Twelfth Imam az-Zaman, Ali Khamenei is the *sipahi* (soldier) who leads the way, and all the *mujtahids* are his friends. Speeches were interspersed with political sloganeering and the recitation of poetry, a popular medium in Kargil to express both personal and political sentiments. Several of the lectures by clerics, Islamic intellectuals and the representatives from Iran dwelt upon the concept of *vilayat-i faqih*. One speaker explained that the *vilayat-i faqih* is necessary to keep the injunctions of Islam alive, weaving the concept into a historical narrative of the Prophet's migration from Mecca to Medina for the survival of Islam. As speakers caught their breath, the audience chanted the IKMT *salawat* (salutation) that appended a line in praise of Khamenei to the liturgy in praise of Prophet Muhammad. Another speaker connected the concept of *vilayat-i faqih* to the context of contemporary politics, arguing that America is creating trouble in Iran to hinder its leadership as it is a country that has the temerity to stand up to Western imperialism. Expressing support for the Iranian cause, he added, 'Bush, America and Israel are seeing what the Iranians can do. Today they cannot budge Iran.' The audience chanted the *takbir* 'Allahu Akbar', raising clenched fists in unison, followed by denunciations of America and Israel: 'Amrika murdabad! Israel murdabad!' (Down with America! Down with Israel!) (Figure 3.1).

A man sang a song condemning George Bush and urged young people to come forward for the cause of Islam. The song couched the theme of martyrdom in a patriotic idiom: 'It is very easy to say *Vande Mataram* [a nationalist hymn from the Indian freedom movement] inside a room', exhorting young people to actively

Figure 3.1   Raising fists, Khomeini's *barsi*, 2008

Source: Photograph by the author.

fight for freedom from oppression rather than being passive spectators from the confines of their homes.

A cleric from the Kashmir Valley, part of the delegation of guests invited from outside the region, told the audience that the work of the *rahbar* (Khamenei) is not to concern himself with small day-to-day matters such as reading *namaz* or giving *zakat*, practices that could not be stopped even during the reign of the Shah of Iran; it is to protect Islam from its enemies. Implicitly directed at what they deemed Sunni fundamentalist regimes, he added, 'Wherever there is no Islamic government, the enemy of Islam becomes successful – see what happened in Afghanistan, Pakistan or Iraq.'

Then a cleric from the Imamia Mission School in Leh, dressed in a modern suit rather than a turban and cloak, recited Iqbal's poetry. Speaking passionately in Urdu, he said, 'Let me tell you what I have learnt from the revolution. It made humans out of people. The rays of Imam Khomeini have even reached a remote place like Kargil. His message was one of *insaniyat* [humanness].' He stressed the importance of education in making better human beings, necessary to the well-being of society and the nation: 'If educated, the children of Kargil will not only keep the flag of Islam flying high, but also become famous in Hindustan. They will work for their country, and people from Kanyakumari [southern-most tip of India] to Ladakh will praise the children of Ladakh!'[7] With each speech an electric current seemed to ripple through the *majlis* that June morning, charged with slogans chanted with mounting intensity. While the men raised their fists ever more dramatically, women beat their chests with one hand more gently, holding their palms out wide to God above when *du'as* invoked blessings for the well-being of the *qaum*, Islam, Iran and Shi'as across the world. Kashmir-based correspondents from SAHR television, an Iranian channel, covered the event.

Traditionally, the death anniversaries of the Imams and the Ahl al-Bayt (the Prophet's family) in Kargil are commemorated through mourning *majalis*, which were predominantly religious in character. Khomeini's *barsi*, like his politics, marked a departure from the traditional *majalis* format. Ritual gatherings became occasions to not only renew a community of faith but also impart social and political messages relevant to contemporary times. Political consciousness was generated through denouncements of regimes considered to be imperial oppressors and perpetrators of injustice towards Muslims. On occasion, this went beyond chanting slogans and raising fists in symbolic protest. On the Day of Quds, when Shi'as around the world express solidarity with Palestine, the IKMT procession swept along a flag of Israel, with men stomping on it to condemn Israeli atrocities against Palestinians and burnt effigies of Western leaders.

The Islamia School criticised the IKMT for converting what it considered to be a religious occasion into a political event. They denounced the IKMT for appending an ode to Ayatollah Khamenei to the standard liturgical praise to the Prophet, the *salawat* – 'Allahuma salli 'ala Muhammad wal-i Muhammad' – which punctuated the ritual syntax of *majalis* as a symbol of their endorsement of the institution of the *vilayat-i faqih*. It was also chanted in a faster tempo. When I expressed curiosity about this difference, a young IKMT supporter told me, 'We have made this modification to suit the faster pace of life in the modern world.' In moments of acute frustration, some Islamia School supporters remarked on the inappropriateness of taking Khamenei's name while living in India, where his commands could not be followed. Those aligned with the school were thus uncomfortable with several symbolic practices vividly on display in the *barsi*. They particularly disliked the act of *takbir* – raising slogans with clenched fists to denounce the oppressor. In the month of Muharram in 1978, Khomeini, while speaking of the martyrdom of Husayn, proclaimed, '[It] ... showed us how the clenched fists of those who seek freedom, desire independence, and proclaim the truth may triumph over tanks, machines guns, and the armies of Satan, how the sword of truth may obliterate falsehood.'[8] Drawing upon the Karbala paradigm, clenched fists became an important symbol of social and political dissent during the revolution and extended to contemporary perceptions of imperial domination and oppression.

While Nasir, whom you met in Chapter 2, supported these gestures of protest, most of his family followed the Islamia School's political orientation. But one of his uncles, a man of gentle demeanour with the kindest of smiles, usually dressed in a *pathan* suit, decided to switch allegiance from the Islamia School to the IKMT. Motivated by 'personal conviction', he became a black sheep in his village. As Nasir affectionately teased him for shyly raising his fists at the *barsi*, his uncle explained to me, 'Giving *takbir* is important for it means you are acknowledging *zulm* [oppression].' Islamia School supporters, while never negating the value of the revolution to Shiʿas everywhere, disliked the vociferous expression of solidarity with Iran, arguing that it was inappropriate while living in Hindustan. Such criticism was in large part borne of local intra-sectarian rivalry and was therefore rhetorical. But it also demonstrated the Islamia School's politico-theological orientation to Ayatollah Sistani in Iraq, who has been a critic of the institution of the *vilayat-i faqih* and did not endorse it at the time of its inception by Khomeini. Both the Islamia School and the IKMT shared the desire to belong to India and to free their region from the subjection they felt as a double minority. But as competitors in the local public arena, each symbolically and rhetorically distinguished itself from the other and also legitimised engagement with democratic politics in India with reference to competing spheres of authority in the transnational Shiʿi world.

Adhering to a quietist stance of traditional Shiʿi political theology, the *ʿulama* of the Islamia School had in the past eschewed active political involvement, at least in theory. Earlier generations of Kargili clerics such as Shaykh Mohammadi, the president of the Islamia School, had supported regional and national political parties from the backstage. In the spring of 2008, Shaykh Mohammadi returned to Kargil after six months of *ziyarat* to Iraq and Iran. A special *majlis* was organised at the Islamia School to welcome him upon his return. A van drove through the bazaar announcing the gathering through a loudspeaker. Islamia School was soon packed to the seams. In an emotional speech, Shaykh Mohammadi recounted the experience of visiting the holy shrine cities. He assured people that their donations – a sum of 3.4 million rupees – had been handed over to their *mujtahid*, Ayatollah Sistani in Iraq, and of the blessings this would accrue. Towards the end of his speech, the shaykh briefly explained the political situation in Iraq at the time. The American invasion of Iraq in 2003 had led to the execution of Saddam Hussein in 2006. 'Finally the time has come for a Shiʿi *hukumat* [government] in Iraq,'[9] he declared, rousing the audience into chanting the *salawat*. While Shiʿas had celebrated the downfall of Saddam, the American occupation meant that Iraq was not yet free.[10] Shaykh Mohammadi was voicing the hope that with American troop withdrawal, a Shi'a government would be elected in Iraq. Indeed, in November 2008, a new pact was approved by the Iraqi parliament that the United States troops would have to withdraw from Iraq's cities by mid-2009. The reference to the political situation in Iraq in Shaykh Mohammadi's speech was not an innocent remark. It signalled the changing political outlook of the Islamia School, which was provoked in part by the IKMT's appropriation of revolutionary ideology to legitimise active involvement in electoral politics.

Since its founding in the 1950s, the Islamia School had followed the political quietism of Ayatollah Husayn Borujerdi, the last of the unanimously accepted *marja'iyyat-i taqlid* (the most learned and supreme exemplar for emulation). As Mohammad Ayatollahi Tabaar writes, 'Borujerdi kept the mosque and the state strictly separate from each other. He established a "board of governance" to settle internal conflicts in Qom and prevent the state's interference in clerical affairs.'[11] In the absence of a unanimously declared supreme exemplar after Agha Borujerdi's death in 1961, at least seven *mujtahid*s had a considerable following, including Ayatollah Muhsin Hakim and Ayatollah Khoi, both of whom were based in Najaf in Iraq.[12] Led by the Islamia School, the majority of Kargilis had taken up the emulation of Ayatollah Hakim, followed by Khoi and then Sistani, like most Shi'as in the Indian subcontinent.[13] Shaykh Mohammadi explained to me in a personal interview: 'Sistani believes that a *hukumat* ought to be Islami, but not directly.' For Sistani, the legitimacy of a government in Iraq rested upon both popular sovereignty and the approval of the grand *ayatollah*s of Najaf. He did not see the sharia and popular sovereignty as being contradictory.[14] In his view, clerics have a role to play in politics but not as direct electors to government. Sistani rejected Khomeini's model of a theocratic government and *vilayat-i faqih*. Keeping in line with Sistani's views, the Islamia School did not accord as much symbolic importance to Khomeini and Khamenei. Instead, gatherings and rallies held by the Islamia School displayed posters of Ayatollah Sistani and Khoi showing their orientation to Shi'i leaders in Iraq.[15] After a couple of months in the field, it was easy to guess whether someone was aligned to the Islamia School or the IKMT from the way they answered questions on the impact of the Iranian Revolution on Kargil. While IKMT supporters immediately extolled the revolution and Khomeini, the School supporters were reticent. As a cleric from the School argued:

> There had always been a religious link between Iran and Kargil even before the revolution. More good books became available after the revolution. But what can be achieved by following Iranian politics here? The law of the land is different. Some people are just using the revolution to sow discord among the people of Kargil.

The Islamia School argued that the concept of *vilayat-i faqih* could only work in a country like Iran, which has an Islamic regime; it could not be applied in non-Islamic states. However, challenged by the IKMT's growing power in Kargil, the Islamia School was compelled to change its proclaimed quietist stance. It is this transformation in the Islamia School's political outlook that was reflected in Shaykh Ahmad Mohammadi's speech, when he mentioned the turn of politics in favour of the Shi'a in Iraq as the School attempted to legitimise the change in its own stance with reference to Sistani's changing political ideology in Iraq. Controlled by clerics traditionally partisan to the Indian National Congress (hereafter, Congress), the Islamia School had never been entirely apolitical. It prided itself for backing the opposition rather than seeking any active role in the government. But the transformation in Sistani's ideology, endorsing clerical intervention in important issues facing society – a middle way between Khoi and Khomeini – was selectively appropriated by the Islamia School to legitimise active entry into politics.[16]

To strengthen their political strategies and shore up their waning legitimacy among many of the younger generation, the Islamia School set up a Youth Wing. It included 'young' men in their thirties and forties from various walks of life, who bankrolled many of its activities.[17] The Youth Wing started organising events, which seemed to mimic the IKMT for mobilising Islamia School followers. Religious discourse mingled with political talk in the Islamia School *majalis*, often with an explicitly political agenda. While never denying the value of the Iranian Revolution for Shi'as globally, the School remained steadfast in its alignment with Sistani's disapproval of the institution of *vilayat-i faqih*. Given the critique that the *vilayat-i faqih* holds no place in a non-Shi'a-majority nation state, how might we understand the IKMT's explicit endorsements beyond the role it played in building an institutional identity? How could this symbolic identification be calibrated with endorsements of Indian secularism?

The IKMT was well aware that the commands of the *vilayat-i faqih* could only be implemented in Iran and not within the framework of Indian secularism. I suggest that invocations of the *vilayat-i faqih* in the Indian context could be read as an endorsement of a more encompassing ideological unity that Khomeini had sought rather than as a blueprint for political action. Moojan Momen succinctly summarises this:

> Previously [before the 1979 revolution], as long as one observed the outward dictates of the religious law, orthodoxy of one's own belief and thinking were not considered to be a matter of concern. But now, Khumaynī was insisting that to be a Shi'i involved not only observance of religious law but also one's own thoughts must be moulded by the socially-active Revolutionary ideology. With Shi'ism now

rigidly defined, for Khumaynī, in terms of both action and ideology, any opposition, dissent or deviation must, by definition, originate from outside Shi'ism (i.e. from U.S Imperialism, Zionism, etc.).[18]

This all-encompassing moulding of thoughts was reflected in the way supporters often explained their allegiance to the IKMT as being a matter of their *aqida* (creed). In practical terms, the differing perspectives of the Islamia School and the IKMT on *vilayat-i faqih* have had little direct bearing on the larger politics of Kargili Shi'as in the national context. Fundamentally, they did not disagree on the overall political stance that they must adopt in relation to a nominally secular Indian state and their commitment to a democratic polity. The difference lay in the way each authenticated this commitment. While the Islamia School followed Sistani's perspective, the IKMT calibrated its endorsement of Khomeinism with nationalist sentiments in two ways. First, like the Hizbollah, the IKMT incorporated the concept of *vilayat-i faqih* into its intellectual structure but not into its political practice.[19] Beyond its role in factional polemics, Amal Ghorayeb's analysis of Hizbollah's politics could perhaps be applied to understanding the IKMT's referential practice: 'The party's intellectual commitment to the Islamic state is profound, but this does not render its political commitment to democracy hollow.'[20] The creation of a 'just' society – the IKMT's stated agenda – rested upon the cultivation of pious, reflective and rational youth who are not passive in the surrounding social and political environment but active agents of change. And one way of effecting change was active engagement with democratic politics. In this way, like the Hizbollah, one could argue that the IKMT incorporated both the categories of the 'religious' and 'secular' into its political practice.[21] Young men aligned to the IKMT would tell me how proud they were of the seats the Hizbollah had won in the Lebanese parliament. Put another way, the secular state may be understood as being 'normatively external and pragmatically internal'[22] to Shi'i politics outside Iran. Thus, strands of the ideological repertoire of the Iranian Revolution were selectively invoked to also actively engage with Indian democracy. Second, IKMT supporters often stressed that Khomeini ultimately privileged the loyalty of believers to the nation state they live in, forbidding non-Iranians living in Iran at the time of the Iran–Iraq War (1980–88) to fight at the front. The intensification of nationalist sentiments in Iran, wherein even non-Shi'i minority communities in Iran willingly sacrificed themselves for the country, also perhaps had a diffuse effect of foregrounding loyalty to the nation among Kargilis who were studying there at the time.[23] The figure of the patriot was sieved through a Shi'i lexicon and epistemology of martyrdom, perhaps indirectly drawing inspiration from a discourse in Iran where 'nation building became synonymous with martyrdom'.[24] This is not to suggest that this is the predominant explanation for the patriotism of Indian Shi'as more broadly or historically; but given Kargil's location along a strategic and contested border, it served to validate a particular form of minority politics, which was not rooted in dissimulation of sectarian identity and ethics.

The theme of martyrdom in Twelver Shi'i political theology was another idiom through which sectarian identity was calibrated with national belonging. This was demonstrated in the way Gandhi, the father figure of Indian nationalism, was deployed in the public sphere. As is widely accepted, ethnography is always the product of an inter-subjective exchange between the anthropologist and her interlocutors.[25] Knowing that I was not a Muslim, people would often attempt to explain Islamic beliefs and practices to me through idioms they assumed I would be familiar with. A recurrent example was the explanation of Imam Husayn and his martyrdom at the battle of Karbala with reference to Mahatma Gandhi. As I spent more time in the field, I realised that Gandhi was not just an allegorical figure, useful for conveying Shi'i Islam to a non-Muslim, but also a significant mediator of their religious and national identity.[26] The display of a banner with a picture of Gandhi carrying a statement by him – 'If ever India desires to be a successful country it should follow the principles of Imam Husayn' – was a striking visual representation of this (Figure 3.2).

Figure 3.2   Poster displayed at a public function in Kargil, 2008
Source: Photograph by the author.

Strands of Gandhi's thought travelled to Kargil from a transnational Shi'i sphere via nodes of Shi'i media production in India. To explain the moral content of Husayn's revolution, that he went to Karbala with foreknowledge of his own death, Lara Deeb's interlocutors in Lebanon told her: 'Gandhi used to say, "I learned from Husayn how to be oppressed and be victorious".'[27] While doing fieldwork in Mumbai in 2013, I stumbled across similar images in Dongri, a Shi'i neighbourhood in the old city of Mumbai. These posters were made as part of a Muharram Awareness Campaign by a Shi'i media outfit called the 'World Islamic Network' (WIN), where a couple of young men from Kargil worked.[28] The repetition of such tropes and images across Shi'i India is an indication of the networks of Shi'i internationalism and growing connections with lesser-known locales of the Indian Shi'i ecumene such as Mumbai. My interlocutors in both Kargil and Mumbai would often cite Khomeini's reverence for Gandhi as a model for applying the political philosophy of Karbala founded upon the idea of martyrdom to nationalist struggles.[29] Repeated references to Imam Husayn and Hasan can be found in Gandhi's speeches, letters and political notices though usually not in any specific context of mobilising Muslim support during India's anti-colonial struggle. The incorporation of the meaning of Imam Husayn's martyrdom at Karbala in Gandhi's philosophy is perhaps best captured in the following quote on *satyagraha* – his creed of non-violent resistance. Explaining his concept of resistance in a letter in 1917, Gandhi wrote:[30]

> The English phrase 'passive resistance' does not suggest the power I wish to write about; 'satyagraha' is the right word. Satyagraha is the soul force as opposed to armed strength. Since it is essentially an ethical weapon, only men inclined to the other ethical way of life can use it wisely.... A satyagrahi bears no ill will, does not lay down his life in anger, but rather refuses to submit to his 'enemy' or oppressor because he has the strength himself to suffer.... Imam Hassan and Husain were merely two boys. They felt that an injustice had been done to them. If, however, they were to submit to injustice, they would disgrace their manhood and betray their religion. In these circumstances they yielded to the embrace of death.... In my view, Islam did not attain its greatness by the power of the sword but entirely through the self-immolation of its fakirs.

How was Gandhi's emphasis on standing up to injustice and waging a non-violent struggle invoked in Kargil to negotiate belonging to India? First, it enabled Kargili Shi'as to emphasise Islam, and specifically Shi'i Islam, as non-violent in the context of the demonisation of Muslims arising from what they deemed 'Wahhabi fundamentalism', acutely abetted by the 'war against terror' discourse. Distancing themselves from the stereotype of Muslims as being violent was critical to their performance of patriotism. Condemnation of violence of any sort recurred in my conversations with Kargil's Muslims, whether it was men or women, young or old, Shi'a or Sunni.[31] They would lament that the meaning of jihad has been distorted by the Taliban, lending all Muslims a bad name, or say that no religion permits violence, be it Hinduism, Buddhism or Islam, citing as an example Gandhi's creed of non-violent resistance.

The discourse on Gandhi's reverence for Husayn was also mobilised by Kargili Shi'as in their practice of secularity through everyday relational ethics. People often mentioned Gandhi's references to Husayn when explaining the significance of mourning for the martyrs of Karbala. As a Balti friend explained to me, '*Matam* [mourning] for Husayn is for *insaniyat*; its appeal extends far beyond Shi'i communities.' Every year the Muharram procession from his neighbourhood, Balti Bazaar, took a particular route to the main bazaar in Kargil town before joining the larger procession. When it passed by the home of Sardar Avtar Singh, one of the Sikh families in town, the men from these families would join the Balti Bazaar procession till the end of their alleyway. One year, when the people of Balti Bazaar contemplated changing the traditional route, the Sikhs are said to have appealed to them to keep it the same. 'They too drown their personal grief in the collective mourning for Husayn,' my friend asserted. In appreciation of this sentiment, the route was not changed. This vignette is another example of the important place that Imam Husayn and Karbala have historically held in inter-cultural and inter-religious spaces in the subcontinent.[32] Besides attesting to the ordinary relational ethics that different religious communities have forged with each other in everyday life, it was also an instance of an important symbolic gesture by the Shi'as towards another minority community living amid them. Kargil's Muslims often presented their amicable relationship with the Sikh families as evidence of their own 'secular' disposition, especially as a counter to their fraught relationship with Buddhists since the communalisation of politics in Ladakh. They prided themselves about the fact that the Sunni mosque and the Sikh gurdwara shared a wall. The presence of a gurdwara in Kargil town was all the more symbolic given the absence of a Buddhist *gonpa*, a point of much contention for Buddhists. In everyday life, both the elders of the Sikh families and especially the older generation of Muslims in Kargil would mention that they always invited the Sikh families to their weddings even though the permissible forms of meat for both communities are different. The Sikhs eat *jhatka*, while the Muslims eat halal, where the difference is in the way the animal is slaughtered. Several of my interlocutors told me on more than one occasion that even though the Sikhs did not consume meat at Muslim festivities, they were given live chickens to take home to fulfil their obligations of hospitality.

Majalis held on the eighth day of Muharram kindle heightened emotions as the martyrdom of Imam Husayn's infant child, Ali Asgar, is commemorated on this day. Certain *matam-sarais* in Kargil, like the one in Balti Bazaar, where Ali Asgar's slaying was enacted, were packed to their seams; even people who stayed away from *majalis* on other days attended.[33] In this highly charged atmosphere, Shaykh Ahmad Mohammadi's narrative of Karbala skilfully wove in the example of Gandhi's emulation of Husayn's *inqilab*, as he called out to young people to give *qurbani* (sacrifice) themselves for their society. Sacrifice as a metaphor for martyrdom did not imply literal martyrdom but alluded to its ethical significance. As a young man explained to me, 'Imam Husyan did not fight for the chair [that is, to gain political office], but to keep Islam alive.' This resonated with Gandhi's concept of an ethical and moral politics derived from religious conviction. In a leaflet on *satyagraha* dated May 1919, Gandhi stressed that all *satyagraha* activity should be guided by the religious spirit.[34] The call to young people to sacrifice themselves for their society and the nation resonated with Gandhi's portrayal of Imam Husayn as a 'great *satyagrahi*' – a model for emulation by the youth in India's nationalist struggle.

It was on this higher moral plane that both the Islamia School and the IKMT sought to ground the legitimacy of their politics. Each promised to deliver to its followers an *adl* (just) government, or *hukumat-i Husayni* (the government of Husayn), which was not driven by the quest for power, of which the *kursi* (chair) is a widely used metaphor in India, but by the quest for justice. 'Khomeini and Gandhi's *inqilab* are comparable,' a group of young men aligned to the IKMT explained to me. They added that Shahid Mutahhari had also written about Gandhi, gushing about how 'people in Iran really love Gandhi'. 'I have heard there is even a market in Tehran named after Gandhi,' said one boy with incredulity. Khomeini's revolution and Gandhi's *inqilab* appeared to transcend the modern separation between politics and ethics. In the search for justice and freedom from oppression, followers of both the IKMT and the Islamia School invested hope in an ethical politics.

Three words – oppression (*zulm*), injustice (*na-insafi*) and freedom (*azadi*) – made a repeated appearance in the speeches of the IKMT and Islamia School leaders. Although this political lexicon echoed the language of mobilisation used by the NC in the Kashmir Valley against Dogra oppression, in Kargil it took on a sectarian hue, framed as it was by the Karbala paradigm. Within the context of local politics each faction pointed to the other as the source of oppression and injustice. From the IKMT's perspective, the old guard of clerics in the Islamia School had misled people to retain power, while the entrenched elite had exploited them historically. From the Islamia School's perspective, the IKMT's ideological discourse of social and political reform had just been a ploy to grab power. Beyond the local level, however, both factions identified the squeezing of Kargil between Leh and Kashmir as the source of oppression and injustice. Each sought legitimacy in their youth base. Projecting the younger generation as the future of Kargil, each roused the youth to become aware, to educate themselves and to fight for the rights of their *qaum*. One man who embodied the tension between the IKMT and the Islamia School was Asgar Ali Karbalai, the political face of the IKMT. He played no small part in stirring the political energies of young people, especially men, either because they hated or because they admired him. But even those aligned with the Islamia School could not disregard his oratorical skills and charismatic qualities. Inspiring something akin to hero worship, many of his youth supporters referred to him as the 'lion of Kargil'.

The 'Lion of Kargil'

> Before the Iranian Revolution, other than rituals there was no awareness among the Shi'a about politics and the modern world. The *'ulama* did not have the thinking that in the modern world a perfect Shi'a can be made. The revolution showed us that life in this world is not oriented only towards *akhiriyat* [the other world]. A good life or a life of excellence can be lived even otherwise. For this one needs to fight for the public.

Asgar Ali Karbalai was among the young men who founded the IKMT along with Shaykh Zakiri. He left school at matriculation. Despite not having a university education, Karbalai's career began as a schoolteacher at the Mutahhari Public School set up by the IKMT. He was elevated into a powerful political position as the chief executive councillor (CEC) of the Hill Council in 2004 and subsequently a member of legislative assembly (MLA) in 2014 in the erstwhile J&K state assembly.

Karbalai's reputation preceded him. I first heard of him in 2007 from a Buddhist friend in Leh as the 'new charismatic leader finally managing to project Kargil to the outside world'. Karbalai's short, stocky build was more than compensated for by his oratorical skills, forthright manner and intensity of demeanour. He provoked strong reactions in Kargilis – either intense admiration or hatred. The first time I met Karbalai in person was while accompanying a foreign visitor, who wanted to call on him in his Council office and asked me to join him. Quickly sidelining the visitor for whom the appointment had been taken, he launched into an interrogation of my research. Sufficiently intimidated by the barrage of questions, I asked him what he thought should be the focus of any research on contemporary Kargil. In his typical forceful manner, he replied, 'The impact of religion on everything – on politics, economics, culture.... The people of Kargil are what they are because of religion.' He threw a question back at me: 'What do you think of Kargilis?' I fumbled and said, 'They are generous and warm. Society seems to be experiencing rapid change.' To this he said, 'A cultural invasion is taking place through new media, and it is only religion that can provide rules and ways of conduct as circumstances change in time [*zaman*] and space [*makan*].' 'I myself am a product of religion,' he added with pride.

The next time I met Karbalai was after he had lost political power. He was at his home in a neighbourhood called Bagh Khomeini, then a relatively new settlement located on the plain overlooking Kargil town. He ushered me into a small side-room for visitors, sparsely decorated with a picture of Khomeini on one wall and a television in a corner. It was Ramadan, but he insisted on offering me a cup of tea. Karbalai spent his early childhood in Karbala (Iraq), where his father was training to become a cleric in the 1970s. He studied at an Iranian school for modern education in Iraq till the age of ten or eleven, when his family had to return to Kargil. 'The communists expelled all outsiders.... Indians were given the option to return to India while the Iranians were forced out, even those who had been living in Iraq for four or five generations,' he recalled. While in Iraq, Karbalai learnt Persian and Arabic, which enabled him to read religious books on his own. He explained that he continued to educate himself on religious matters even while studying in a government school upon his return to Kargil. The years spent in Iraq remained vividly etched on his memory: 'In Iraq we studied in coat and pant, but when I returned to Kargil we were not allowed to wear this. We were told by religious leaders to dress in the *pathan* suit and not keep hair.' Many elderly men in Kargil continued to shave their head, covering it with a cap, while the young sported trendy locks, marking the generational difference. This remark on the sartorial differences between Kargil and Iraq seemed to be another expression of the way many Kargili Shi'as uphold Iran as an exemplar of modernity. Iran returned yet again in references to modernity, illustrating that in the late nineteenth and twentieth centuries, ideas of modernity were not simply a Western import.

Talking about the IKMT's agenda for bringing progress to Kargil by learning from Iran, Karbalai repeated the now-familiar discourse of IKMT supporters on the importance of 'empowering' women. Mid-conversation, switching on the television to an Iranian news channel – beamed through dish antennae into many Kargil homes and installed, in particular, by those who have returned from Iran and are able to understand Farsi – he pointed to the woman news anchor, 'See, she is wearing the hijab and is like any other foreign news presenter. Women in Iran can take up any occupation as long as they are in hijab.' He added,

'In Iran the religious dress code for women is not like many other places in India where women have to wear the full burqa.' The head of Zainabia – the IKMT's women's wing – spoke of Karbalai as their very own Mahmoud Ahmadinejad, the president of Iran (2005–13). Once while walking past his house, she remarked, 'See, Karbalai's wife continues to do all the household chores and even works in the fields like any common woman.' Others praised him for living his ideology 'just like Ahmadinejad', saying that despite being politically powerful he lived humbly and was not corrupt.

In the early years of his political career, Karbalai appeared to make it a point to deliver most of his speeches in Urdu rather than Purigi, the local Tibetan dialect. This indicated his main support base – educated youth, more at ease with speaking Urdu than the elders. Karbalai would often call out to young people in his speeches that they must make all of Hindustan proud of Kargil. His political speeches often had the cadence of religious sermons. This appealed to his followers as he skilfully cast contemporary politics into a moral idiom. Local politics was linked to a larger humane cause. In one such speech, Karbalai expounded from the mosque pulpit:

> A good person is one who does a lot for people, who thinks about other people, thinks about *insaniyat*. He thinks about what one's thinking should be, and when, where and how common people can be benefited. An exemplary role model for this is Imam 'Ali. If there is any role model it is 'Ali, and if there is anyone who experienced severe injustice it was 'Ali. Even now we have not been able to understand 'Ali and his life.... Try and come to the path of 'Ali, try and come into the *maktab-i 'Ali* (school of 'Ali).

A popular quote across the Shi'i world – 'Live like Ali! Die like Husayn!' – was ubiquitous, stamped on stickers in buses, cars, the bazaar and homes, capturing the spirit of the broader message – to engage in action for fighting against injustice. Reiterating Imam 'Ali as a model emphasised his active political engagement upon becoming the fourth Caliph, following the death of Prophet Muhammad. The belief that the previous three Caliphs were illegitimate successors to the Prophet is foundational to Shi'ism. Imam 'Ali was upheld as an exemplar of a just politics, one founded upon values of humanness. For Karbalai's followers, at the time, this politico-moral discourse suggested that politicians need not necessarily be corrupt, ruthless and power-hungry. Instead, they could be capable of practising a moral and ethical politics.[35]

This was a departure from the widely held notion of *siyasat* (politics) as being intrinsically corrupt and corrupting. Perhaps it was no coincidence, then, that Karbalai, who proclaimed that he would enact this message in Kargil, came to be popularly and playfully known as the 'lion of Kargil'. The lion is a symbol of 'Ali. Often called by the surnames Haydar or Ghadanfar, both of which mean 'lion', 'Ali is extolled as Asad Allah, 'God's lion'.[36] He is upheld as the exemplary statesman and practitioner of ethical politics. I was often advised to read his philosophical treatise, *Nahj al-Balagha*, in order to truly understand Shi'ism. As one young man put it, the book provides a 'formula for politics'. It struck me later that the designation 'lion of Kargil' also echoed the popular reference to Sheikh Abdullah, the leader of the NC, as 'Sher-e-Kashmir' before he lost credibility in the Valley. Coincidentally, he, too, had worked as a schoolmaster before entering politics. And like him, some years later Karbalai's image of a just politician lost sheen among some of his fans. 'He was too proudy', meaning arrogant, they said. I often heard that people shuddered to enter his office for fear of reprisal. Others blamed him for indulging in a politics of revenge.

In fighting for 'the public' and creating the conditions for a 'good life' – a life of justice, a life free of oppression – as the extract from his speech here declares, Karbalai launched a crusade against the traditional elite of society. He argued that until political power and economic wealth remained vested in these groups, there would be little chance of progress and equality in Kargil. Invoking Khomeini's call to dissolve the boundaries between religion and politics, the IKMT jumped into the political fray by directly getting involved in the elections to the Hill Development Council with Karbalai as their candidate for the position of the CEC in 2003.

Engaging with Indian Democracy

The acquisition of power through control of the Hill Development Council became pivotal to factional identity and a conduit for tackling the region's (under) development. The Ladakh Autonomous Hill Development Council (LAHDC) is an autonomous governmental body, which was granted to Ladakh by the central government in 1995. It was offered as a compromise with the struggles being waged by Buddhists in Leh for autonomy from J&K and UT status. The provision to set up the Hill Council with separate and independent branches for Leh and Kargil was modelled on the Darjeeling Gorkhaland Hill Council. The Council held powers of development, planning, implementation and administration through a separate budget, control over allocation of land, rights to levy taxes and a say in the hiring and firing of government employees.[37] As discussed in Chapter 1, although Kargil had shared the grievance in Leh that Ladakh was being marginalised within J&K, it rejected not only the demand for declaring Ladakh a UT but also the provision to set up a Hill Council in 1995. This was underlined by two contradictory fears. On the one hand, Kargil feared alienation from Kashmir. The NC party, which for long had enjoyed a strong following in Kargil, had refused to support the passage of the Hill Council bill. On the other hand, the rejection of the Hill Council was also an expression of distancing themselves from Kashmir. A Kargili ex–member of parliament explained to me, 'At the time militancy in Kashmir was at its peak and we feared that accepting the Hill Council might be construed as endorsing the separatists' demand for *azadi* [freedom].' There appeared to be confusion on the difference between autonomy within the nation state and freedom from it.

In 2003, however, Kargil reversed its rejection of the Hill Council. By then the Leh Council had been functional for a few years; the control over developmental decision-making and the monetary power vested in it became apparent to Kargilis. People became aware of the power that could be wielded by winning a seat in the Council. The recognition of Kargil's loyalty to the nation state during the Kargil War after 1999 may also have implicitly influenced this decision. In hindsight, Kargili political leaders admitted that the earlier rejection of the Council was tied to a more complicated regional politics, wherein Kargilis were caught between the Kashmir Valley and Buddhist Ladakh with little space for their own political voice. Most common people, however, simply stated, 'We did not really understand what the Hill Council meant and the benefits it offered at the time.' Perhaps this general naivety made the first election to LAHDC (Kargil) in 2003 a relatively muted affair. It was primarily fought along political party lines between the Congress and the NC. Individuals from the religious factions were aligned with the parties but neither faction played an overt political role. This reflected a general pattern of Shi'i politics in other parts of the country.[38] By 2008, the second elections to the Hill Council became a locus of intra-factional rivalry. The passionate politics aroused by the elections spilled beyond the event.

In the 2008 elections, both the IKMT and the Islamia School for the first time fielded clerics as candidates in the elections. The School also justified its direct involvement in electoral politics by employing the lexicon of justice and freedom. Shaykh Ahmad Mohammadi explained to me:

> It is never possible to get hundred per cent justice. But neither should there be *zulm*.... We laid the foundation of the Hill Council on the concept of *azadi*, when there were no parties. Then when the parties came, they destroyed everything. People are very angry with the Council just now because it is an illegitimate Council.... They are ruining Islam by telling lies, deception, and corruption.

Shaykh Mohammadi was not referring to political parties in this statement. By 'parties' he meant the religious factions. His critique was directed at the IKMT, which had seized power from the NC-elected Hill Council in the previous elections in 2003, through an irregular process. At the time, the Congress, which had entered an alliance with the IKMT, had been in power at the state level. It gave the nominated members of the Council voting rights, which led to the ouster of the NC and Karbalai's ascendance to the position of the CEC. It was thus deemed an 'illegitimate' Council by the Islamia School.

The involvement of religious institutions in the Council led to the emergence of a 'political society', where governmental functions of development and welfare overlapped with the workings of community institutions.[39] Despite disavowals, nearly every individual from the Shi'i community in Kargil was aligned with one or other religious institution, whether out of *aqida* (creed), ego or older social ties. Given the control it wielded on local development, the Hill Council continued in subsequent years to be the locus of people's aspirations for acquiring power and monetary resources and for actualising a developmental vision for the region.

Alliances forged between the religious institutions and political parties led to a widening of the arena of political mobilisation. Politics around the Hill Council elections lend insight into not only local social dynamics but also Kargil's relationship with the Indian state. In laying out an argument for a more expansive understanding of the political in anthropology, Jonathan Spencer criticises resistance studies, including the subaltern school, for its broad exclusion of organised politics as a way of engaging with the state. He writes, 'In the literature on resistance, the state is never a resource, or a place to seek justice, let alone a zone of hope, however distant or deferred, in the political imaginary.' Further, it posits too radical a break between the state and the local social order.[40] I build upon this point to suggest that precisely because of Kargil's captivity, the civil face of the state – as long as it included local participation in decision-making – for a long time represented a space of hope for people in this borderland to make a life that was more than just bearable. In contrast to the Kashmir Valley, Kargilis did not boycott democratic processes, be it the Hill Council or the state assembly or the national parliamentary elections. Rather than resisting the state, the Hill Council was seen as an avenue for inhabiting the state, of building a relationship with it, of finding some room to manoeuvre within a broader context of voicelessness. Since Ladakh was declared a UT in 2019 against the explicit desire of Kargil, people fear that the power of the Hill Council will be diminished to make it an impotent entity. In light of this, the sense of ownership over the Hill Council among the people of Kargil becomes ever more critical to understand negotiations of belonging in the future.

I present here an ethnography of the 2008 elections to illuminate political consciousness in Kargil that refused to be misled by religious leadership. People became critical of the involvement of religious institutions in politics for this led to an acute politicisation of society. By permeating its very core, splitting families and villages, elections to the Hill Council created 'ripples' beyond the event.[41] Criticism came as much from the moral concern with preventing conflict (*fitna*) in society as by the worry that religious leaders with little experience of 'secular' governance would hold back its progress. The desire for freedom from any form of shackling was held in the tension between hope and cynicism that suffused the Council elections every five years.

Passionate Politics

On 29 August 2008, the frantic summer life that characterises the Kargil bazaar was replaced by a sudden eerie quiet. The town had emptied out. Everyone but the permanent inhabitants had returned to their native villages in order to cast their vote in the Hill Council elections the next day. For more than a month, election gossip suffused peoples' talk, even entering children's play. The slogan of Karbalai's supporters – 'Jeetega bhai jeetega, sher ka baccha jeetega' (He will win, he will win, the son of the lion will win) – was picked up by my neighbour's children in their games, much to the chagrin of their elders, who were staunch supporters of the Islamia School. People kept close daily tabs on candidates coming forward or stepping down, rumours of money circulating to buy votes, the motivation behind standing for the elections or who would vote for whom on what basis. I recollected being told earlier in the year, 'Madam, this year you will see a lot.... Kargili society will become visible to you through the elections.' Indeed the elections laid bare the tensions that the religious factionalism ignited in every social unit. The tension between emotion and reason in deciding which side to vote for surfaced in the political realm, too. Politics entered the space of the family and neighbourhood, blurring the strict boundaries between the private and public, spheres that are commonly assumed to be separate, especially in representations of Muslim societies.[42]

Family, Neighbourhood, Village

There were numerous cases of families in Kargil split between the Islamia School and the IKMT, brother against brother, father against son and, in rare cases, even husband against wife. When brothers followed different factions, they were usually heads of nuclear households, and the children and the spouse tended to follow the father in their allegiance. While in daily life most siblings appeared to have an amicable relationship, 'coming and going from each other's households', they were torn when it came to voting. A man aligned to the IKMT explained the conundrum he would have faced if his brother, who supported the Islamia School, had decided to stand for elections as originally planned. He would have been pulled between his mind (*zahan*), which would tell him to vote for the IKMT and his heart (*dil*), which leaned towards the brother. Yet strong filial sentiment did not guarantee a vote. The difficulty in making a decision was heightened when the candidate in question happened to be an agha.

Sayyid Hussain, an elderly agha, who performed death rituals for many inhabitants of Kargil town, had been fielded by the IKMT in this prestigious town constituency (Figure 3.3). He was revered as a *pir* (saint or spiritual guide) by many and held immense religious authority. Several people told me they would vote for him as a form of giving *sadqa* (offerings to earn merit), thereby not only ensuring accrual of merit for the afterlife but also his services at the time of death. But this decision was not so simple for Sayyid Hussain's relative who was a powerful sayyid in his own right but was aligned with the Islamia School. He confided in me that those aligned with the School told him that they would follow whomever he directed them to support. 'I didn't tell them who to vote for. But I went to cast my vote with Sayyid Hussain.' Kinship ties overrode political allegiance in this case.

Figure 3.3   Agha Hussain on a victory parade, 2008

Source: Photograph by the author.

But this was not true for many younger men. There were also cases where sons did not follow the allegiance of the father. This usually happened when young men claimed to be drawn to the 'rational thinking' of the IKMT, while their parents continued to follow the Islamia School, unwilling or unable to break away from traditional affiliations. 'The Trust began to appeal more to my emotions,' said one such young man. The difference between the younger and older generations extended to ties within neighbourhoods, too.

Neighbourhood unity held immense value for Kargilis, drawing both from an Islamic discourse on the importance of good neighbourly relations and from Ladakhi traditions of social support. The neighbourhood had increasingly started replacing the *phaspun*, which was the traditional unit of material and moral support during key lifecycle events across Ladakh.[43] Over the years, with increasing migration from villages to the town or transfers of government employees to other parts of the region, the *phaspun* got geographically dispersed, making it difficult for its members to be present in times of need. As a result, the neighbourhood acquired greater importance, stepping in to perform the duties of the *phaspun*. The Islamic value accorded to neighbourliness was also reinforced by reformist clerics. In the Chigtan region, a popular religious leader, Shaykh Amir Ali, instituted a new system called the *schu khak* (*schu* – ten) in 1985. Neighbourhoods were divided into groups of ten households to do all the work that marriages and deaths in a particular household necessitate. Good conduct towards and cooperation with neighbours was a frequent subject of sermons.

Neighbourhood solidarity usually extended to factional affiliation, wherein entire neighbourhoods were often associated with either the School or the IKMT. Yet during the Council elections a new line of fragmentation appeared within some neighbourhoods between the younger and older generation. Unlike many parts of India, where there is a high level of political apathy among urban youth, young people in Kargil have been getting more engaged with the political process. Many young men came forward to stand for elections, when the initial notification was made. As I mentioned in the previous chapter, both the IKMT and the School placed the responsibility for the progress of their *qaum* and *khitta* (region) upon young people. Thus, at least in theory they encouraged young men to stand for the elections. In practice, however, some of these young men were eventually forced to make way for religious leaders, who continued to hold sway over people's emotions. Each faction tried to ensure that no more than one candidate contested the elections on their behalf to prevent votes from being divided, forcing several young men to withdraw their candidature.

At the level of the village too – the last sphere of close contact and reciprocity across Ladakh – solidarity was disturbed by factional politics. Several villages became divided between the two factions. Tensions produced by such divides reached a crescendo in Pashkum village, where Karbalai had filed his candidature. Supporters of the Islamia School were angry that those aligned with the Congress party in this village, which had entered an alliance with the IKMT at the time, were supporting an 'outsider', someone who did not belong to their village. When I asked some IKMT supporters about this, one of them retorted, 'It's a free world and anyone can stand from anywhere.' When Karbalai won in Pashkum, defeating the local candidate of the School, violence broke out and a case was lodged in court. This indicated the level of tension for a premium is placed on resolving disputes within the village across Ladakh. Animosity coloured social relations and occasions for several months after. People refused to say *salam* when passing by or to attend *fatiha* readings in the home of their factional opponent. Thus, the IKMT and the School's direct involvement in the Hill Council elections and the politicisation of society resulting from this tugged at its affective core. Over time this disruption of everyday social relationships became a matter of concern. People feared that factional politics had begun to sow discord in their society.

'Party-*bazi*'

Although the election animated life in Kargil, it left in its wake a sense of disquiet. Regardless of whether factional allegiance or other forms of social solidarity managed to claim their vote, everyone in Kargil was aware of the divisive impact that 'party-*bazi*' (politicking) was having on their society. In common parlance 'party' refers to a political party and *bazi* means politicking; people started using 'party' to refer to the Islamia School and the IKMT. They began to question the justness of both the School and IKMT's politics, disgusted that it had deteriorated into mere politicking for personal and institutional gains. Dark humour expressed the intensity of sentiment: 'If this level of tension continues, there might be a murder or two by the next elections,' remarked one man. The joke about murders in society was a euphemism for a deeper concern with the maintenance of its moral unity. This concern emanated from both a regional as well as religious premium placed on preventing conflict. At the regional level, ties of reciprocity and maintenance of amicable relations take on additional meaning in the context of Ladakh's geography and climate, which necessitates cooperation. Any form of conflict is considered harmful to the community, including the expression of anger by a person.[44]

Others felt that Kargili society was not 'mature' enough to have a Council of its own, arguing that people got carried away by *jazbat* (emotions), that along with having young and educated candidates, you also need educated and aware voters.

Yet others bemoaned that the Council had become a locus of everything but what it ought to be – the development and progress of Kargil. The son of one candidate, and therefore deeply involved in politicking himself, after an hour of speculative gossip, laughed and said that no one was really thinking of development but simply 'having fun out of the elections'. When I asked an agha (who chose not to wear the turban and cloak and worked for the district administration) in jest why he was not standing for elections, he replied, 'Oh, the elections are only for people looking for a pension.' He clarified that he did not need one as his government job guaranteed that. Another man satirised the whole scene with a possibly fictive anecdote about a young man running to the election office in his village one day to file his candidature. He was in a rush to get there before his uncle, who was also planning to stand for the elections. Elections had become a free-for-all, a subject for mockery.

Several people blamed the entry of religious leaders into politics quite explicitly. A record number of them had contested the 2008 elections, and many played an active role in campaigning and strategising backstage. The Council elections confirmed the cynicism of those who felt this was an avenue for religious leaders to retrieve their diminishing power in society. Though some of these critics had themselves voted for aghas, they admitted in private that it was out of political compulsion related to their factional affiliation or religious sentiments. They were under no illusion that a religious leader was capable of doing any developmental work. A young IKMT-aligned man grumbled that the 'ulama became serious only during elections rather than paying attention to societal issues prior to that. Perceptibly annoyed, he added, 'They just speak during the ten days of Muharram and not with any seriousness. They should say they will boycott weddings if someone asks for jahez [dowry] or will not read the nikah (to marry). Instead, during the elections, they threaten people by saying, I will not bury you.' The younger generation's sentiments were captured by a popular mixed Urdu–Purigi proverb: 'Gni mullah khatre iman, gni hakim khatre jan' (Less educated mullahs are like bad doctors, dangerous to one's health). Fielding old or uneducated aghas as candidates in the election was often perceived as fooling people in the name of religion. A politically canny, elderly man remarked, 'What can the 'ulama say in the parliament of Hindustan? They have only religious education.' Not only was he restating the importance attached to modern education but also turning the tables back on the old clerical class, which in the past had discouraged modern education saying it would not guarantee a place in heaven.

When factional politicking began to threaten social solidarity and be seen as a source of fasad (conflict), criticism became even more widespread. From an Islamic perspective, fasad or fitna in a society signals the breakdown of the moral fabric of the community. Denoting conflict internal to the Muslim community, the concept of *fitna* evokes the foundational conflict between the companions of the Prophet over the battle for succession. This intersection of regional and religious disapproval of conflict was expressed in the use of the word *tsokpo* (bad or dirty) in Purigi to describe *fasad*. In the early days of fieldwork, when I referred to the factions as *firqa*, the Urdu word for 'sect', I would immediately be reprimanded: 'This is just party-*bazi*; we are all Shi'a.' 'There is no fundamental difference between us.' My interlocutors did not want the factionalism in Kargil to be seen as a breakdown of sectarian unity.

The concern with protecting unity was reflected in the endeavours of Kargili scholars studying in Qum to overcome factional allegiances that lingered even in Iran. A brief visit to Qum in 2009 was enough to discern this. Friendships seemed to be forged along lines of factional allegiance. One cleric denounced the factionalism, saying, 'Political and religious leaders get bought off.' Another explained that different *mujtahid*s have different perspectives: 'One might say sighting the Eid moon through a telescope is legitimate, while another might insist on seeing it with the naked eye. Here difference in perspective is accepted, but it becomes a big issue in Kargil. Exaggerating issues there is a pre-revolutionary habit.'

Even as clerics continued to characterise Kargil as 'backward', many parents wanted to free their children of the stranglehold of this factional politicking. A man educated in the IKMT's Mutahhari Public School told me that he had sent his children to study in Srinagar for he did not want them to grow up absorbing the 'atmosphere' of Kargili society. It was precisely the mixing of religion and politics that churned emotions in Kargil that this man wanted to protect his children from. Thus, 'progress' was articulated both in developmental terms as well as the inculcated dispositions of people: 'party-*bazi*' was not only seen as detrimental to development but also a way of living life. It related to a widely held sentiment that only external oppressors could not be blamed for Kargil's 'wretched' condition; they must hold themselves accountable, too.

Criticisms of the effect of emotions and passions churned by religious belief on 'progress' uncomfortably echoed European Enlightenment discourse which made the modernisation of a society contingent upon the retreat of religion to the private sphere. I contend, however, that what appears to be a tension between rational and emotional considerations that people faced while voting in the elections reflected a growing and widespread critical and questioning attitude among Kargilis. Even when people voted based on emotional ties, governed by their concern to accrue merit for well-being in the afterlife, or by kinship obligation, many were conscious that this went against their *'aql*. For many, especially women, the secret ballot of the elections in fact offered an opportunity to break free of communitarian logics of kinship.

A lady teacher at the Mutahhari Public School confided in me that she chose not to follow her family's choice of candidate because she was exercising her right to think independently, based on her own intelligence. The passions aroused by party-*bazi* did not leave women untouched despite their relative invisibility in public-political space. Even those women who appeared to be illiterate and rustic quietly absorbed the political temperature of the day. They discussed the merits or deceptions of different candidates as they sat on their terraces, knitting for the upcoming winter season or cooking for the family in the kitchen.

Campaigning during the elections took place among the menfolk within the largely male space of the Islamia School or the IKMT or private all-male meetings. Typically, talk of politics pervaded men's conversations much more than those of women, as they socialised every evening after work in the bazaar where certain teashops were associated as the hangouts of either School or IKMT supporters. Fathers, husbands and brothers would, however, carry political talk from the bazaar into their homes. As families sat down to eat the evening meal together in the kitchen, women would either engage in active discussion or at least be privy to this talk among the men. Usually, the head of the household would instruct all family members to vote for a certain candidate, and it was assumed that his decision would be binding on them. This expectation came into question in the Council elections. As one man complained to me, in good humour, 'Now one cannot even trust one's wife.' Election day saw a large turnout of women, queuing at the polling stations from early in the morning (Figure 3.4). Long hours of waiting did not diminish their enthusiasm. When I asked one woman whom she would vote for, she told me off, saying the ballot is secret, and asked me why should she reveal her choice.

The passions aroused by politics and politicking thus became another arena for quotidian expressions of *'aql*. There is no doubt that education and exposure to the outside world through radio, television and travel also played an important role in the development of this questioning disposition. A critical attitude expressed in the register of cynicism towards politicking was equally shaped from within the discursive tradition of Shi'ism, which is founded on a distinction between moral and immoral politics. It was not the legitimation of political participation through religious ethics per se that came under attack after the elections; it was the immorality or lies behind the candidature of religious leaders unsuited to navigating the modern world. Making a 'rational' voting choice implied making a truthful choice for a candidate capable of working for the well-being of Kargili society. There was no disagreement on the 'common good' for Kargil across factional allegiances. Everyone shared the same vision for Kargil's progress and development.[45] This became clear when the biggest blow to democracy was dealt

Figure 3.4   Women voting in the Hill Council elections, 2008
Source: Photograph by the author.

with the creation of the UT of Ladakh. As I will discuss in the Epilogue, both the Islamia School and the IKMT transcended their differences to jointly raise their voice against the UT.

While people in Kargil were embarrassed by the factional politics, conscious of the detriment it posed to presenting a united Kargili face to the outside world, their commentary on the election and its afterlife went much beyond narratives of deception on the part of either politicians or voters that have dominated ethnographies of elections. Their cynicism displayed an acute understanding of the very nature of the real *politik* and the workings of democracy. Cynicism became another affective register to reiterate the importance of exercising *'aql* in quotidian realms, of exercising the faculty of moral discrimination when seeking to balance affective social bonds with idealised aspirations of modern governance.

☙❧

The involvement of religious factions in politics contributed to a certain openness of debate in Kargil's public sphere that was muted in the past. The contestations between the IKMT and the Islamia School, even if dismissed by people in Kargil as 'party-*bazi*' was part of a wider trend of internal democratisation of Islamic movements.[46] The disenchantment with factional politicking did not lead to political apathy or the death of the 'public man' in Kargil.[47] Rather, it led to a honing of political sensibilities. Polemics between the IKMT and the School on the value of applying the political ideology of the Iranian Revolution and the institution of the *vilayat-i faqih* in India were not merely internal debates but reflected their negotiations of belonging to the nation state.

Political subjectivity in Kargil can be subsumed under neither the generic dichotomies of Shi'i quietism in a non-Islamic state nor communal assertion in a secular state. Instead, Kargil lends a more nuanced insight into how Shi'i minorities in contemporary India have navigated nationalist discourses and ideologies. This becomes clearer through a historical comparison with Muslim politics in the subcontinent, particularly in the late colonial period. Islamic revival and reform movements in the subcontinent during the colonial period turned 'inwards',[48] identifying 'religion with the private sphere'.[49] In contrast, contemporary modernist Shi'i movements, such as the IKMT and the School, turn outward. These institutions have become key mediators between the state and people. In the aftermath of the bifurcation of J&K, their support has become even more important in fighting for justice and freedom from oppression.

This outward orientation of Shi'i modernist reformists in Kargil resonates with trends in the politics of other sectarian groups in post-colonial India, such as the Jamaat-e-Islami. Its stance towards secularism and democracy changed from the time of its formation in 1941, as later generations of ideologues no longer regarded secular democracy as alien to Islam.[50] Rather than engaging in an oppositional politics or shunning any kind of political activism altogether in order to protect the community, Muslims in post-colonial India have attempted to find a place for themselves within the mainstream, albeit with little success. This is an outcome of both the declining tolerance for them in a violent Hindutva state and the difficulty of building solidarity across sectarian divides, historically. In post-colonial India, Shi'i politics became less ecumenical. During the anti-colonial struggle, Shi'as from different denominations came together to carve out a space for themselves within the Muslim League that increasingly came to be dominated by Sunni groups,[51] with signs of Shi'a–Sunni tensions becoming visible in parts of North India from the early decades of the twentieth century.[52] After the creation of Pakistan, however, Shi'as who stayed back in India developed a stronger denominational identity and adopted different strategies to mark themselves as distinct from the Sunni majority. Their politics also became deeply grounded within regional contexts.

As discussed in Chapter 1, Kargil's relationship with the Kashmir Valley was a complicated one. Experiences of sectarian discrimination in the Valley and the impossibility of imagining a viable future with Pakistan underlay a feeling of alienation and the need to project a distinct political subjectivity. Kargili Shi'as embraced the negligible freedoms that India offered and denounced calls for *azadi* from India. They have tried to build a relationship with the Indian state, not least through an engagement with electoral democracy. Since 2019, Kargil's Muslims are confronting further entrapment with the creation of Ladakh as a UT. The crystallisation of political consciousness, which I have examined in this and the previous chapter, is manifesting in a new politics of rejection. Kargilis have raised their voices condemning the discriminatory policies of the UT administration. They are also publicly denouncing the Indian state's violence in the Kashmir Valley. This has undoubtedly been influenced by Khamenei's call to the Islamic world to support the people of Kashmir.[53]

Despite the captivity imposed by a security state, Kargil's political horizons have extended beyond the bounds of the nation state. They have negotiated belonging by calibrating ideologies from a transnational Shi'i sphere with nationalist idioms – seen, for example, in the parallels drawn between Khomeini and Gandhi's revolution. Such discursive connections bring to the fore anti-imperial and post-colonial axes of solidarities that shape political consciousness in ways that complicate the dichotomy of resistance and submission. Borderlands like Kargil offer rich insights into post-colonial internationalisms beyond the dominant scholarly foci on textual, artistic and institutional domains of left socialism. The calibrations between discourses of piety, politics and patriotism that I examine in this book also quietly shatter illusions of nationalist idioms being culturally sealed or pure in the way that majoritarian political ideologues wish to impose. States seldom succeed in fully colonising people's senses of place and inner consciousness for these are more capacious than the demands and desires of national belonging.

Practices of place-making and belonging in Kargil draw upon not only ideologies that travel from West Asia but also longer historical connections with Central Asia and Tibet in their location within a trans-Himalayan ecumene. The next chapter turns to practices of translation through which the Shi'as of Kargil calibrate their Buddhist past with the Islamic present to foreground the importance of place in thinking about patriotism beyond the binds of nationalist ideologies and the communal fissures these have fomented.

Notes

1. Instances of Shi'ite political activism could be found in Iraq and Lebanon. But even in these cases, national, ethnic and linguistic identities tended to be

foregrounded over the religious in the context of Arab nationalism. Cole, *Sacred Space and Holy War*, 175.

2. Iran is the exception due to the rise of Shi'i states from the sixteenth century onwards. These states were, however, underlined by a constant tension between 'government' and 'religion', seen in the division of power between kings and clerics. Momen, *Introduction to Shi'i Islam*, 170.

3. Arjomand, 'History, Structure, and Revolution'.

4. Saad-Ghorayeb, *Hizbu'llah*, 61.

5. The *faqih* plays a direct role in government in Iran: He appoints the Council of Guardians, composed of the heads of the judiciary, military and the revolutionary guards, and also has the last word over the president and the prime minister. Esposito, *The Iranian Revolution*, 27.

6. The Iranian Cultural House in Delhi sponsors Shi'as from different parts of India, including Ladakh, to travel to Iran for this occasion very year. See Pinault, *Horse of Karbala*, 94.

7. 'From Kashmir to Kanyakumari' is a popular geographical epithet of India's nationalist discourse of 'unity in diversity'.

8. Khomeini, *Islam and the Revolution*, 242.

9. With Saddam Hussein's downfall in 2003, new hope emerged among the majority Shi'i population of Iraq which had been facing decades of repression under the Sunni Arab Socialist Baath party.

10. For insight into the sentiments of Iraqi Shi'as who celebrated Saddam's downfall but also condemned the American occupation and sectarian politics, see Antoon, *Corpse Washer*.

11. Tabaar, *Religious Statecraft*, 36.

12. Mottahedeh, *Mantle of the Prophet*, 242.

13. On the Shi'a in Hyderabad, see, for example, Howarth, *Twelver Shi'a*, 35.

14. Cole, 'Ayatollahs and Democracy', 10.

15. In subsequent years, based on images circulating on the internet in 2010 and later, I found that the School had even started displaying pictures of Khomeini. Iran tried to bring about a reconciliation between the School and the IKMT but with little success. However, Shaykh Mohammadi's son, Shaykh Nazir Mehdi, the current president of the School, who had studied in Iran, instituted changes in the School that reflected reformist discourses of rationalisation.

16. R. Gupta, 'Experiments with Khomeini's Revolution'.

17. Even though the factions' political rhetoric was couched in an Islamic idiom, it bore striking similarities to the Youth Wing set up by the Ladakh Buddhist Association (LBA) in Leh in 1989. The School's Youth Committee's role was similar to that of LBA's Youth Wing in relation to its senior cadres – that by virtue

of being more educated and aware, the youth would perform the 'difficult tasks' that the elders could not. Aggarwal, *Beyond Lines of Control*, 72.

18. Momen, *Introduction to Shiʻi Islam*, 294.
19. Faisal Devji argues that Khomeini, through his explication of the institution of the *vilayat-i faqih*, lays the ground for a theory of global popular citizenship that rests on political action effected through the power of civic ideals that the Prophet comes to represent. He suggests that for Khomeini, ideals were more powerful than origins and were therefore able to effect political action within a total system in which 'historical events become equivalent, each one exchangeable with the other'. Devji, 'Imitatio Muhammadi', 367.
20. Saad-Ghorayeb, *Hizbu'llah*, 58.
21. Crooke, *Resistance*, 173; Shaery-Eisenlohr, *Shiʻite Lebanon*, 6.
22. Bowen, 'Beyond Migration', 890.
23. See Bolourchi, 'Sacred Defense.'
24. Varzi, *Warring Souls*, 6.
25. Jenkins, 'Fieldwork and the Perception'; Rabinow, *Reflections on Fieldwork*.
26. Husayn's martyrdom had been applied to anti-colonial mobilisations in North India since 1857. Imam Husayn's mobilisation as an '"exemplar for all humanity"' was used to establish cross-religious dialogue with Indian nationalist leaders in the 1940s. Jones, '"Shiʻism, Humanity and Revolution,"', 424.
27. Deeb, *Enchanted Modern*, 151.
28. See Eisenlohr, 'Media, Citizenship, and Religious Mobilization', on the Muharram Awareness Campaign of WIN.
29. In the current geopolitical environment it is all too easily forgotten that the Iranian Revolution was successful and continues to be endorsed in Iran across the social and political spectrum, including those in opposition to the clerical regime, for it was above all a nationalist revolution. National identity holds pre-eminence for a vast majority of Iranians. The debate instead revolves around what role religion should play in this national identity. Aghaie, *Martyrs of Karbala*, 86.
30. Gandhi, *The Collected Works of Mahatma Gandhi*, vol. 16, 6–7.
31. Praise for Husayn and other members of the Prophet's family can also be found in classical Sunni literature, especially of the Shafi and Hanafi schools. In new Sunni literature he is glorified as the 'rebel and the prototype of all those who challenged the false consensus'. Inayat, *Modern Islamic Political Thought*, 184.
32. Hyder, *Reliving Karbala*, 172.
33. The martyrdom of those who accompanied Husayn to the battle of Karbala – his standard-bearer (Abbas), sons (Ali Akbar and Ali Azgar) and nephew (Qasim) – provoke intense mourning for these figures are seen as the symbols of courage, piety and truth. Aghaie, *Martyrs of Karbala*, 9.
34. Gandhi, *The Collected Works of Mahatma Gandhi*, vol. 17, 16.

35. Islamia School supporters disagreed, pointing to the 'coup' that brought Karbalai into power when voting rights were given to nominated members of the Council by the state government, which was formed by the Congress party at the time. They argued that the very basis of Karbalai's *hukumat* (government) was therefore 'unjust' because it did not come into power based on the original rules laid out in the Hill Council Act.

36. Schimmel, *Two Coloured Brocade*, 103.

37. van Beek, 'Act of 1995'.

38. See, for example, Pinault, *Horse of Karbala*.

39. Chatterjee, *Politics of the Governed*, 73.

40. Spencer, *Anthropology, Politics, and the State*, 45–46.

41. See Govindarajan, 'Electoral Ripples', on the afterlife of an election in Uttarakhand.

42. See Menon, 'What Do Polemics Do?', 142, on Sunni intra-sectarian polemics in Kerala and its effects on blurring the lines 'between private and public, personal and political, friend/brother and enemy', portending dire consequences for the maintenance of the *qaum*.

43. Common to the wider trans-Himalayan region, pieces of land in Kargil, despite the conversion to Islam, are associated with a protector deity. Families sharing a piece of land constitute a *sa phaspun* (*sa* – earth). Fragmented households are referred to as *mgo phaspun* (*mgo* – head).

44. Pirie, *Peace and Conflict in Ladakh*.

45. Similarities in the dissolution of factional differences between the modernists and traditionalists on the engagement with modernity and progress can be found in other Muslim communities in India. See, for example, Osella and Osella, 'Islamism and Social Reform'.

46. See, for example, Ahmad, *Islamism and Democracy*; Devji, *Landscapes of the Jihad*; Eickelman and Piscatori, *Muslim Politics*; and Hefner, *Civil Islam*, on this trend of democratisation within Islamic movements in other contexts.

47. Sennett, *Fall of the Public Man*.

48. Zaman, 'Modernity', 254.

49. Metcalf, *Islamic Contestations*, 279.

50. Ahmad, *Islamism and Democracy*.

51. Devji, *Muslim Zion*, 66.

52. Hasan, 'Sectarianism', 219.

53. Majidyar, 'Khamenei's Kashmir Remarks'; Nayar, 'Iran's Ayatollah Khamenei'.

4

Talking about Culture

Often befuddled by the typically open-ended nature of anthropological inquiry, people in Kargil would ask me, 'But what is your topic?' Sometimes, the easiest answer to proffer was 'the culture and history of the region'. My response elicited a variety of reactions and suggestions. The most common was, 'If you want to study culture go to Chigtan or Dartsigss–Garkone. People there have preserved their culture.' The cultural qualifications of Chigtan lay in people continuing to wear traditional clothes, such as the *goncha* (Ladakhi tunic), maintaining their houses as in the 'olden' times or being one of the sub-regions of Kargil district where a few elders could still recite the entire *Kesar Saga*.[1] Similarly, the famed mythic 'pure Aryan' villages of Dartsigss and Garkone in the Batalik region were offered as the seats of 'original culture'. Elaborate floral head adornments, blue eyes and fair skin mark the inhabitants of these villages in the imagination of locals and outsiders alike as exotica.[2] When talking about 'culture', comparisons with Leh would also invariably surface, confirming the well-established anthropological insight that culture is always a category of difference and hierarchy. A teenage boy remarked, 'Leh is more developed because people there have kept their culture. They whitewash their houses and decorate them with prayer flags. That is why outsiders come to see their place and tourists do not come to Kargil.' His friend added, 'The culture in our region has died because religion has got mixed up with it.' When I asked for an example, he lamented how Losar (Tibetan New Year, celebrated in Ladakh in the month of December) was no longer held in his village, Chanegond. 'Till recently, say about 2000, it was celebrated with so much enthusiasm that every household slaughtered an animal,' he explained, but also said that animals had become more expensive, and people did not have the time anymore. Conversely, a cleric, somewhat sceptical of my interest in studying the 'culture' of Kargil, commented, 'There is no *makhsus* [distinct] Kargili culture. What might constitute a culture for Kargil is defined by religion.'

Culture had become a frequent topic of discussion and debate in Kargil's public sphere, particularly in urban areas such as Kargil town, as consciousness of regional and sectarian identity strengthened since the 1980s. Often used in English, the word 'culture' was easily absorbed into conversations conducted in Purigi, Balti or Urdu. It was invoked in diverse contexts and frequently used as a metaphor for 'our identity' (*gnati pai'chan*) and 'our language' (*gnati skad*). People also used the Urdu words *saqafat*, *tamaddun* and *adab*, the meanings of which draw upon a wider Persianate imaginaire, referring to an Islamic ethos of refinement, etiquette and civilisation.

This chapter will examine the cultural politics of place-making seen in the vibrant and ongoing debates on differences between regional and religious culture.[3] I analyse these debates both on-stage through cultural performances that feed into negotiations of belonging to India and off-stage. The latter become visible in practices that cannot easily be slotted into either the category of the regional or the religious. I deploy the interpretive strategy of translation as a 'search of equivalence' between a past essentialised as Buddhist and the Islamic present in Kargil.[4] Following Tony Stewart, I eschew the concept of syncretism to avoid presenting the encounter between Islam and Tibetan Buddhism as complete and, therefore, relegated to the past. This encounter is a dynamic and ongoing process that shows how Islamic rituals and doctrines are creatively translated into the material conditions of dwelling in a place. These off-stage practices underscore Kargil's location in the trans-Himalayan ecumene by illustrating people's deep affective relationship to their land. Cutting across religious and political boundaries, this attachment is integral to the language of belonging on this frontier. It challenges the discursive captivity imposed on Kargil by external representations of Ladakh and exacerbated by communal politics. Cultural practices of belonging on this frontier transcend both the constraints of religious orthodoxy and national categories.

Cultural Activism

Culture talk articulated both symbolic and material concerns. It was underlined by the desire to project a regional Kargili identity envisioned as being independent of both Buddhist Ladakh and Sunni Kashmir and yet irrevocably tied to both.

It was also linked to the desire to situate Kargil on the tourist itinerary which had historically bypassed it. Since Ladakh was opened to tourism in 1974, it became a popular destination for Western travellers seeking the Tibetan Shangri-la. Buddhist Ladakh easily stood in for Tibet that remained officially closed to outsiders;[5] it satiated the Western imagination of Tibetan Buddhism nestled peacefully in rugged mountains dotted with remote monasteries, monks and prayer flags fluttering across high passes. In this representational repertoire several features of a trans-Himalayan regional culture that cut across religious differences – be it salty butter tea or mud-brick homes – were essentialised to being Buddhist in the eyes of outsiders, including some scholars.[6] This perception was exacerbated by the fact that monks and monasteries had given way to turbaned clerics and mosques. Also, Kargil's relative proximity to the Kashmir Valley made it more susceptible to its cultural influences.

The discursive captivity perpetuated by such external representations and communal politics was not lost on Kargili Muslims. It has fed into their endeavours to foreground ideas of place that challenge singular and homogenising external representations of Kargil as a war zone or a conservative Muslim backwater. Yet Kargili Muslims have simultaneously tapped into the representation of Ladakh as a Buddhist land for the pragmatic purpose of attracting tourists. This has led to further encapsulation of the region within the cultural terms set by the nation state through its rhetoric of integration. Cultural politics thus illustrate another dimension of the paradox of freedom in captivity that Kargili Muslims inhabit.

The separation between the 'culture' of Buddhist Ladakh and Muslim Kargil was not merely an outcome of external representations. The communalisation of Ladakh since the 1980s instigated a consciousness of religious identity that had to grapple with cultural markers distinguishing among the Buddhists and Muslims. This was brought home to me on a quotidian level, when a Buddhist friend from a mixed Muslim–Buddhist village, living in Kargil town, remarked that she only wore a firan (woollen tunic from Kashmir) here for people at home would tease her for dressing like a Muslim. Back in her village, in order to mark herself out as a Buddhist, she wore a goncha. In Kargil, in both the town and most villages, the majority of Muslim women have taken to wearing the firan in winter on a daily basis. As a result, an association has emerged between Buddhist women and gonchas and between Muslim women and firans.

It is difficult to trace with certainty when internal debates on the distinction between regional and religious cultures in Kargil arose. These were triggered in part by the influence of Islamic reformists and by feelings of inferiority to Leh. The concern for protection of regional culture was also manifested in the activism of Balti intellectuals, who sought to preserve their language from the influence of

Urdu, and Purigi that they deemed to be a bastard dialect.[7] Their cause was taken up by the elite Munshi family, to whom you were introduced in Chapter 1. Some of these Balti intellectuals along with the Munshi brothers and their friends formed an organisation called the Kargil Social and Cultural Organization (KASCO) in 1997.[8] Together with other creativity enthusiasts, the Munshi brothers and other KASCO members became the mouthpiece of a simmering debate on what constitutes Kargil's culture. Their ability to speak the language of 'culture' itself was a reflection of their exposure to a wider world. This included interactions with scholars and anthropologists like myself for whom they became the first mediators of insights into Kargil. These cultural activists, as I will refer to them, came from different walks of life. Cutting across class differences, some worked as schoolteachers, and others were employed in the district administration. A motley group, they shared the concern that the influence of reformist Islam would strip the region of its cultural heritage and disapproved of what they considered the uncritical acceptance of certain injunctions made in the name of Islam. They also bemoaned the decline of traditions of architecture, dress or food habits in Muslim villages that had become synonymous with Buddhist identity, though devoid of Buddhist religious symbolism. These activists sought to reclaim and revive Kargil's regional heritage.

With the conversion from Islam to Buddhism, facets of Kargil's regional cultural past gradually transformed, faded or disappeared. The deeming of music to be haram became a pervasive trope of this sense of loss. Sighing, one of these activists said, 'This has influenced the ethos of occasions such as weddings and seasonal festivals.' The *surna* (double reed) and *daman* (kettledrum), traditional Ladakhi instruments, are no longer played in Kargil except during state 'cultural' festivals and sporting events such as horse-polo and archery matches, and then, too, the musicians are Buddhists. Nevertheless, young people danced to Bollywood music at weddings, but only after the clerics invited for the feast had left and often in a separate room. During Muharram, shops selling music albums covered posters and counters with black cloth, black being the colour of mourning. For many years music and dance were not legitimate extracurricular activities in the Jaffaria Academy and the Mutahhari Public School for Modern Education.

Emblematic of this concern with losing history was the loss of the repertoire of Purigi and Ladakhi folksongs in the region. Besides epics like the Kesar Saga and Api-tso, a trove of *glu* (folk songs) for every occasion, relationship and sentiment is said to have existed in Ladakh – for big people like kings (*che glu*), children's songs (*phru glu*), for ordinary gatherings (*zhung glu*), songs related to religion (*chos glu*) and wedding songs (*bag ston glu*), and so on. These songs not only encoded the history of the region but also were said to constitute a 'secret language' of communication. An aged Apo (grandfather) from Chigtan recalled bygone times when they would go to the Mon[9] to correlate tunes with particular songs. He explained, 'Then songs were taught as education.' When I asked if he had imparted this education to his own children, he replied in a matter-of-fact way, 'No, because there is no need. They go to schools and have jobs.' Cultural politics of the present betrayed his nostalgia for the past. When the younger man, who had accompanied me to meet Apo, urged him to sing a few stanzas of the Kesar Saga, he steadfastly refused. Apo descended into silence, concentrating instead on turning his string of prayer beads. Cultural activists pointed to conscious forgetting among those they labelled as 'orthodox'.

The repertoire of folksongs in Kargil has not been dated with any certainty. Ladakhi intellectuals suggest that since the songs speak of the times of the kings, they must go at least that far back. Some claim that no new songs were written after the fifteenth century. Regardless, folksongs have come to be associated with Kargil's pre-Islamic past. As Islam gained popularity, a new genre of religious music became prominent in social life, bringing with it the influence of Persian and Arabic on the Purigi and Balti dialects. This was the music of majalis – *nauha* (rhythmic dirges), *qasida* (odes), *marsiya* (Muharram elegies) and *na't-e-sharif* (songs in praise of the Prophet).

One of KASCO's main activities over the years was the production of music as a medium to preserve the region's poetry and language, though much of their focus remained on Balti verse. They set traditional religious poetry such as *qasida*s scripted by poets in Baltistan to modern rhythms and also produced music videos that became quite popular among young people. To indicate the success of these music albums, one of the cultural activists pointed out, 'Earlier at weddings only Bollywood music would play. Now these songs are also played.' Indeed, I enjoyed this music many a time on long journeys in shared taxis, attesting to the popularity of its revival.

A younger member of KASCO rued that with the entangling of religion and politics, 'the shaykhs are becoming more powerful. But the thinking of these shaykhs is still quite small'. He felt that it was very difficult for cultural activists to break their stranglehold over people, lamenting, 'Through mosque sermons, in majalis during Muharram, and so on, they indoctrinate people.' Against this background, music for these cultural activists was not merely a source of creative impulse and entertainment but an important medium of change, of resisting orthodoxy at the time. Yet there were others who were also resisting the old clerical guard but challenged music and dance being made an index of the decline of regional culture. Karbalai articulated this view for me in an interview:

Saqafat [Culture] is that which you find in the mahaul [social environment] in which you have grown up; you adopt those traditions. If some go against *mazhab*, leave those. But Islam is not against culture. Culture is not just song and dance. It is a way of life – marriage and death rituals, the way crops are cut, how you behave with your wife, children, relatives and neighbours.... Unfortunately here, when Islam came, limitations were imposed on song and dance. So people have started thinking that only this constitutes culture. But we have many cultural traditions here – Mamani, Mendok Tanmo ... people give *khatak*s [*btag*s – ceremonial scarves] to each other; Islam is not against this.

While betraying a hint of defensiveness, Karbalai offered a more expansive conception of culture, challenging too clear-cut a dichotomy between orthodoxy and heterodoxy that continues to haunt many anthropological studies of Muslim societies. This has often led to locating culture within the realm of Sufi Islam, fetishising it to be consumed like other cultural commodities. It was not as if the more 'orthodox' individuals who championed certain Islamic norms disavowed their Ladakhi identity. Nor did the cultural activists disavow a Shi'i Muslim ethos. This was perhaps best expressed in the way Nasir Munshi, a staunch supporter of the IKMT and one of the founding members of KASCO, explained their take on music:

From an Islamic point of view, *lahu-lahab*, music, alcohol, ... are all haram. But I myself am of the opinion that if music so completely absorbs a person that it interferes with their daily work then it is bad. But if music and sport are seen as being important for mental rejuvenation and relaxation, then there is nothing wrong – this is a fatwa given by Khomeini.

Such statements reveal how those cultural activists who subscribed more broadly to the reformist agenda nonetheless sought to preserve regional culture – in this case, legitimising it with reference to Khomeini and the reformist discourse itself.

Another location for cultural activists' anxieties of cultural loss was the disappearance of traditional architecture. In a survey of the region in the 1970s, David Snellgrove and Tadeusz Skorupski pointed to what they considered to be the absence of a 'higher Islamic culture' in Kargil, noting: 'The village mosques are mostly simple adaptations of normal flat-roofed stone and mud Tibetan-style houses. In Kargil and Leh one sees a rare dome and small minaret.'[10] Perhaps they would have been glad to see the much-changed religious architectural landscape of shiny steel and asbestos domes and concrete minarets that became ubiquitous two decades on.

Most villages either razed to the ground the traditional mud-brick flat-roofed mosques and rebuilt them in concrete, incorporating Perso-Arabic styles, or built new mosques and *matam-sarais* (spaces for mourning [*matam*]). The bigger and more concrete a mosque or *matam-sarai*, and the more elaborately adorned it is with Persian-style floral motifs and Arabic calligraphy, the greater the pride of the village. Not only do people voluntarily contribute large sums to rebuild mosques, but they have also received support from MP funds in the past. While most of these mosques and *matam-sarais* are 'off-stage', a few are now advertised to tourists, of which the most prominent is the Trespone *imambara*. While cultural activists extolled the splendour of sites such as the Trespone *imambara* as examples of material culture that incorporate both trans-Himalayan Tibetan and Islamic motifs, they also lamented the destruction of the older mosques and *matam-sarais* as the loss of tradition.

At stake in these debates on regional and religious cultures was the character of Islamic ethos considered desirable by cultural activists and those they labelled 'orthodox'. Culture talk, debates and activism in Kargil reflected a broader process of place-making that grappled with giving due weight to the *longue durée* of their history, a history that brings together a past essentialised as Buddhist and the Islamic present. Whether activist or orthodox, everyone deplored the insufficient recognition given to Kargil and Muslim culture in outsiders' representations of the cultural heritage of Ladakh. The frustration with Kargil's invisibility in external representations came to a head in 2021, when the first tableau of the UT of Ladakh at the Republic Day parade in Delhi only showcased Buddhist culture. Kargili outpouring of anger was noted by the national media.

Culture on Display

The revival and preservation of regional culture in Kargil was also underlined by the desire to develop and promote Kargil as a tourist destination. Mimicking the Leh festival organised every year in the month of September to prolong the tourist season, Kargil too started organising the Kargil Tourism festival. The festival puts on display troupes from different ethnic groups (Balti, Shina, Brogpa) to perform dance and music in traditional attire along with horse-polo and archery matches. The name of the venue – the Khree Sultan Cho sports stadium – itself harks back to its *qadim* (ancient) past. This event began to be replicated through smaller festivals like the Aryan festival in Dartsigss and Garkone and the Youth Cultural Festival organised by the Kargil branch of the J&K Cultural Academy. In 2019, the latter included painting, poetry and storytelling competitions. Such events illustrate the pedagogical role of the state in producing a citizenry with a cultural consciousness that fits the state's formats of identification. This is a form of slow encapsulation that over time renders other expressions of self-identification illegitimate. Although Kargilis embraced these festivals quite uncritically, both for the meagre material benefits and for the sense of inclusion within the nation state such events appeared to offer, they also attempted to break free from discursive captivity.

Cultural activists made efforts to institutionalise the display of regional culture in ways that do not conform to the templates provided by the nation state. One of the more well-known initiatives has been a private museum, the Munshi Aziz Bhatt Museum for Silk Route and Central Asian Trade. It was established by Gulzar and Aijaz Munshi in the annex of their home in 2005 at the bidding of anthropologist Jacqueline Fewkes, who alerted them to the importance of material objects in the preservation of the region's history.[11] Named after their grandfather, Munshi Aziz Bhatt, who was a prominent trader, the museum displays objects retrieved from Aziz Bhatt's *sarai* (inn) for traders. Some of the objects were solicited as donations from families across the region, while others were allegedly bought off cheaply. The museum was re-curated in 2014 with the help of an art historian from Delhi, when it was also renamed 'Munshi Aziz Bhat Museum of Central Asian and Kargil Trade Artifacts'. Inspired by a visit to the Pitt Rivers Museum in Oxford, the museum was originally designed as an ethnographic museum along the lines of the classic 'cabinets of curiosities' model. A motley collection of objects ranging from animal accessories to coins and currency, textiles and clothing to a rich collection of personal and trade correspondence dating to the 1870s, and old volumes of the Qur'an are displayed in its cabinets.[12] By foregrounding Kargil as the centre of a historical network of trade routes between Ladakh and Central Asia, the museum projects the region beyond its contemporary border location even as its success increasingly depends on the hordes of Indian tourists for whom the lure of Kargil lies in it being a 'theatre of war'.[13]

For many years the Munshi brothers had been at pains to find funding to build a separate building for the museum, a larger space that would accommodate their entire collection. They told me about having refused offers of financial support made conditional on shifting the museum to Leh. Underlined by their complaint that all external attention and funding had been focused on Leh, their refusal illustrated that the museum represented a small space for political negotiation. The Aziz Bhatt Museum was implicitly positioned in a relation of competition with the better publicised Central Asian Museum designed by the Tibet Heritage Fund in Leh. The museum's location is another reminder of the centrality of Kargil within a trans-Himalayan ecumene, forged in part through trading networks that stretched across the high mountains from Central Asia to Tibet.

Such displays of regional culture are a window into a more eclectic cultural history than that afforded by ahistorical nationalist representations.

The model of displaying everyday objects used in the past was replicated in another smaller museum, Unlock Hundarman: Museum of Memories, an initiative taken by the Delhi-educated, savvy nephew of Gulzar Munshi in 2015. It is located in Hundarman, a village that was (re-)incorporated into Indian Territory during the 1971 war with Pakistan. The idea for this museum emerged from an architectural workshop that Muzammil had organised for a group of students from the Western Indian city of Ahmedabad as part of a larger commercial enterprise to develop education tourism in the region. Housed in the abandoned mud-brick home of his local partner, Ilyas Ansari, they discovered war debris (shells, helmets, guns) that was put on display along with letters from families torn apart in 1971 and antiquated objects of everyday use. Advertised as 'unlocking the past', the Museum of Memories is a palimpsest of sorts. It displays layers of the region's history from the mundane to the monumental through the serial partitions that this frontier has experienced from 1947. This museum has received significant coverage in the Indian media as Indian tourists and journalists have suddenly discovered the nation's periphery with the Indian state encouraging tourism in border areas. Such connections to the heartlands of India contribute to re-inscribing the region as a battlefield in the national imagination and perpetuate the discursive captivity of Kargil. The Museum of Memories, however, also narrates the ruptures and disconnections that get written out of official histories by lending a glimpse into the stories of families splintered by the 1971 partition. It is an example of the dynamic between freedom and captivity that the inhabitants of this borderland inhabit.

Although elites such as the Munshi family continued to dominate the cultural (re)presentation of the region to the outside world, museum ideology filtered into popular consciousness. During my long stint of fieldwork in 2008, one day, a shopkeeper in the Kargil bazaar beckoned me and handed a piece of paper that a young man, Naqi, from the village of Apati in the Batalik sub-region had left for me. Below a coloured print of the Buddhist statue (*chamba*) located in his village were his phone number and a note on the cultural heritage of his village. When I called him, he told me he had heard I was doing research and invited me to visit his home in Apati, where he hoped to open a small museum. Inspired by the Munshi Aziz Bhatt Museum, but also critical of its elite owners for allegedly exploiting poor people, Naqi led me up to his home one hot summer afternoon. We trudged up the steep, winding road to his village as there was a transport strike that day. I became tired and irritable, but Naqi was not deterred. At home, with quiet pride, he showed me his collection of everyday 'traditional' objects such as utensils, agricultural implements, wool and thread used for weaving, which had been stored in the loft. Soliciting suggestions for establishing and marketing a potential museum, Naqi had made sure that I was carrying my camera before we set out. He invited me to photograph his collection of objects while goading his aged father and sister to demonstrate the use of various traditional implements for my photographic benefit. Relating the history of his family as belonging to the lineage of a man popularly known as Apo Si Si, who used to be a *surna* player in the court of Tha Tha Khan, Naqi told me, 'Even now our family is known by the name of *tang-pa* or *dang-pa*', referring to the *surna* players in the courts of ancient kings. Naqi, again, illustrated to me just how widespread the perception was among Kargilis that, for outsiders, 'culture' must be authenticated with reference to its ancient past.

A decade later in 2018, I tried to locate Naqi to see what had become of his museum dream. I could not track him down anywhere. He earned his living as a lorry driver and was probably on the road somewhere. So I decided to visit Apati only to find stillness around Naqi's home. On knocking, we found his wife, who graciously invited us in when I told her about my visit in 2008. Responding to the enthusiasm of my companions, who were undertaking a survey of Kargil's intangible heritage for the Indian National Trust for Art and Cultural Heritage (INTACH), she took out and dusted off some of the objects I had seen many years ago, but with a certain weariness. These objects lay wrapped up, stored away, neither of use to contemporary life nor displayed in the museum that Naqi had dreamt of. Although Naqi did not succeed in opening his museum for reasons I did not succeed in finding out, his forsaken dream indicated that the archiving and presentation of 'culture' no longer remained the prerogative of the outsider: the colonial explorer, the anthropologist and the post-colonial state in search of the exotic and primitive. Local communities are themselves becoming 'actors in the world of anthropology'.[14] Their histories do not need external authorisation. Their memory-keeping is also a site of freedom, even if it often remains invisible.

Furthermore, just as the Munshis had refused to shift their museum to Leh, Naqi claimed to have refused the possibility of merging his collection of objects with the Munshi museum. This indicated his awareness of the power relations that inhere in museum collections, of how personal wealth and elite status facilitate the acquisition of objects through expropriation or purchase.[15] Though his effort did not come to fruition, it reflects attempts to extend the custodianship of projecting and commodifying Kargil's 'culture' for the outside world beyond the elite of Kargili society, gesturing to an inner confidence inculcated, in part, through the diffusion of modernist reformist ideas. Naqi was aligned with the IKMT.

Naqi's house in Apati happened to be located between the village mosque and the path leading to the *chamba*, one of the three monumental Buddhist statues – approximately 30–40 feet in height carved into rock faces – still extant in Kargil district. When I had started my research in Kargil, very few people knew about the Apati *chamba* (Figure 4.1). Of the three, the *chamba* in the Buddhist majority village of Mulbekh was the most well-known, where the tourist itinerary of those not making their way farther to Zangskar typically ended. Mulbekh implicitly marked the transition from Buddhist Ladakh to Muslim Kargil in tourist representations of the region.

Figure 4.1   The *chamba* in Apati, 2008

Source: Photograph by the author.

Clearly possessing a sharp business acumen, while leading me to the *chamba* in his village, Naqi had added, 'When people visit the *chamba* they can go to the museum on the way. The entire village will benefit from this as visitors can also be requested to make small donations to the mosque.'

Naqi's ideas echoed ongoing discussions among cultural activists and the tourism department in Kargil on how to make Kargil a more attractive tourist destination. They complained about the trickle of tourists at the Kargil festival compared to the throngs in Leh and were seeking new ideas to advertise Kargil. One of these was to develop a 'Buddhist trail' in Kargil, which would market the material heritage of the region's pre-Islamic past that had remained intact but had gone largely unnoticed or unacknowledged.[16] The three *chamba*s (in Mulbekh, Apati and Kartse Khar) were envisioned as being highlights of this trail along with the ruins of the *khar*s (palace-fortresses) of the small kingdoms that ruled the region before the Dogras. Besides the *chamba*s, the Hill Council also advertised smaller Buddhist images of the Maitreya and Avalokiteshvara carved in relief on stone blocks on the way to Drass and Buddhist rock engravings in Sankoo.

Besides serving the instrumental goal of attracting tourists to Kargil district, highlighting the *chamba*s also contributes to Kargili Shi'a negotiations of belonging to India.

Translating the Aura of Ruins

Given the dearth of research on early Buddhist artistic heritage in Ladakh, little work has been undertaken on the *chamba*s, and these have not been dated with certainty.[17] In an unusual visit by an outsider to the Karste Khar *chamba* in the Suru Valley in the mid-1970s, Jan Fontein found two large square holes besides the *apsara*s that appear above the shoulders of the Maitreya, suggesting that this statue was protected by a wooden roof.[18] Having lost significance for the surrounding Muslim population, the fact that the *chamba*s are nonetheless intact was aligned with global politico-cultural discourses by Kargili cultural activists. They discussed the possibility of marketing them as next only to the destroyed Bamyan statues in Afghanistan. Tapping into an international geopolitical discourse surrounding the Bamyan episode, these activists denounced the destruction of the statues by the Taliban, repeating, 'Such acts are not Islamic, but just give Islam a bad name.' 'The preservation of the *chamba*s is an example of the "*aman pasand*" [peaceful] nature of Muslims in Kargil,' one of them remarked, using a phrase frequently deployed by the Indian army in its framing of civil–military relations in the region.

In this generalised denouncement of the Taliban's actions within their own negotiations of belonging, Kargil's activists had also picked up a global heritage discourse that Finbarr Barry Flood has critiqued in relation to the Bamyan episode. Flood argues that it was the conversion of the Bamyan statues into a fetish of Western modernity by a Western cultural discourse that drove the Taliban's actions rather than religious iconoclasm – that religious otherness has not been the sole determinant of iconoclasm historically, even when ordered by rulers. The defacement of the Bamyan statues, he writes, 'indexed not a timeless response to figuration but a calculated engagement with a culturally specific discourse of images at a particular historical moment'.[19] The Taliban, he suggests, attacked not the literal worship of the Bamyan Buddhas but rather their appropriation into a Western cultural heritage discourse, which made them into cultural icons, an example of 'contemporary iconolatry' of which the modern museum is a locus par excellence. It was this shift from *cult image* to *cultural icon* that was targeted by the Taliban. They attacked the melange of values attached to a complex of Western modernity, premised on a false and often hypocritical separation of the spheres of the religious and the secular, which legitimises the protection of *global* heritage. It does not recognise or allow for the inhabitants of certain places as being capable of 'curating their own patrimony', Flood writes. This discourse also overshadows the 'coexistence between Buddhists and the Muslim population that marvelled at them for a millennium before they were obliterated by the Taliban'.

Kargili cultural activists reproduced this Western heritage discourse in their desire to market the *chamba*s as evidence of the region's *cultural heritage*, offering evidence for Flood's argument of the conversion of a cult image into a cultural icon. Furthermore, by seeking to foreground the *chamba*s as a symbol of the peaceful disposition of Kargil's Muslims, they also deployed the grammar of belonging demanded by India's politics of state security. The invocations of 'peace', 'silk route' and 'cultural heritage' have been the only legitimate representations available to Ladakh. The Kashmir Valley itself has for long been trapped in this frame, as sarcastically illustrated in Malik Sajad's graphic novel *Munnu*, on the experience of growing up in one of the world's most militarised places.[20] In a telling scene towards the end of the novel, when Munnu is invited to represent the youth of Kashmir to a visiting delegation from the European Union (whom he sardonically refers to as 'programmed mannequins'), he ruminates that the only 'authentic arguments' that would be palatable to the delegation must invoke this global cultural heritage discourse. Its focus on destruction and reconstruction of heritage that is unquestioningly owned by the 'global' would help to detract from the real geopolitics that might have led to the destruction. The incorporation of the *chamba*s into the category of regional cultural heritage in Kargil illustrates how local cultural politics of place-making are embedded within global geopolitics of heritage.

In invoking the resemblance between the *chamba*s in Ladakh with the Bamyan Buddhas in Afghanistan, cultural activists in Kargil demonstrated an acute, if implicit, understanding of their place in a right-wing nation state and an Islamophobic world as a double minority. They appropriated the same Western discourse on culture that the Taliban attacked to position themselves on a representational map in legitimate and acceptable terms. Kargili activists' focused on the *chamba*s in Kartse Khar and Apati not merely because these lay deep in Muslim villages, but also because, unlike the *chamba* in Mulbekh, these were no longer active sites of worship or consecrated contexts. This safely allowed for the *chamba*s to be relegated to the region's past with little significance beyond their instrumental value for tourism and self-representation as peaceful, cosmopolitan citizens. Their negotiations of belonging to India bring to the fore the murky intersections between the politics of state security that manipulates sectarian identities and global heritage discourses.

What happens to the image of the destroyed Bamyan statues once they begin to circulate in other locales? Besides the easy comparison and readily available geopolitical cultural discourse that Kargilis could tap into, could the comparison between the *chamba*s in Kargil with the Bamyan statues in Afghanistan allow us to think about the aura of ruins? The word 'aura' immediately brings to mind Walter Benjamin's discussion of authenticity in the mechanical reproduction of works of art in the modern age. Benjamin argues that authenticity lies outside the sphere of technical reproducibility. The moment a work of art is reproduced in a photograph, something of it is lost. Authenticity is not an issue in the invocation of the Bamyan in Kargil. As a means for advertising the *chamba*, the invocation is one of resemblance (akin to Ludwig Wittgenstein's idea of family resemblance[21]). The Bamyan statues are invoked through their received images circulating in the global media, not through direct viewing or contemplation. It is precisely the loss of authority of the Bamyan, the diminishment of the aura of the *original* Bamyan, that allows for the flexible invocation of these ruins for incorporation into heritage discourses in another place and time. The lack of need for authenticity in Benjaminian terms is reflected not only in the circulation of the mechanically produced image out-of-context, but also in the comparison as kin and not as copy of the original. Kinship is invoked not only in physical similarity, but also in the severing of both the Bamyan statues and the *chamba* from any link to the past in terms of the basis of both monuments in ritual and tradition. This effects a double displacement such that the aura of the ruin lies not in its authentic essence but emanates from its incorporation into the realm of heritage. However, while the Western heritage industry obfuscates the politics underlying the invention of heritage since the Renaissance, the double displacement that we see in its invocation in

Kargil illustrates the political functions of art that, Benjamin argues, emerge from the loss of authenticity. The invocation of the Bamyan statues by cultural activists in Kargil is a kind of reactivation of the 'object reproduced', as Benjamin put it, except here it is not a literal reproduction. It could be interpreted as a practice of translation that is germane to the production of heritage and yet is seldom acknowledged as such.

Translations between past and present, the regional and the religious, are not merely strategies for representing Kargil to the outside world to challenge singular, homogenising representations of their region. Searches of equivalence between a Buddhist past and an Islamic present can also be discerned in everyday practices that are not always on-stage. Rooted in a trans-Himalayan ecumene, these lived traditions lend insight into social and cultural horizons of belonging that do not conform to static or reified categories of region or religion. It is to ethnographic vignettes of these off-stage translations that I now turn.

Living Culture

Mendok Rgyaspa

In the month of June, Kargil is resplendent with wild pink and yellow roses, and the fields are carpets of fecund green of ripening barley and wheat. Every year, during this month, a seasonal festival celebrating fertility, abundance and the availability of pasture is held across Ladakh. In Buddhist villages, it is called Sngo-lha. Celebrated over three days, boys born in the Tiger Year (Stak-lo) would traditionally go to mountain tops to collect flowers in the night, while young unmarried girls born in the Sheep Year (Lug-lo) gathered roses in areas around the village; the flowers are for propitiating the *lha*, the spirit deity that protects the village.[22] In an evocative ethnographic account of the festival in a mixed Muslim–Buddhist village in Leh district, Ravina Aggarwal describes the atmosphere of merriment as villagers gathered in the night to celebrate with *chang* (local alcohol made from fermented barley), music and dancing. She also notes how villagers described the festival to her in terms of the importance of preserving tradition and authentic culture, mandating Ladakhi attire and traditional music. This cultural consciousness among her informants, she explains, arose from the perceived threats to their tradition by Muslims that were instigated by a request one particular year to postpone the festival to after Muharram. A young man she spoke with referred to Muslim customs as *go-log* (inverted) and further insisted that she correct the misperception that Muslims and Buddhists in his village intermarried. Aggarwal writes: 'I was instructed to take down the "true history" of Mingchanyul, one in which there had been no inter-dining between different faiths and no intermarriage without conversion. I had not bargained for being selected as the chronicler who would disavow a history of religious plurality.'[23]

A few months into my own fieldwork, perhaps a decade or more after Aggarwal's study of the Sngo-lha at Mingchanyul, early one morning in the beginning of June 2008, I received a phone call from one of the Munshi brothers. He invited me to come to his family cemetery with my camera, telling me I must not miss an opportunity to document an important example of the region's culture – the festival of Mendok Rgyaspa. When I arrived at the cemetery, women, children and a few men from their extended family were spreading wild rose petals collected in wicker baskets over the graves of their ancestors amid bunches of incense sticks. Some of the ladies carried large platters of cooked food and fresh fruit, including traditional delicacies like stewed apricots. Slowly, children from surrounding neighbourhoods arrived and seated themselves in a neat row to partake in *tabarruk* (consecrated food), which the family was giving as *sadqa* (alms). The offering of *sadqa* holds dual meaning; it is believed to earn merit for the afterlife as well as convey a gesture of thanksgiving. *Sadqa* is offered across South Asia at Sufi shrines and *khanaqah*s when a wish has been fulfilled or a misfortune averted. While a couple of elderly ladies quietly read the *fatiha* (the opening chapter of the Qur'an) at the graves of their loved ones, others enjoyed the fragrance of the flowers, the crispness of a summer morning and the special food for the occasion. This, too, was a ritual of thanksgiving and celebration of the season of abundance, albeit without singing, dancing and *chang* to keep with Islamic injunctions.

Later in the day, while travelling to the Suru Valley, I saw a man in the bus holding a wild rose in his mouth (Figure 4.2); several other men ambled along the roadside or village pathways in a similar fashion, enjoying the fragrance of the flowers. However, when I asked one of them to explain the significance of Mendok Rgyaspa, he denied knowing much about it and conjectured, 'It is the one day when we remember the dead, who tend to be forgotten otherwise in our busy lives.' Another young man said, 'The flowers have a nice fragrance and are placed on graves to impart happiness to departed souls.' Evidently, people in the Suru Valley, at least, seemed hesitant to acknowledge the regional historical meaning of this ritual. Or perhaps these young men genuinely did not know.

A year later, I heard rumours that some Ahl-i Hadis clerics had begun to discourage the festival, telling people it was not part of Islamic culture.[24] But a few years later, on a visit to Kargil in 2014, an old Shi'a cleric from Akchamal, one of the founders of the Islamia School, too, told me, 'Customs like Mendok Rgyaspa are finished because they are not in our religious books.'

Figure 4.2   Man in a bus on Mendok Rgyaspa, Suru Valley, 2008
Source: Photograph by the author.

This denial of a long-standing regional tradition had clearly accounted for the keenness of my hosts in Kargil to 'document' the festival, as a tradition that risked fading away.[25] The celebration in Kargil appeared to be a modified version of the Sngo-lha, but not referred to as such because of its association with the Buddhist practice of venerating spirits that reside in the land. Referring to the festival as Mendok Rgyaspa instead of Sngo-lha, I suggest, reflects translations of this regional tradition into the Islamic imaginaire. The shift in nomenclature stripped the occasion of overt references to a fair – singing, dancing and drinking – associated with a Buddhist ethos. The use of *mendok rgyaspa*, I was told, simply means taking out flowers. In Tibetan dialects, *rgyaspa* suggests auspiciousness and wealth. For many common Kargili Muslims, it was a festival for remembering their departed ones by imparting fragrance to their souls. From this perspective it aligned with the practice of remembering ancestors in the Islamic and especially Shi'i tradition. When situated within the context of Ladakh's regional culture, however, one can also interpret Mendok Rgyaspa through the idea of 'refraction', wherein the 'translation reflects the original idea but refracts it in the process', introducing significant distortions in the semantic field.[26] The festival of

Mendok Rgyaspa is thus an example of seeking equivalence between the Buddhist past and the Islamic present. Contrary to Aggarwal's experience with her Buddhist interlocutors in Mingchanyul who, too, presented it as an example of preserving tradition but communalised it, I was invited to the festival by a Shi'i Muslim family to document it as an example of the region's 'composite culture'. They had put on display for me a regional tradition that was off-stage.

Landscape Veneration

Although Kargili Muslims disclaimed celebrating Sngo-lha, I found that respect for the sacral qualities of the landscape persisted. The resilience of long-held beliefs and practices relating to the power of the landscape underscore that the Islamic imaginaire in Ladakh is not external to the trans-Himalayan ecumene.

Tibetan Buddhists believe that spirits 'of place' reside on mountains (*lha*) above and in land and water below (*lhu*) and must be appeased to ensure good fortune and protection.[27] Small white earthen structures called *chorten*s (reliquaries), also known as *lha-khang* (*lha* – spirit; *khang* – room) in Tibetan dialect, are often constructed on high mountainsides to offer protection to villages below. Relics of ancestors are placed inside *chorten*s. A white prayer flag called *tarchog*, attached to a pole, fluttering atop these structures makes them visible from afar. With conversion to Islam, the practice of building *lha-khang* continued in Muslim villages across Ladakh. However, it was not referred to as such, thus disavowing a belief in *lha*. Furthermore, the *tarchog* in Tibetan dialect came to be referred to as *'alam* in Perso-Arabic. The *'alam* is an emblematic crest or flag that is central to Shi'i material culture and is carried during Muharram processions. Usually crested by a *panjitan* – the hand representing the family of the Prophet (Ali, Fatima and their sons, Hasan and Husayn) – it is a material mediator of the connection to the divine represented by these five spiritual exemplars of Shi'ism. During Muharram and other rituals of mourning, women and children in particular seek to touch *'alam*s and other votive banners, as they believe these to have intercessory power.

One crisp autumn afternoon in 2008, while sauntering around aimlessly just enjoying my beautiful surroundings, I stumbled across a small structure, painted white (the colour of *chorten*s) with a padlocked door clinging to a high rock in the village of Shiliktse, perched next to the Suru River, a few kilometres outside Kargil town. When I asked a passer-by from the village about it, he referred to it as a *khanaqah*[28] and explained that amulets (*ta'wiz*) had been placed in it by an *'alim* (cleric) to protect the village from flooding that the canal (*nallah*) above the village was particularly prone to, leading to landslides. Over the years, I came across similar structures in several other Muslim villages typically located in their higher parts. Mountaintops hold a heightened significance in Tibetan Buddhist cosmology for it is there that the highest Gods, those who give life, reside.[29] Despite the transition to Islam, the construction of protective structures in high places for protection is another example of the absorption of a regional and pre-Islamic or Buddhist cultural practice into the Islamic imaginaire through the use of an Islamic lexicon. But this is not merely a lexical shift. The use of *'alam*, accompanied by the placing of old copies of the Qur'an and amulets in these structures, also signifies a different conceptual system. Nevertheless, cutting across theological differences, a shared belief in the value of the practice – seeking protection for the land – lives on, whether through invocations of the divine or the appeasement of spirits.

Specific situations necessitate the special placing of *'alam*s on high-mountain spots above villages, for these spaces, removed from the activities of daily life, are considered pure. When a village collectively places an *'alam* on a mountain, this is also referred to as *'amal karna* (in Urdu); *'amal* means both 'hope' and 'expectation'. Every winter in the drought-prone area of Sot, if snowfall had been scanty, people would go to an open space on top of a mountain in their village to do *matam* (mourning ritual) to make invocations for more snow, led by a shaykh who read a prayer called *namaz-i istisqa* (rain prayer). Also referred to as *zikr karna* (to remember), this *matam* could continue for as long as a whole month. The prayer for rain was casually, but without specific reference, attributed by a few laypeople to the Qur'an. However, as Steve Caton has argued in his fascinating account of similar 'rain invocations' in Yemen, this ritual is more likely an example of 'metapragmatic discourses' rather than 'authorizing discourses' that can be validated by the Qur'an.[30]

When I was visiting Kargil in the late summer of 2014, as floods ravaged the Kashmir Valley, the month of August had been unusual with heavy intermittent rains, posing a threat to the wheat waiting to be harvested. One day in the second week of September, much to everyone's relief, the rain finally stopped. And I noted in my fieldnotes: 'Ladakh has been restored to its full glory, to all that I love about it – a blue sky, snow on the high mountains, the play of light and shadow and a gorgeous sunset', after returning from the Batalik region. This image bore little resemblance to Batalik of the Kargil War fame even though one cannot miss the remnants of bunkers jutting out of the land in this area. On our way back from Silmo, a friend and I had stopped by at a teashop on the road just above the village of Apati for a break. It was a quiet evening, and as the day was winding down, we were the only customers. As we waited for our Lipton tea (sweet tea) and Maggi noodles, standard travel fare across the Himalayas, conversation turned to the unusual weather. The men running the shop that evening told us that two days ago, on a Friday, all the households in Apati had got together and slaughtered a few goats. The meat was distributed as *niyaz* (supplication), as an offering for the rains to stop. Here was an example of another Islamic ritual of making an offering to God for clement weather. In Apati too, as we learnt from the young men in the teashop, every year in the month of July, an *'alam* inscribed with a *du'a* is placed on a high spot above the village, where people go to do *matam* and *ziyarat*. Pointing in the distance, they told us, 'there is a structure up there that was built in *qadim* times with old amulets and a Qur'an placed in it, for such spaces above every village are *paak* [pure] places'. Such practices of landscape veneration that ensure well-being transcend contemporary communal fissures. These regional cultural practices are integral to Ladakhi Muslim modes of belonging without necessarily needing to be authenticated with reference to an Islamic text.

Over the years, while travelling to and fro between Kargil and Leh, I noticed many a time that a Muslim bus or taxi driver turned down the music in the vehicle, much in the way that it is switched off during the *azan*, as we snaked our way up the Namika-la and Fotu-la passes. There were also a few journeys in buses when some people spontaneously chanted the *salawat* (benedictions to the Prophet) as we safely crossed a pass. Crossing points are transitional spaces where danger lurks, requiring that the *lha* be appeased, regardless of your religious identity. Prayer flags in the five colours of the elements are thus hung in dense profusion at thresholds – bridges over rivers nestled in steep gorges and wind-swept high passes. On our way to Silmo village, my friend had driven his car clockwise around a chorten, respecting the directionality of Tibetan Buddhist *kora* (circumambulation).

Integral to both the 'semiotic and aesthetic character of landscape',[31] structures such as *lha-khang* foreground affective geographies that challenge the captivity generated by the political communalisation of belonging. Given the ubiquity of off-stage practices that illustrate the seeking of equivalences between the regional and the religious, I was hardly surprised one cold dark winter evening to find a Muslim woman in Kargil town desperately looking for the site where a Buddhist monastery once stood. She needed a handful of soil from the site to take to an *amchi* (Tibetan medicine doctor) to cure an ailing member of her family. Resonant with cross-faith healing traditions found across India, it is common practice for Muslims and Buddhists in Ladakh to seek the services of allopathic doctors, Muslim healers, Tibetan medicine practitioners and even oracles, when struck by illness or psychological distress.

As observed in other parts of India, such practices point to 'a world of shared ethics and cosmology that transcends the visible differences of Hindu and Muslim' in Kargil, too.[32] Anand Vivek Taneja shows us how his interlocutors, who write petitions to *djinn*s that they believe inhabit the ruins of Feroz Shah Kotla in Delhi, establish hermeneutic equivalences between Islam and Indic traditions. In Kargil, these equivalences are not hermeneutical but rather everyday practices of dwelling in the land. Even as people debated the distinction between religious and regional culture, it was in the process of translating across these slots that shared life-worlds were both embraced and rejected. The case of the *lhamo* of Trespone whose healing practice appeared to bring together both Islam and Buddhist oracular traditions was particularly illustrative of these practices of equivalence and the tensions surrounding them.

The Lhamo of Trespone

During a visit to Kargil in 2014, I heard passing mention of a Muslim woman in the village of Trespone in the Suru Valley being referred to as a *lhamo* (female spirit medium). I was struck by this for there were scarcely any Muslims practitioners of Tibetan Buddhist healing left in Ladakh. A few Kargilis said they had heard of the *lhamo* in Trespone but had never been to see her, while a couple of other friends reluctantly admitted going to her for treatment. This was not surprising given the reformist maligning of traditional healing practices as 'superstitious'. The *lhamo* of Trespone was a public secret. So, one rainy morning, a Kargili friend, who was a PhD scholar in history, and I decided to seek out the *lhamo* of Trespone. As we made enquiries about her in the village, someone pointed to a woman wearing a traditional maroon *goncha* with a shawl wrapped around her head, walking a little ahead in the distance. People in the village referred to her as Cho Cho Bilqees. We managed to catch up with her, and on that first meeting, she stepped into the car and was happy to tell us a little about herself.

Cho Cho Bilqees was a lean woman around the age of forty with a glowing face that seemed to emanate light. Speaking rapidly and animatedly in Purigi, she recounted her journey of becoming a healer. When she was around nineteen–twenty years old, she fell very ill and went to an *akhun* and a doctor. The doctor said she had tension, and the *akhun* said that a *djinn* or *bhoot* (a Hindustani word meaning ghost, which she used) had entered her. Then, one day, she fainted and while she was unconscious, she met the *djinn*. Trying to explain what had happened to her, she took the metaphor of writing with a pen, 'in the same way the *djinn* spoke to me'. This was a *karamat* (miracle) for her.

The *djinn* compelled Cho Cho to do *bismillah*, to read *marsiya* and do *matam* of Zainab (Imam Husayn's sister). After that she also learnt the *hadith-i qissa* (stories from the Hadis). Until then she was a completely illiterate woman. She did not know the Qur'an or Urdu. The *djinn* revealed to her that she must do *tawassul* (supplication to get close to God), take *qasam* (oath in Urdu) of

Hazrat Imam Husayn, Hazrat Fatima and Hazrat Imam Sajjad, and heal people. The *djinn* also revealed to her the method of heating a knife and rubbing it on her tongue as part of the treatment she gave. 'If I rub the hot knife on my hands or feet, it hurts, but not on the tongue,' she explained, elaborating that different diseases have different *du'a*s, which were also revealed to her by the *djinn*. Cho Cho's eyes lit up as she wistfully recalled that the *djinn* had told her that she would definitely go to Iran someday to the shrine of Imam Reza. She also quietly mentioned that there was a lot of opposition to her in the village. Some people degraded her. But the *djinn* told her, 'Even if someone is your enemy, treat them with compassion.' During the first three years, she treated people in secret, revealing cautiously that she had even treated many aghas, naming a couple of well-known clerics from Kargil town who had come to her secretly. Our curiosity piqued; we decided to return a few days later to experience her healing first hand. I reproduce here an excerpt of that visit from my fieldnotes:

> When we arrived at Cho Cho's house, which is a typical farmer's house (*zamindar*, as they call them here) – made of mud and stone bricks, with a pen for a cow – we were told that Cho Cho is asleep although it was nearly noon. While waiting outside, we heard someone wake her up. Soon we were led inside, into a carpeted room with quilts piled up on shelves lining the wall. A part of the roof was leaking rainwater. Cho Cho was dressed in a pink *salwar kameez* and had a draped a black *chador* with white embroidery casually over herself. She looked tired and was yawning loudly, saying in Purigi that today *zermo yongs* (she was ill [*zermo*]). Her husband hovered around us, and she asked him to give us tea. In the meanwhile, Cho Cho gathered herself and emerged from her sleepy state in a few minutes. She started preparing for the healing ceremony. She first took out a bundle from the cupboard, which she unwrapped, and placed some incense sticks and a *tasbih* (rosary) on a green cloth in the centre of the room. Starting with 'bismillah-e-Rahman-e-Rahim', she tied a red band around her head with a solemn air. Cho Cho slowly started recitation in Purigi, with intermittent short sobs, all the while rotating her *tasbih*. Just like matam, the tempo of the recitation and sobs rose gradually as she remembered the martyrs of Karbala. At some point she stopped rotating her *tasbih*, and as the *matam* intensified, tears rolled down from her now closed eyes. She then paused with hiccups, saying 'salam alaikum', taking a black scarf with a gold border and wrapping it around her neck, and then continued with the *matam*, calling out the name of Husayn repeatedly, and holding on to the end of her scarf with her hand along with the *tasbih*, chanting again 'bismillah-e-Rahman-e-Rahim', then taking the name of Fatima Zahra. At this point her husband, who had been watching from the side of the room, got up and asked Gulzar [the friend who had accompanied me] if he had a matchbox. The *matam* continued, and Cho Cho's crying intensified with the *matam* of Zahra. She kept saying 'hay', sobbing in staccato bursts.

As the volume of these sobs increased, her husband lit more incense and started rotating the bunch around her head and then placed it in an incense holder. The intensity of *matam* grew with tears freely flowing down Cho Cho's face. She wiped her running nose with her *dupatta* and said that she had made contact (*rahbita*) with Hazrat-e-Zahra. She then stopped the *matam* and wiped her face. Her husband told Gulzar to sit next to her for he was the one looking for *ilaj* (cure). She asked Gulzar what *zermo* (illness) he had. After this she asked him his name and took hold of the middle finger of his right hand with her left as she continued holding the *tasbih* in her right hand. She whispered something about *bagsthon* (marriage) and tension, and taking his pulse, she asked if his blood pressure was okay. She then chanted a *du'a* and asked Gulzar to chant along with her. In between her husband brought a knife which Cho Cho asked him to heat. Then she held Gulzar's hand and blew on his face, while rotating the *tasbih* and chanting. We could hear the *azan* going off in the background. Gulzar was looking noticeably nervous at the sight of the knife. Cho Cho took hold of the heated knife and touched it to her tongue, blew on it and placed the handle of the knife on Gulzar's head. She rotated the knob on his head and around the edges of his face while holding his hands. She asked Gulzar if it was hot and then whispered something to him about his mother and sister. After her diagnosis she told him that his cure required him to get some cow dung and place it in a plastic bag along with some blades, and then to place the whole packet in some high mountain place. She told him to take the name of Hanifa (Hanifa *phyakpo*) and asked him to do *'aqida* of Ali and Husayn, to give *sadqa* to a sayyid and drink the water of *zam zam* and *ab-e-neesan* (the first water of spring rain considered to be pure), and also advised him to take the name of the imams during travel. In the end she recited a *du'a*. Cho Cho explained to Gulzar that the evil eye (*mikha*) had struck him while on a journey. But it was not inside him. If it had been inside him, he would have fainted during the procedure.

In our conversation in the car a few days earlier, Cho Cho had told us that the *tasbih* aids her in diagnosing illness. The votive headscarf that Cho Cho had tied around her chest was printed with Qur'anic verses and apparently brought from Iran. On her right-hand ring finger, she wore the *dur-e-najaf* stone ring. Reflecting on the healing practice, she explained that when a patient comes with a problem she fights with the *djinn* in them, explaining that everyone has a little *djinn* in them. Sometimes the patient has to be made unconscious. Her husband interjected that Cho Cho gets very tired when she performs these rituals of healing. In the midst of this conversation, Cho Cho suddenly broke into a recitation of the sura *yaseen*, an important Qur'anic verse.

Achieving an altered state of consciousness through the elegiac liturgies of Muharram was something that I had witnessed during Muharram *matam*. Some women would suddenly start swaying, crying more loudly and hoarsely as the mourning for the martyrs of Karbala gathered momentum. This same Muharram liturgy structured Cho Cho Bilqees's healing practice. The performative trance-like state was reminiscent of what I had seen among the women who eventually fainted and had to be revived by sprinkling water on them. But what was striking and perhaps different from the ordinary fainting of women in *majalis* was that Cho Cho made contact with Fatima Zahra, the revered daughter of Prophet Muhammad through the *matam*. It was at this point, once the contact had been made, that she turned to her patient to perform the curative actions.

Several equivalences can be discerned between Cho Cho's healing practice and Buddhist oracular traditions and yet elide encompassment within them. First, the process of making contact with the divine and a changed state of consciousness that Cho Cho Bilqees achieved through Shi'i liturgy was akin to the trance of Buddhist oracles in Ladakh. Oracles have the power to make enlightened beings manifest in their body.[33] Possession by the gods gives them the power to cure sickness. In the case of Cho Cho, possession by *lha* was replaced by making contact with Fatima Zahra, an important female figure for Shi'as. Second, Buddhist *lhamo*s possessed by specific gods can often name them during the trance.[34] The specificity of contact with Fatima Zahra by Cho Cho echoed this naming of gods. However, it also bore similarities with the calling forth of the 'agents of God' in healing rituals by Muslim healers in other parts of the Indian subcontinent.[35] Third, a common practice within the repertoire of oracular healing is *shrakches*, the burning of troublesome demons inhabiting the bodies of afflicted persons. Cho Cho Bilqees's use of a hot knife was similar to *shrakches*. But what I did not witness was the practice of extracting substances from the body of the client that Buddhist oracular healing is known for. Finally, just like Buddhist oracles, Cho Cho Bilqees also became aware of her powers after a period of illness.[36] Miraculous deeds confirm an oracle. In the case of Cho Cho Bilqees, these miracles were demonstrated in her knowing the *hadis* and liturgy without ever having studied or being literate. Finally, in Cho Cho's cure for Gulzar, we see again the importance accorded to high mountain places, where she tells him to leave the packet with cow dung and blades.

Cho Cho Bilqees's healing practice also incorporated Islamic healing rituals, used by *akhun*s, such as chanting *du'a*s and blowing air on the face of the afflicted person. Cho Cho, however, did not dispense amulets. In this, she conformed to a widespread tradition among Muslims in India, where writing is usually the preserve of male healers, while women recite the Qur'an and blow healing prayers.[37] Cho Cho's practice also bore resemblance to *haziri* rituals in Shi'i shrine culture in North India, where the supernatural intervention of judges, who are usually key Shiʻi figures, enter dialogue with the spirit possessing the ailing person.[38] Her contact with Fatima Zahra seemed to also perform this function.

Cho Cho Bilqees's practice thus crossed various boundaries between Buddhist oracular healing practices and Islamic healing cultures. It defies easy classification into either religious culture or regional culture. There was an equivalence with Ladakhi oracular traditions in the form of the ritual, while the content was suffused with Shiʻi liturgy, materiality and aesthetics. The translation between Buddhism and Islam embodied by the *lhamo* of Trespone pointed to a mode of being that resists the dictums of reformist Islam and communal boundaries. Firmly rooted in a local geography and a trans-Himalayan way of life, such equivalences are another dimension of relational ethics that imbue belonging in Kargil.

A Second Muharram

Perhaps the most curious example of a tradition that is both regional and Islamic and yet cannot be understood as an act of translation with certainty is Asad Ashura.

Asad Ashura commemorates the martyrdom of Imam Husayn at Karbala in the summer in addition to the annual mourning during Muharram that is held in accordance with the lunar Islamic calendar.[39] It recalls the actual season in which the battle of Karbala took place in 680 CE. Asad Ashura falls under the Borj-i Asad, the constellation of Leo in relation to the zodiacal calendar, between 21 July and 21 August every year, when the summer heat is at its peak in the trans-Himalayas. Commemorating the martyrs of Karbala at this time is meant to recreate the actual conditions of the battle and the intense suffering of Imam Husayn and his followers induced by the heat and absence of water in the desert of Karbala. Ever since then thirst has been a key motif in Shiʻism. During Muharram, the experience of thirst is evoked through dramatic enactments of the scene in which the water bag being carried by Abbas (the standard bearer of Imam Husayn) from the river Euphrates for the children in the camp is pierced by the arrows of Yazid's army on the ninth day of Muharram mourning.

In the villages of Leh district, Asad Ashura is referred to as Yaum-i Asad, or the 'Day of the Lion'.[40] It is predominantly a rural event across Leh, Kargil and Baltistan. People in Kargil echoed what David Pinault's interlocutors told him in the 1980s – that to the best of their knowledge it is not held in any other part of the Shiʻi world. In Kargil district the Ashura of Asad is held only in villages in the Suru Valley and in the Fokar region, which is home to several mixed Muslim–Buddhist villages. Unlike Muharram, mourning does not take place for a full ten days but only for a few days leading up to Asad Ashura. Since it is not determined by the Islamic lunar calendar, the day on which it is held is flexible. Most villages try to organise Asad Ashura on a Sunday to enable people from across the region to participate. They typically hold the event on successive Sundays to avoid an overlap. Asad Ashura is marked by a sense of competition between villages over the number of participants, the fervour surrounding the event and the presence of preachers from Iran. Every village liked to claim for itself the status of being the oldest site of the tradition. It is, however, difficult to put a date to the origins of this tradition; while some people said it started as recently as two or three decades ago, others claimed to remember it from the time of their forefathers.

Just as in the month of Muharram, *majalis* are held in village *imambara*s, where clerics narrate episodes of the battle of Karbala. After the *majalis*, men take out a procession replete with votive banners, Zuljenah (the horse of Imam Husayn) and coffins (*tabuts*) of the key martyrs. Most of these processions start from the new *imambara* of a village, typically a concrete cement construction imitating mosque architecture in West Asia, and wind their way to the old mud and stone *imambara*, carving out local ritual geographies. Large vats of food, often yellow rice, are prepared to offer as *tabarruk*, which people jostle to receive after the completion of the *matam*. Those who come from Kargil town or other villages then make their way to a relative or friend's home for the late afternoon meal. It is another occasion for people to socialise and renew the bonds of community.

Though an event of commemoration, the Asad Ashura that I witnessed was marked by a sense of festive gaiety. As the hot summer and harsh mountain sun bore down upon people, they took shelter under the poplar and willow trees, squatting by the small irrigation streams in villages before a *majalis* commenced. Children ran around with merry abandon while their parents too enjoyed popsicles purchased from the numerous ice cream carts that parked themselves along the village pathways. Were it not for the predominantly black clothes worn by people, the scene could easily have been mistaken for a picnic. Pinault too mentions the atmosphere of gaiety in Chuchot village (Leh), where he experienced Asad Ashura.[41] While watching the flagellation in Tambis village in the Suru Valley in 2008, a friend of mine remarked, 'See how much *raunak* [gaiety] there is over here today ... really, the Asad Ashura of Tambis is one of the best.' 'Even Kashmiris come to Tambis for *matam*,' she added. Later in the day, one of the doctors on duty from the district administration – to tend to the wounds of the men doing *zanjirzani* – remarked in passing that this was the first time that people from Kashmir had also joined the procession. This was another reminder of the relative freedom that Shi'as in Kargil were granted by the state to practise Muharram in contrast to the Kashmir Valley.

How do we make sense of this festive atmosphere of Asad Ashura given that it is a commemoration of the martyrs of Karbala? I suggest that it would be fair to conjecture that this is a cultural tradition that is deeply anchored in a trans-Himalayan ecumene. Asad Ashura coincides with the onset of the harvesting season in Ladakh and Baltistan. Harvest fairs called *strubla* (*srublha*) are held in villages with a substantial Buddhist population. They celebrate the bounties of the land and offer prayers for the smooth completion of the harvest. With the advent of Islam in Kargil and Baltistan, the tradition of holding a *strubla* was discontinued as it came to be seen as a Buddhist cultural practice. Yet the gaiety surrounding Asad Ashura and its seasonal timing suggest an affinity with the tradition of harvest fairs.

In the mixed Muslim–Buddhist village of Fokar, which many believed is the oldest site of the tradition of Asad Ashura, the *katilga* – a site designated for *ziyarat* – was located on top of a mountain overlooking the village. Almost all villages where Shi'as live have a local *katilga*, where the Muharram procession on the day of Ashura ends. Its literal meaning – a place of slaughter – indexes the battlefield of Karbala where Husayn and his followers were slain. The village *gonpa* was also perched on this high spot above the village. The site was referred to as *chomo shukpa* in the Tibetan dialect, deriving its name from the shrubs of juniper (*shukpa*) found on mountainsides. Incense made from juniper is extensively used in Buddhist monasteries and rituals. Both Muslims and Buddhists thus shared the sacred space of the village, even though their homes could be clearly discerned from a distance by the absence or presence of prayer flags.

None of my interlocutors compared Asad Ashura to the *strubla*. For them, it was only an occasion for remembering the sacrifice of Imam Husayn and his companions in Karbala through the somatic experience of the suffering induced by intense heat. This nonetheless begs the question of why Asad Ashura is indigenous to Ladakh and Baltistan. Although Asad Ashura and *strubla* do not share a vocabulary, the shared experience of a life-giving season among Muslims and Buddhists suggests the plausibility of discerning an equivalence between these two traditions. The *matam* of Asad Ashura could be interpreted as performing the same function of invoking blessings for a good harvest as the *strubla*. By doing *matam*, a believer remembers the family of the Prophet and their descendants. And to remember them is to invoke their blessings. People would often explain to me that *matam* is important for it leads to *sawab* (reward). In contrast to the sobriety of the ten days of Muharram mourning, the festivity of Asad Ashura is perhaps borne from offering prayers for a successful harvest.

The equivalences discernible in Asad Ashura illustrate the dynamic process of interaction between Islam and Tibetan Buddhism within the trans-Himalayan ecumene. This also means that some of these traditions may change or disappear over time if the purveyors of doctrine further consolidate their power. Reformists did not criticise Asad Ashura openly, and yet the disapproval of some was quite evident. Hajji Amina, for instance, brushed it off as 'excess', saying, 'Islam does not encourage excess.' This was somewhat paradoxical given that Kargili preachers from Iran were invited to preside over the *majalis* on this occasion, too. Variegated strands of thinking thus exist even among those who look to Iran and modernist reform more generally, contributing to culture talk.

CRSBO

Animated by the debate on what ought to be the distinctions between 'regional culture' and 'religious culture', talking about culture in Kargil reveals the labour involved in fitting national slots. The projection of Kargil's Buddhist past for material gains through tourism as well as symbolic recognition of being peaceful, 'good' Muslims were expressions of negotiating belonging on the terrain of culture. Yet these did not entail an erasure or dissimulation of the Islamic present. All the off-stage lived traditions that I have described in this chapter testify to Stewart's argument that language (lexicon) does not always faithfully reflect the traditions behind it.[42] Translations of regional traditions into an Islamic imaginaire in Kargil spilled over doctrinal limits and revealed a shared world that is hidden by the dark clouds of communal politics, nested within an increasingly intolerant national public. I argue that the equivalences established between region and religion are a mode of belonging on this frontier. Lived traditions also underscore the place of Islam within a trans-Himalayan ecumene that is typically reduced to Tibetan Buddhist culture in external representations, perpetuating a discursive captivity with concomitant political effects. Debates on the difference between regional and religious cultures, and translations between these slots, illustrate how Kargili Muslims creatively negotiate the captivity produced by artificial boundaries of both nation and religion.

The ethnographic examples of off-stage practices also foreground the deep attachments of Kargilis to their place of dwelling in all its materiality: ranging from considering high mountain spaces to be pure to an implicit respect for the spirits that reside in land and water to celebrations of seasons of abundance. Even though they regularly talked about the difficulties they faced due to the absence of transport connectivity, leading to a feeling of being entrapped within the harsh mountains, especially in the winter, I also noticed that they increasingly express appreciation of their landscape – the clean air and rivers are contrasted to the putrid atmosphere of the plains. The landscape they speak of cuts across political borders and is integral to their feelings of connection with Gilgit–Baltistan. But how do people sustain these cross-border affective attachments to people and places in the face of closure of cross-border mobility? How has the congealing of the LoC shaped the negotiations of belonging among those who live on its edges? The next chapter turns to these questions to discuss the dynamics of connection and disconnection that the gradual encapsulation by India is producing.

Notes

1. The *Kesar Saga* is a mythical legend popular in Tibetan cultural areas in the Himalayas, sung or related over several days.

2. Friese, 'Liver is Not Mutton', provides a witty travel account of searching for the 'pure Aryan' in the villages of Dha and Hanu in Leh district.

3. In the anthropology of Muslim societies, Marshall Hodgson's concept of 'Islamicate' has been widely applied to describe the encounter between Islam and regional cultural traditions. Shahab Ahmed argues that the Islamicate has been framed by a long-standing 'foundational logic' of differentiating 'religion' from 'culture'. This, he asserts, ends up reducing Islam to an essentialist core of personal piety while the sociocultural sphere of religion becomes less Islamic. See S. Ahmed, *What Is Islam?* It is important to note against the background of this critique that Kargili Muslims do not make a distinction between 'religion' and 'culture', but rather seek to differentiate between 'religious culture' and 'regional culture'.

4. Stewart, 'In Search of Equivalence'.

5. Ahmed and Harris, *Ladakh at the Crossroads*, acknowledge this perception of Ladakh as a 'Tibet in microcosm' and have made a notable contribution towards including non-Tibetan historical influences on Ladakh's material culture.

6. Snellgrove and Skorupski, *Cultural Heritage of Ladakh*, xiii, for instance, write:

   > Since we are concerned ... with Ladakh's cultural heritage, it is with the Buddhists that we are almost exclusively concerned, for it is Buddhist culture which remains typical of Ladakh. Even where it has been largely effaced in the Moslem areas, no higher Islamic culture has come to take its place.

7. For a detailed discussion of this, see Chapter 5.

8. Aggarwal, *Beyond Lines of Control*, 202. KASCO was initially registered under the name BASCO (Balti Social and Cultural Organisation). The name was changed later as people objected to it being restricted to Balti culture in the context of simmering intra-ethnic identity competition.

9. At the lowest rung of Ladakhi caste hierarchy are the Mon – the musician caste who played the traditional instruments, the *surna* (double-reed) and the *daman* (kettledrum). For more on caste in Ladakh, see Aggarwal, *Beyond Lines of Control*.

10. Snellgrove and Skorupski, *Cultural Heritage of Ladakh*, xiii.

11. See Fewkes, 'Living in the Material World'.

12. L. Gupta, 'Making a Museum'.

13. See, for example, *DNA*, 'Theatre of War'.

14. Stocking Jr, *Objects and Others*.

15. Stocking Jr, *Objects and Others*, 5.

16. For example, an INTACH report, Sharma, 'Architectural Heritage', contains no reference to Kargil and generalises all western Himalayan culture as Buddhist heritage.

17. While Snellgrove and Skorupski, *Cultural Heritage of Ladakh*, date these statues to sometime between the sixth and tenth centuries, Luczanits, 'Early Buddhist Heritage', 67–68, contends that based on stylistic comparisons and the dating of the Alchi monastery, the *chamba*s may have been built only in the eleventh century.

18. Fontein, 'Rock Sculpture', 8.

19. Flood, 'Between Cult and Culture', 642, 651–54.

20. Sajad, *Munnu*, 339, 344.

21. Wittgenstein, *Philosophical Investigations*, 65–71.

22. Aggarwal, *Beyond Lines of Control*, 88. For an elaboration on *lha*, see Day, 'Embodying Spirits', 58–60.

23. Aggarwal, *Beyond Lines of Control*, 90.

24. The Ahl-i Hadis have a very small following in the Drass region, the predominantly Sunni area of Kargil district. Their condemnation of Mendok Rgyaspa is, however, not a great deterrent to the practice.

25. After the formation of the UT of Ladakh, Mendok Rgyaspa was included in the 'Toursism Vision' document for Ladakh, indicating its imminent commodification. Administration of Union Territory of Ladakh, 'CEC Feroz Khan Chairs Meeting Regarding Tourism Vision Document for Ladakh Emphasizes Inclusion of Adequate Data Related to Kargil District to Ensure Holistic, All-Inclusive Vision Document', 30 November 2021, https://ladakh.nic.in/cec-feroz-khan-chairs-meeting-regarding-tourism-vision-document-for-ladakh-emphasizes-inclusion-of-adequate-data-related-to-kargil-district-to-ensure-holistic-all-inclusive-vision-document (accessed on 24 June 2022).

26. Stewart, 'In Search of Equivalence', 277–79.

27. Day, 'Embodying Spirits', 113.

28. *Khanaqah* is a Persian word. It refers to spaces where Sufis take retreat. People in Kargil would use the word *dargah* sometimes to explain it to outsiders, believing that it has similar intercessionary powers as a *dargah*.
29. Day 'Embodying Spirits', 61.
30. Caton, 'What Is an "Authorizing Discourse"?'
31. Mitchell, *Landscape and Power*, 7.
32. Taneja, *Jinnealogy*, 153.
33. Day, 'Embodying Spirits', 9, 23.
34. Day, 'Embodying Spirits', 511.
35. See, for example, Flueckiger, *In Amma's Healing Room*, 69; and Ewing, *Arguing Sainthood*, 132–38.
36. Day, 'Embodying Spirits', offers an inventory of village oracles to point to commonalities or patterns. Buddhist oracles are often recognised after a period of illness.
37. Flueckiger, *In Amma's Healing Room*, 66.
38. Bellamy, 'Person in Place', 38.
39. The Islamic calendar moves forward by approximately twelve days every year in relation to the solar, Gregorian calendar.
40. Pinault, *Horse of Karbala*.
41. Pinault, *Horse of Karbala*, 205–06.
42. Stewart, 'In Search of Equivalence', 270.

5

Living on the Edge

When I reached Skardu, I was received like Nelson Mandela when he got out of prison. I touched the soil of my ancestral land.

When the RAW [Research and Analysis Wing, India's foreign intelligence agency] tried to question me on my return from Pakistan, I told them I'm not a 1947 type of person. I'm not a trespasser; I have a passport.

This is how a prominent Balti cultural activist in Kargil described his arrival in Baltistan in 2007 and then his return to Kargil. A fragment from a longer narrative of his first visit to his ancestral homeland, the first quote, by invoking the metaphor of Nelson Mandela's release from prison expresses the sentiment of freedom in being able to visit Skardu. Yet, as we read in the second quote, he unequivocally expresses a sense of belonging to India through the possession of a passport considered a key document of citizenship while remarking on his interrogation by the Indian intelligence agency upon his return to India. By saying 'I am not a 1947 type of person', he was perhaps alluding to the difficulties experienced by Muslims seeking to return to India in the years following the partition when India introduced the emergency permit system in 1948.[1]

This Balti poet is an example of 'cross-border settlers' – a category of people whose location on one side or the other of a border between two nation states was not shaped by the 'new border'.[2] This category, I suggest, also includes those who were already living on one side before the drawing up of the de facto border and chose not to go back. Their predicaments of belonging are distinct from 'partition refugees' who voluntarily migrated to the other side. Cross-border settlers embody seemingly contradictory emotions, of longing for one place but belonging to another. Liisa Malkki points to the 'metaphoric practices' that make identity between people and place appear 'naturalised'.[3] A recurrent practice and motif is to demonstrate loyalty to the nation through emotional ties to its soil. Cross-border dwellers in Kargil challenge this naturalised identity between people and place. The poet touches the soil of his ancestral land, Baltistan, but expresses belonging to India. His sentiments highlight the dialectical entwinement of longing and belonging, if we follow Susan Stewart's exploration of one of the meanings of longing as 'belonging or appurtenances'. She writes, 'Here we might remember the meaning of the appurtenance as appendage, the part that is a whole, the addition to the body which forms an attachment, transforming the very boundary, or outline of the self.'[4] Longing for one place but belonging to another are, then, not contradictory emotions. Narratives of the other side lie at the core of cross-border dwellers' sense of self, such that they can never be bound by the territorialities of nation states. Even though their emotions are seeped with nostalgia for their ancestral homelands, they have no desire to return permanently. Evident in statements such as 'We would be happy to die here', the final resting place where one has lived for long becomes a marker of a sense of belonging rather than the place of birth.[5] Drawing upon this distinction between the place of birth and where one dies, I refer to Gilgit–Baltistan as 'homeland' and Kargil as 'home'.

In her discussion of Tamil displacement from northern Sri Lanka, Sharika Thiranagama notes that home and homeland are not 'congruent emotive and political concepts'.[6] This applies to cross-border settlers, too. However, in contrast to displaced Tamils, home and homeland for cross-border settlers in Kargil did not have 'parallel lives involving different moments and senses of self' but rather shaped and infused each other in both imaginative terms and lived realities *across* a temporal span. Their social connections and communitarian identifications proceeded at a different tempo from the demarcation of the political and military border.[7]

In this chapter, I turn to the history of cross-border settlement in Kargil, which includes not just the Balti community but also the villages that experienced multiple partitions during the 1947–49, 1965 and 1971 wars between India and Pakistan – a history that finds little mention in partition historiography. Displacement for those who live on the edge – in villages located close to the LoC – was not confined to a singular event in 1947–48 with which the partition of the Indian subcontinent is typically associated. Those who experienced multiple displacements inhabited a liminal space long after territorial occupations by nation states. This chapter examines encapsulation within India as a *process* and the dialectic of connections–disconnections that is particularly heightened for those living on the edge. I argue that borderlands are not homogeneous spaces. Internal spatial demarcations, through their institution and dismantling, are crucial to the politics of state security.

Despite the captivity generated by the absence of cross-border movements, linkages with the other side shape negotiations of belonging to India. Cross-border settlers' refrains of homeland are formed by both the stories that people tell and the journeys that they have undertaken via more circuitous routes.[8] Narratives of those who managed to journey to Gilgit–Baltistan, which through retellings take on a life of their own, produce imaginative renderings of the other side. The affective horizons sustained by these journeys and narrations are, however, inflected by perceptions of the political and material challenges of life in Pakistan. Thus, the politics and desire to belong to India is constantly refracted through the 'other' side, illustrating a particular dynamic of post-colonial belonging that is not unique to this borderland.

Living along the Shifting LoC

Narratives from Punjab and Bengal and the violence accompanying the large-scale migration of people across the border in 1947 have dominated the historiography of the partition. Ladakh and Gilgit–Baltistan only find mention with reference to the 'tribal invasion' of the Gilgit Scouts in 1947 and the victory of the Indian army in forcing them to retreat. After the revocation of Kashmir's special constitutional status in 2019, the Indian government included a new holiday on 26 October in the public holiday list of J&K called 'Accession Day', marking the day that the Dogra maharaja Hari Singh signed the instrument of accession to India. This is a tactic of captivity through another form of discursive erasure. It negates the fact that the LoC was supposed to be temporary, pending a referendum, and that it shifted even after 1947–48. Nationalist historiography of the partition in Kashmir in its focus on the 'territorial contests between India and Pakistan over the Kashmir Valley' has always elided the experience of people from other sub-regions.[9] There is scarce mention of the stories of people living along the LoC in Kashmir who abruptly found themselves in Pakistan in 1947–48 or those who had to silently acquiesce to their homes suddenly being re-captured by India in the subsequent wars of 1965 and 1971. Linked to Bangladesh's war of liberation from Pakistan, scholarship on 1971, in turn, has been dominated by a focus on the eastern borderlands of India.[10]

Before 1947, people circulated between Baltistan and Kargil and farther beyond to other parts of Kashmir and India for trade, education, work, marriage and religious services. As a result, many Baltis came to live in Kargil, Leh, Kashmir and parts of Uttaranchal and Himachal Pradesh. The Baltis in Kargil town, for instance, are descendants of traders from the Kharmang region of Baltistan. Even today referred to as the 'shop people' (*hatti-pa*), this trading community formed a neighbourhood known as Balti Bazaar, which is the oldest part of the main bazaar of Kargil town. Goods from all directions – Changtang, Zangskar, Baltistan and Kashmir – exchanged hands in Balti Bazaar. Evoking its cosmopolitan atmosphere at the time, renowned local historian and poet Sadiq Ali Sadiq (d. 2020) described it as a 'beautiful time' (*khubsurat zamana*) in Urdu, when traders would gather in the evenings to hold *mahfil*s (gatherings), where much poetry and music would flow. Another Balti activist wistfully recalled seeing a book in Skardu that contained a song from Purig to convey the intermingling of cultures that took place in the caravanserai and shops of Balti Bazaar.

Hardas and Karkichu, villages located on the right bank of the Drass River, a couple of miles south of Kargil town, are also predominantly Balti villages. These were settled by the raja of Kharmang to act as halting points on his journeys between Skardu and Kargil and later left to him as endowed estate (*jagir*) by the Dogras.[11] In 1901, Baltistan was divided into two *tahsil*s: Skardu and Kargil; Kharmang was placed within Kargil *tahsil* for administrative purposes due its geographical proximity. Consequently, the land records of people from Kharmang were stored in Kargil. When the ceasefire line was drawn in 1949, these Balti habitations in Kargil suddenly found themselves on the 'wrong' (Indian) side of the LoC, separated from their families, fields and orchards in Pakistan. But their land records remained in government offices in Kargil. This was also the fate of several Balti labourers working in the hill states of Uttaranchal and Himachal Pradesh at the time of partition. Many of them ended up settling in the Kalsi Gate area near Dehradun in Uttaranchal. There was a regular traffic of Baltis between Uttaranchal, Kargil and Turtuk (in Leh district), another area that was annexed to India in 1971. Community ties were maintained through marital exchanges.

Many Baltis from Uttaranchal also come to Kargil in the summer months, setting up Balti *dhaba*s (small restaurants) that are immensely popular with locals, migrant labourers and low-ranking army personnel, especially for food like *aloo paranthas* (potato pancakes) that are typically associated with Punjab and the northern hill states. While the odd Balti *dhaba* remains open throughout the year, most close down in the winter season. Their owners return home to Uttaranchal, complementing the seasonal migration of road builders and other labourers from Jharkhand who work in Ladakh between the spring and autumn seasons. I would frequent one such *dhaba* fairly regularly, and through scattered discussions over time with the uncle (as I took to addressing him) who ran the *dhaba*, I came to learn about the particular predicaments of Baltis settled outside J&K, too, and the allure of the erstwhile state of J&K for them.

Uncle Mahdi's village in Baltistan was captured by India in the 1971 war with Pakistan along with others in the Turtuk area in the Nubra Valley in Leh district. His father originally hailed from Thanu village in the Chorbat area of Baltistan; his family continued to be identified as Chorbat-pa even after their incorporation into India. When these areas along the LoC were partitioned, Uncle Mahdi was running a business in Dehradun. Narrating how he came to settle in Uttaranchal, he recalled:

> In 1947–48 when India did *kabza* [capture], people got left on one side or the other. The Baltis in the Dehradun area were kept in army camp number nineteen for a while. However, the Kashmir issue remained unresolved. They were then shifted to Karanpur camp with full *suhuliyat* [facilities]. When it became clear that the Kashmir issue was not going to get resolved so quickly, the Baltis in Dehradun were given a choice to return to Pakistan or stay. Those whose *karobar* [business] was doing well stayed; others left.

Claims to ancestral land in Baltistan remained unresolved for many Baltis who stayed on in India. Getting land deeds out of the district administration offices in Kargil or Leh (for those in the Nubra Valley) echoed the unsurprising experience of wrestling with bureaucracy to search for files weathered by time and neglect in state archives. The inhabitants of Balti Bazaar in Kargil town lived in leased properties and had for long been lobbying for the allocation of land to them. According to Master Sadiq Hardasi, a Balti journalist and writer, author of an independently published book on the history of Balti settlement, Kargili *muhajir*s (the term used for refugees) in Baltistan had been allocated twenty *kanal*s of land,[12] in contrast to the Baltis of Balti Bazaar, who in this context also referred to themselves as 'refugees' in processes of claim-making. Although the government allocated a few *kanal*s of land in Kumbathang, a barren plateau-like plain overlooking Kargil town to people from Baltistan, it was of poor quality, unfit for cultivation, an unsatisfactory substitute for the fecund agricultural lands and orchards they had owned on the other side. Despite not receiving satisfactory land, they chose to continue living in India, apprehensive of their security and well-being in Pakistan.

Baltis in Uttaranchal also struggled to acquire state-subject status of J&K for the many privileges that it conferred in comparison to residents of Uttaranchal. After many years of trying, Uncle Mahdi succeeded in getting state-subject status for both his children on the basis of proof of ownership of a small piece of land close to the border on the Nubra side, which was captured by India in 1971. It was, he explained, a way of insuring the future of his children. Though the refrain for their homeland lingered among Baltis, much of their labour of belonging within India was directed towards accessing Indian constitutional provisions accorded to J&K. But from the time of the partition(s) to some success in this struggle to belong, cross-border settlers inhabited a liminal space. Some villages and families experienced multiple fragmentations and serial displacements between 1948 and 1971. It is to these histories that I turn to in order to highlight the specific experiences of the long partition in this region.

Badgam

Badgam is a mixed Dard–Balti village which was shuffled between India and Pakistan twice. Half the village, lying on one side of a stream running through Badgam (Figure 5.1), was captured by India in the 1965 war, while the other half continued to remain in Pakistan. Both parts of the village were reunited in the 1971 war, when the other half was brought within the territory of India. The time between 1965 and 1971 was one of fraught fluidity between the two sides.

Figure 5.1   The stream that marked the erstwhile 'border' in Badgam, 2008

Source: Photograph by the author.

I was told that people covertly continued to marry or go to the mosque on the other side of the stream that marked the border.

The heavy surveillance of this village and its surrounding areas after the 1965 war disrupted people's daily lives. Zulfikar from Badgam recalled:

> When our livestock strayed over to the other side, the army did not allow us to go and fetch them. When the border ran through Badgam till 1971, the army was suspicious … that people were going into Pakistan and therefore would not allow them to go beyond the picket. But the Indian government gave us rations, since between 1965 and 1971 the whole area was virtually under siege. The whole area remained shut for six years. At that time we would eat our own crop and were therefore strong and fair. So the Indian army used to say that these people are from Pakistani *fauj* [army]. Now with outside food, people have become weak and dark.

This narrative alerts us to micro-spatiality within wider borderlands that are homogenised in both nationalist representations and in claim-making upon the state that demands regional coherence. Attending to these micro-spatial narratives of cross-border settlers foregrounds the process of encapsulation of a contested frontier region within the nation state, producing uneven geographies of captivity within the borderland – an unevenness that was experienced as suspicion in racialised registers such as 'looking like the Pakistani army' to being denied a return to their homeland. This was poignantly expressed in the story of the much-respected, elderly shaykh of the village, Shaykh Ghulam Hussain, who was in his mid-eighties, when I met him:

> Before 1971, when one side of the *nallah* [stream] was under Pakistan and the other in India, we could see people on the other side but were not allowed to go there. Our people have to travel between India and Pakistan using passports. Even though the road from Srinagar to Muzaffarabad has been opened, the Kargil–Skardu road remains closed. No one asks about us. They could have made us meet people there out of human compassion. Are there no human beings here?

Shaykh Ghulam Hussain's anguish of being so close and yet so far from his kith and kin, arbitrarily split between two nation states, welled from being separated from his brother, who lived in Pakistan. His brother was away on pilgrimage to Iran and Iraq when the 1971 war broke out. Since he had a Pakistani passport at the time, he could never return to Badgam, as his village was captured by India. While cross-border settlers were entrapped in India, some became caught in such bureaucratic gaps that denied them return to their homes. Many families, the shaykh lamented, were divided in this way.

Beyond the pathos of separation from kin, the story of Shaykh Hussain's brother also reflects the arbitrary exclusions made by post-colonial states on the basis of identity documents, long before the passing of the Citizenship Amendment Act (CAA) in 2019, and the imminent extension of the National Register of Citizens to all of India. Though Shaykh Hussain did not live to see the growing threat to Muslim belonging in India, in hindsight one can only read his response to my naïve question on whether he preferred the Pakistani regime or Indian as deeply ironical: 'We like that place where there is freedom of *mazhab* [religion]. There is freedom [*azadi*] in Hindustan. There is *aman* [peace] in Hindustan.' His appreciation for this freedom masked the price that had to be paid for it.

One fine summer day, Nasir's cousins, men in their early twenties, took me on a tour of Badgam village. As we walked around enjoying the greenery, they told me that their family still had some 40–50 *kanal*s of land divided between India and Pakistan – land which was either occupied by the army or had been mined. Till ten to twelve years ago (1998–99), they used to get compensation (*mu'awaza*) for this, but not anymore (2008–09). The period the young men mentioned coincided with India's victory in the Kargil War, when the Indian state conceded that the Muslims of Kargil were loyal to India. The inhabitants of Badgam were rewarded for their loyalty, it seems, through the loss of compensation. They also complained that the mobile phone network was still not allowed in the whole Badgam area because 'the network would be caught in Pakistan'. Despite the freedom to practise their faith and the reunion of the lands of the village in 1971, the residents of Badgam remained in a state of captivity wrought by such disconnections for long after. Several people living in other villages situated along the LoC shared a similar sense of being held captive, illustrating the long afterlives of post-colonial wars.

Latoo

The Balti village of Latoo was less fortunate than Badgam. Temporary displacement from their land in the time of war became a permanent condition. The people of Latoo lost their ancestral land in the 1971 war. Until then they lived in Drelung village, which was approximately 4 kilometres from the LoC. The village pasture, Babachan, where people took their livestock for grazing in the summer, was captured by Pakistan in the 1965 war along with 30 per cent of Drelung. People living in the remaining 70 per cent of Drelung village that lay within the territory of India were temporarily evacuated by the Indian army and sent downstream to other Balti villages, Karkichu and Hardas, during the 1971 war. They were never able to return to Drelung: The part that remained in India was laid with land mines and converted into an army picket after the 1971 war ended.

The inhabitants of Latoo thus lived in a state of limbo, scattered across different Balti villages in the region for several years. They were eventually re-settled on land allocated to them on a wind-swept barren plain overlooking the deep gorge of the Shingo River. But they were never compensated for the lost pastures and orchards.

Until the 1999 war, Babachan, said to be visible from the army picket in Drelung, was still inhabited according to people in Latoo. Heavy shelling in 1999 forced people in Babachan to migrate to Skardu and Karachi. The original village that comprised of Drelung and Babachan was thus not only split between India and Pakistan but also eventually lost to its dwellers on both sides of the LoC. Eager to narrate their story, a few men in Latoo took me on a tour around the village on my first visit, taking pains to reiterate the proximity of the LoC. Pointing in the direction of the army picket, farther up the mountain, they told me that although Babachan was deserted, people on the other side returned occasionally to collect wood and apricots from their orchards. It is not the verity of occasional return of people to these areas abutting the LoC that matters. These narrations gesture to the place that lost land and its bounties continued to hold in people's imagination, becoming a resilient motif in their refrains of homeland.

To get to Latoo one had to cross a non-motorable wooden bridge and then walk for a few kilometres along a narrow mule path along the edge of the Shingo gorge. For many years, the people of Latoo had lobbied both the district administration and the army for the construction of a motorable bridge to improve connectivity to the village. The civil administration finally replaced the old wooden bridge with a steel one in 2016. But households in Latoo had to pool resources to macadamise the mule path themselves, after repeated petitions to the government yielded no response. In 2018, Latoo had a case pending in the J&K high court, filed against the government for not undertaking requisite developmental work in their village.[13] Requests for a lift irrigation project that would allow them to pump water from the swirling Shingo River below to make the barren land of their village more arable had also gone unmet. People in Latoo felt they were invisible to the district administration. As we walked to see the earthen tank (*zing*) that collects snow melt, while passing women lined up next to a handpump with empty urns, a young man rhetorically remarked that perhaps the administration was not even aware that Latoo lay within India. Latoo's inhabitants were also cynical about the army and complained that it only constructed roads to access border posts and not out of any concern for the well-being of the village. This small Balti village, politically insignificant because it did not have a large vote bank, exerted tremendous labour to be recognised by both the military and civilian faces of the state. Their desire to make life viable detracted from the blurred boundaries between democracy and militarism.[14]

Latoo experienced low-intensity shelling from 1988 onwards. It only became a 'big issue', as they put it, between 1996 and 1999. In 2008, I spent the night of Shab-e-Barat, when Twelver Shi'as celebrate the birthday of Imam Mahdi, in Latoo. As dusk darkened into the night, young and old gathered to light candles in their homes and at the village cemetery. Old tires were lit and placed at a distance from homes along hillsides. As the fires flickered in the wind, people recalled other more ominous nights, when cross-border exchange of fire between the Indian and Pakistani armies threatened another displacement. During the shelling the residents of Latoo would go and hide in a cave. For them, unlike for the rest of India, the Kargil War was not confined to a few summer months in 1999. They were rattled and displaced by shelling for many years before.

I narrate the experiences of border villages such as Latoo and Badgam in some detail for these challenge the temporality of war produced by statist histories, forcing us to reckon not only with the aftermath or afterlives of conflict but also a pre-life, beyond causal security analyses. We see how LoC villages, even after their encapsulation within India, remain suspended in a state of uncertainty, yearning for freedom associated with infrastructural connectivity and the ability to physically see the people and lands from whom they have been separated.

Hundarman

Similar to Latoo, Hundarman is another village that was recaptured by India in the 1971 war. It lay within Pakistani territory between 1948 and 1971, and was said to be a no man's land for a while during the 1965 war. People in Hundarman recalled how they were reverted to India in 1971, literally overnight. They woke one morning to find their village captured by the Indian army. Shaykh Ali from Hundarman related the travails of returning to his village in 1977 after completing his studies in Najaf. In possession of a Pakistani passport, he was unable to return to his village until the Indian consulate in Baghdad gave him new nationality papers.

Hundarman is located atop a steep mountain overlooking the Kargil–Skardu road, approximately 10 kilometres from Kargil town. It was part of the old territory defined as Purig, which stretched all the way to Brolmo and Bilargu (now in Pakistan). Recurrent references to these places gestured to how large the 'other' side looms in the mental maps of borderland dwellers. After 1949, when Hundarman came under Pakistan's control, villagers lost access to the land they owned in Akchamal village (Sot) in India, where they would traditionally spend six months every year. According to local accounts, the raja of Sot had built a water channel in Hundarman to feed drought-prone Sot, where, as I have described in the previous chapter, people performed ritual lamentations to make invocations for rain. That is how some inhabitants of Akchamal came to settle in Hundarman. The *phaspun* of some families in Hundarman were therefore in Akchamal even after the partition in 1948–49. As Akchamal was incorporated into India in 1949, and Hundarman into Pakistan, these traditional networks of support were ruptured by the LoC.

A small part of Brolmo, comprising seven households, lay in Indian territory until 1999. These households fled farther into Pakistan during the 1999 war to rejoin the rest of their village. The shrine of locally renowned Shaykh Ali of Brolmo, visible from a high perch in Hundarman, continues to hold an important place in the sacred geography of the region and people's sentiments all across Kargil. It was to Shaykh Ali of Brolmo that clerics like Shaykh Ahmad Mohammadi of the Islamia School traced their intellectual genealogy before heading to Iraq. Even though these scholarly genealogies were also sundered by the partition, the continued fame and reverence for Shyakh Ali of Brolmo reflects the resilience of local historical memories, overriding the amputations of nation-state formations. These memories hold little significance to the colonial or post-colonial official archive but constitute alternative archives of place-based understandings of belonging.

The abruptness and lack of volition with which villages on the edge found themselves as part of one nation state, and then another, meant that for a long time they were liminal spaces from the perspective of both the state and people. An elderly man from Hundarman, who ran a small grocery store in the Kargil bazaar recalled, 'For a year we were kept blind-folded', a metaphor for surveillance through ocular control. Confined in their movements within the 'new' nation state, the elderly in Hundarman remembered being escorted in an army truck to the bazaar once a week for nearly a year, treated as outsiders in what was their original homeland before 1948. After 1971, they shifted from their original homes in Hundarman Thang (the lower part of present-day Hundarman) farther up the mountain to Brok. It was only in 2012 that Hundarman was connected telephonically by landline.

Until 2014, entry to Hundarman Thang was prohibited, while one had to show an identity card at the army checkpoint to go up to Hundarman Brok. The Indian army built a macadamised road up to Brok only after the 1999 war. Even as the inhabitants of Hundarman went about their daily lives, more integrated into the district with the concretisation of the road, the village remained unconnected to public transport. During the war, heavy shelling from Pakistan forced people in Hundarman to flee to other villages. Unlike Latoo, where temporary displacement turned into permanent resettlement, for the residents of Hundarman, displacement in 1999 was temporary, albeit shrouded by the fear that there might be no return.

Even as 'peace' in the military sense has reigned on this borderland since 1999, cross-border villages remain affectively suspended between peacetime and wartime. A profound uncertainty lurks in the shadows of these high mountains. The tension that comes with living on the edge is reflected in the fear that engulfs them every time there is news of heightened exchange of fire between India and Pakistan, portending for them possible war. Small boards warning of land mines dotted the edges of the steep road that snakes its way up to Hundarman. Makeshift electricity poles bore the marks of bullets along village pathways while tin fuel canisters used during the war were repurposed for carrying water from handpumps. The debris of war and military presence was everywhere, constituting 'affectively charged matter'[15] within the lives of the residents of Hundarman.

The landscape bears testimony to the region's shuffled history. Weathered petroglyphs of *stupa*s harking back to its pre-Islamic past can be discerned on boulders along the Kargil–Skardu road on the Kharul side of the Drass River, which was under Pakistan till 1971, but later occupied by an Indian army post. Other rocks along the same road are inscribed with the names of Pakistani soldiers in Urdu, betraying the region's more recent history of being divided between two nation states. And fluttering in the distance, a saffron flag on a Hindu temple built by the Indian army marks the current political location of this region's double minority.

The stories of villages like Badgam, Latoo and Hundarman make visible minor shifts in the LoC that are left out of the annals of official history made available to the national public. The radical displacements experienced by these villages, but considered so *passé* from the perspective of the security state, have led to the naturalisation of frontier geographies in national cartography. The concomitant invisibility of the violence of being held captive can only be discerned in embodied memories that are not always easily voiced. Suspension in a liminal space that came with gradual incorporation into India rewired the meaning of freedom for those living on the edge. Freedom came to be expressed in demands for greater connectivity to both India and Pakistan – a demand for freedom in captivity.

(Dis)Connecting Baltistan

It was only four decades after the partition that some people from Kargil were able to travel to Baltistan. The first person to go to Skardu was Hajji Ghulam Hussain from Balti Bazaar, in 1985. According to Bashir Wafa, 'Hajji Hussain had to cross the border by taking a visa. He came back with news for the first time of who was still alive on the other side.' The closure of the Kargil–Skardu road meant that anyone travelling to Baltistan had to take a long circuitous route: Kargil to Delhi or Amritsar (across the Wagah border), and then on to Islamabad or Lahore by air or road, followed by the long journey up the Karakorum Highway to Skardu. A journey of six hours along the Kargil–Skardu road extended to over two days and considerable extra expense.

Despite the inability to travel overland across the LoC, references to places in Gilgit–Baltistan and the splendour of its landscape suffused nostalgia for the other side. Even people who had never been to Skardu or beyond talked about the plains of Deosai, Rondu Valley, the forts at Shigar and Khaplu, the Sadpara Lake and the Maqpon Polo Ground in Skardu with a vividness that was striking. People would spend hours scouring the web for photographs of Baltistan, correlating them with fragments of stories passed mouth-to-mouth and sites mentioned in Balti poetry. With the arrival of mobile phones, and in later years WhatsApp, youth in the community would regularly exchange photographs, enabling them to conjure the other side as if they had been there. Attachment to the landscape and its bounties – the gushing rivers, orchards, vast plains and valleys – constitutes an affective repertoire that knits both sides. The inability to travel by road to Skardu deprives cross-border dwellers of the experience of a precious sense of place. Roads hold meaning beyond the instrumentality of direct connectivity. As pathways that anchor life, they lend particularity to place, which is central to sustaining a moral community defined by 'networks of personal, genealogical, familial, and status relationships'[16] in contradistinction to the notion of national territory. The closure of pathways leads to a flattening of the landscape.[17] Over time, this can lead to a loss of sense of place, an emotional disconnection that virtual travel diminished a little, but could never compensate for embedded sensory connections to the landscape.

The road to Skardu held importance not only for cross-border settlers longing to meet their relatives in Gilgit–Baltistan; it became an important rallying point in the politics of belonging within India for the Kargil region as a whole. Opening the Kargil–Skardu road was part of a package of longstanding demands raised by the people of Kargil for better connectivity through infrastructure development. The closure of the Zoji-la pass over the long winter months, of the Kargil airport to civilian traffic and of the road to Skardu were material disconnections that contributed to feeling entrapped. Lobbying the central government to open each of these points of closure found its place in the election campaigns of every politician. Of these demands, the government of India finally approved the construction of the Zoji-la tunnel in January 2018. But the process ran into trouble when the National Highway and Infrastructure Development Corporation abandoned the project for financial reasons.[18] Discussions to open the Kargil airport to civilian traffic were also underway. Demands to open the Kargil–Skardu road, however, largely seemed to fall on deaf ears. In February 2019, prior to prime minister Narendra Modi's visit to Ladakh, the Islamia School led a procession in the Kargil bazaar demanding that the road be opened on 'humanitarian grounds', to enable 'divided families' to meet. Kargilis articulated their demands for opening the Kargil–Skardu road with reference to the Srinagar–Muzaffarabad road, connecting the Kashmir Valley with Azad Kashmir, and the Kartarpur corridor in Punjab. The Srinagar–Muzaffarabad road was opened for limited cross-LoC trade in 2013 along with a passenger bus service as part of diplomatic efforts between India and Pakistan around the Kashmir conflict.[19] While lauding this initiative, Kargilis felt slighted by the Indian state's refusal to open the Kargil–Skardu road, lamenting that despite their patriotism to India, the state did not trust them enough to open the road. In the procession in 2019, the president of the Islamia School urged the government to 'take up the issue with Pakistan ... which is ready to open the route'.[20] Holding the Indian state responsible for the sustained closure of this route was a refrain I had heard repeatedly over the years. Some people conjectured that the Indian government was reluctant to accede to this demand of theirs because it felt threatened by potential Shi'i unity across the LoC. This, despite the fact that Kargilis, as they put it, had not engaged in any 'anti-national' activities. Underlying the demand was a canny understanding of the politics of state security – the blocking of potential cross-border solidarities along militarised frontiers. The Kargil–Skardu road thus became a choke point. Insecurity relating to cross-border infiltration along some sections of the frontier in Kashmir was extended to its entirety, while within the frontier, the state manipulated sectarian differences.

The political stalemate between India and Pakistan over the Kashmir issue made not only travel but also phone calls to Baltistan neigh impossible. While people in Kargil could receive calls from Pakistan, they could not dial out. In 2014, a Balti friend had installed a new landline in his home in Balti Bazaar. Quite thrilled about this, he announced, 'The Pakistanis have put this because it is cheaper to call on the landline', making it easier for his family and friends in Skardu to call. According to him, phone calls to Pakistan were not allowed only from J&K: 'The moment you cross into Punjab from Jammu, calls to Pakistan go through.' Prior to phone calls being allowed from the Pakistan side, people in Kargil, especially the Balti community, managed to pierce the captivity produced by limited telecommunications, to feel a connection with Baltistan, by listening to Radio Skardu.

On one of my visits to Karkichu village, a middle-aged woman of Brogpa ethnicity broke into a Balti song to convey her sense of belonging to this predominantly Balti village. As we sat listening to her sing, a group of women who had been washing utensils in the nearby stream gushing with ample glacial melt that summer got distracted. They joined us outside the newly renovated village *imambara*. Listening to the woman sing, they started talking about the programmes they enjoyed on Radio Pakistan (Skardu). The programmes were more systematic and related to their daily lives, they explained. 'Since the pronunciation is the same, we understand it,' one woman added. 'Here the Kargil station is not so good.' The women unanimously extolled the dramas relayed on Radio Skardu, especially the *jazbati* (emotional) ones and the old *qasida*s. It was a jovial scene outside the new *imambara* and even attracted a few teenage boys who joined us. 'He sings *ghazals*,' a lady pointed to one of them. As if this was the cue he was waiting for, the lanky young man promptly ran off to fetch a diary in which he had transcribed the lyrics of *ghazal*s broadcast on Radio Skardu. He did not need much cajoling to sing one of these, mesmerising us with his strong, plaintive voice. Everyone gathered was enjoying the music, until two women interrupted saying that there should not be singing in front of the *imambara*. A minor argument broke out as others retorted that this was not a *gunah* (sin) as it was being sung for my benefit. Since I was doing research for gaining *'ilm* (knowledge), they argued, there was no harm. This intervention echoed the debate on the boundaries between 'regional' and 'religious' cultures that I discussed in the previous chapter. While the airwaves of All India Radio Leh reached these border villages in Kargil, I was told that people here did not listen to Leh radio so much because Leh had started Tibetanising the Leh dialect. Kargilis found it difficult to understand the Leh broadcast. A separate radio station in Kargil was only inaugurated in 1997, two years before the Kargil War became a national matter but had already disrupted the lives of borderland villages through frequent shelling from the Pakistani side.

Tsering Angmo, ex-station director of All India Radio (Leh), who had also spent a considerable amount of time in Kargil, told me that Radio Kargil had played an important role in countering all the propaganda on Radio Pakistan during the war. 'It was creating a lot of confusion. For example, some people had thought that Pakistan had entered Kargil. Pakistan had very accurate information on Kargil.' Officials at All India Radio (Kargil) confirmed that it played a major role in the 1999 war. Initially, the Kargil radio station was only 10 KW. Its power was enhanced to 200 KW in 2005. Subsequently, Radio Kargil reached Baltistan. A young man who had been appointed to work in the news editorial section of Kargil radio reiterated this point to me: 'We heard that in Skardu there was a news magazine called *Siachen* which conducted a survey in 2003 on the impact of

Radio Kargil on Skardu. Radio Kargil reached till Astor.' Its increased frequency was apparently successful in countering the 'propaganda' of Radio Skardu. Just as with other borderland infrastructure such as roads and bridges, state investment in radio was driven by security and surveillance but packaged as addressing the needs of locals.[21] In the process, borderland dwellers were sonically encapsulated further within the nation state, through the airwaves war launched by India. The women in Karkichu lamented that after 2005, the reception of Radio Skardu lost its sharpness; they had to strain to listen to it.

With the establishment of an All India Radio station in Kargil, poets and intellectuals from the Balti community lobbied hard to be granted a slot as part of their endeavours to preserve and promote the Balti language, a defining feature of their ethnic identity. A half-hour slot was granted on grounds of national security after Balti cultural activists claimed they had persuaded intelligence agencies that a programme in Balti was essential to counter Pakistani propaganda on Radio Skardu. One day, a prominent Balti poet excitedly told me that after three stalwarts of Balti poetry in Kargil had delivered their weekly Sunday programme, they immediately received phone calls from Baltistan when their friends across the LoC heard their voices.

Infrastructures of connectivity and communication are integral to the 'border work' of the state.[22] These materialise degrees of captivity through a dynamic between connection and disconnection. On the one extreme, complete disconnection is instituted (like the closure of the road to Skardu). At other times, borderland dwellers are oscillated unpredictably between connection and disconnection, when, for instance, the Internet in Ladakh, too, was cut off in times of heightened state insecurity in the Kashmir Valley. This digital oscillation is another facet of the structural conditions of belonging on Kashmir's frontiers that, I argue, manufactures affective states of freedom in captivity.

Narrating Baltistan

Gilgit–Baltistan of the mind and heart remained strong in Kargil despite varying forms of material and sonic enclosure. Stories related by the few who managed to travel to Baltistan played no small part in sustaining an imagination of the other side. I was fortunate to be able to meet the last of a few elders who had lived through the partition of 1947–48. Among them, Apo Hasan from Balti Bazaar was one of a handful of that generation that had managed to visit Baltistan. Apo (grandfather in Balti) hailed from Pari village in Kharmang. His father was a *nambardar* (headman) who often visited Kargil as Kharmang came under Kargil *tahsil*. Apo came to Kargil at the age of twelve to study 'worldly education' but got stuck there when the fighting between the Gilgit Scouts and the Indian army broke out. He had four brothers and one sister. When I met him in the winter of 2008, he had recently returned from his second visit to Pakistan to meet one of his brothers, who still lived in Pari. Apo was hard of hearing. Sadiq Ali Sadiq, who was related to Apo through marriage, had warned me that my meeting with him might be futile. Quite to our surprise, Apo was very animated and talked at length despite his fragility and hearing problem.

Apo had been to Pakistan twice after the partition: once via Amritsar in 1987 and the second time via Delhi in 2007. His recollections of Baltistan were filled with nostalgia for Pari. He reminisced about his departure from Pari:

> When I left Pari, I took 10–15 litres of water with me so that I could continue to drink the water of Pari till I was in Skardu. The water there is very tasty, not like the hand-pump water here. The water of Pari is the best in the whole *ilaqa* [region].... Even black people become white when they drink it. When I reached Pari, I became clean and white. In Skardu also I drank only the water from Pari. The water supply there has increased over the years. Earlier people on top had water in the morning and left it for people downstream in the afternoon. Now both get water simultaneously, because of the freezing of snow by the Agha Khan Program.

The quality of water – sweet and clean – is a common motif in nostalgic renderings of the past and places people hold dear. Water is a metaphor of longing for place, an element of the landscape, propitiated across religious divides in the trans-Himalayas. Apo's description of becoming white upon drinking the water of Pari was a metaphorical evocation of the purity of his homeland, retained as such in his heart. He described life in Baltistan as being pleasurable and comfortable (*aish duk, aram duk*). His face lit up when I asked him about the *mazhabi mahaul* (religious environment) in Skardu. With an awestruck expression, he told me that on the day of *jum'a* (Friday) thousands of people gather in the mosque. Adding to his impressions of Pakistan, Apo also recalled his stay in Rawalpindi for a month, gushing:

> What a beautiful city ... full of flowers and greenery. The roads are so wide that six cars can go simultaneously ... such is the extent of open space. What is the Kashmiri Dal [lake] in comparison? The Masjid-e-Faisal in Rawalpindi is so big that 4–5 lakh people can gather there to read the *namaz*. Zia-ul-Haq's *qabr* [grave] is there. But what did he give to the people of his country? Why are people reading the *fatiha* at his grave?

Apo had confused Rawalpindi with Islamabad where Zia-ul-Haq is buried. Apo's nostalgia was punctuated with perceptions of the more prosaic realities of life in Pakistan. In the midst of all the praises he heaped on Baltistan, he said, 'But things are expensive there, because the value of money is less.... After 1947, things became very expensive in Pakistan. In the big cities there is no electricity. It is okay in Skardu and Pari, but there is shortage in Lahore.' Quiet for a few moments, he added, 'In Kargil there is *aram* ... it is *azad*.' Even though Kargil had for long suffered electricity shortages until the construction of the Chutak hydroelectric project on the Suru River that commenced in 2012–13, Apo's comment reflected a widespread sentiment among Baltis, but also more widely among people in Kargil of being free in India in comparison to Baltistan. As I have discussed in previous chapters, this sense of freedom typically referred to religious freedom and political representation within a democratic system. Despite being closely tied to the Kashmir Valley and having experienced everyday sectarian discrimination, unlike Baltistan, Kargil had not been clouded by sectarian violence. Apo's passing disapproval of people reading the *fatiha* at Zia-ul-Haq's grave was an oblique comment on the Sunni Islamisation of Pakistan since the 1980s, when violence against Shi'as escalated.

Apo's recollections of his first and second visits no doubt melded into each other. Yet, despite his age, he had a sharp memory and mentioned some changes he had witnessed in Baltistan in the twenty years between 1987 and 2007: 'There was nothing there then.... In the last twenty years there are now machines to take out oil, wood ... and there is twenty-four-hours electricity.' He also noted the similarities between Kargil and Skardu – that most people in Skardu, too, were shopkeepers, coolies or government employees. Apo noted the progress he had observed in Baltistan but was quick to qualify, 'People have progressed, not the Pakistani government.' His comments on India and Pakistan, worthy of praise in one context but of condemnation in another, could be interpreted as another affective expression of the betwixt-and-between subjective state that borderland dwellers embody. Stuck in-between two states, geographically and politically, emotional narrations of Baltistan are political allegories. While bidding him goodbye, I asked Apo when he would visit Baltistan again. With a gentle smile, he handed me some dried red berries from Pari from the depths of his trouser pocket and replied, 'If the road opens, it will only take a few hours. *Inshallah*, the road will open.'

A well-known poet, Bashir Wafa, would often reminisce about his visits to Baltistan, especially the first one. In one of these recollections, he told me the story of an old lady, Api Hayabi, who came to Purig from Baltistan after getting married. She would regale Wafa with stories about places in Baltistan, stories that conjured the landscape in his imagination. When he finally visited Baltistan, to his and others' amazement, he was able to identify many places without ever having seen them before. After his second trip to Baltistan in 2014–15, Wafa started work on a *safarnama* (travel memoir). Poignantly titled 'Wo Jharna Ab Bhi Bahti Hai' (That Stream Still Flows), it was inspired by the story of a woman who got left in Kargil at the time of partition and had asked Wafa to bury her upon passing and sprinkle the water of a particular stream in Baltistan over her grave. This story, too, reiterated the importance of the bounties of land such as water in evocations of loss.[23] We see here how storytelling becomes 'a vital human strategy for sustaining a sense of agency in the face of disempowering circumstances'.[24] The imagination of Gilgit–Baltistan sustained by such narrations is also a site of freedom.

People in the literary circles of Skardu were already acquainted with Wafa when he first visited. Wafa had made contact with poets in Baltistan through Radio Skardu. After hearing a romantic drama penned by Ghulam Hasan Hasni, a much-loved Balti poet on the radio, he became an ardent fan. While some cross-border settlers from the Indian side managed to obtain visas to visit Pakistan from the mid-1980s onwards, it was only in 2005 that the first visitors from Baltistan were able to get Indian visas. Ghulam Hasan Hasni was among a small group of Baltis who visited Kargil in 2005 on the occasion of the conference of the International Association of Ladakh Studies. It was a time of high excitement for Baltis in Kargil. The conference sessions scarcely held their attention, as they gathered around Hasan Hasni and the other guests from Baltistan, showering them with hospitality, staying up late into the nights, exchanging poetry and stories. A documentary film produced in Baltistan in 2014 includes recorded clips of some of these moments in Kargil.[25] Hasni subsequently wrote a *safarnama* of his visit to Kargil. After Hasni's death in 2010, Wafa penned an elegy titled 'My Poet Has Died', which was published in Baltistan, and moved people to tears on both sides of the LoC. Ismail, Hasni's son, continued to keep in touch with Wafa after his father's death. It was not just kinship by blood that sustained cross-border connections within captivity. Friendships forged through a vibrant cultural exchange pierced through the disconnections.

Post-partition Circulations

A vast literature inspired by the partition expresses the loss of the composite culture that thrived prior to the division of the subcontinent. A good example is Qurratulain Hyder's much-acclaimed novel *The River of Fire* (1998). It evokes the pre-partition world among the elite of Lucknow and the subsequent defiance of ruptures caused by the partition. Kumkum Sangari's analysis of the novel offers a useful analytical lens to view the cultural activities of the Baltis in Kargil.[26] She argues that the novel shows that it was not culture per se which was disrupted by the partition, but the webs of human affect woven by it. In Sangari's view, after 1947, cultural transmission became the 'gesture of the scholar, the Indologist, the anthropologist, the state and its museums' and a gesture of political protest against the artificial separation of 'national' heritages. The world evoked in Hyder's fiction challenges these ruptures. In the real world, however, Sangari feared that this shared world may only remain in the 'alienable experience of the generations in transition but may disappear with them'.[27] Cultural exchanges between Kargil and Baltistan challenge this anticipation of loss. Given the recurrent shifts of the LoC in Kargil, not only are many of the 'transitional generation' still alive, but the shared world of culture did not disappear with the demise of the generation that directly experienced the partition in 1947. Cultural dialogue between Balti and Shina cultural activists on both sides of the border flowed through a variety of media.

Kargili poets from the Balti community who had visited Baltistan extolled the intellectual ambience of Skardu, judging it by the prolific culture of poetry there. Poetic expression is considered to be the 'hallmark of intellect' in Gilgit–Baltistan.[28] Kargili poets returned from Baltistan with recordings of *musha'iras* organised in their honour, which were eagerly watched by everyone in the community. Photograph albums of their visits were prized possessions. 'Soft cloth' (Karachi cotton) to stitch *salwar-kameez* that they brought back for their wives and sisters were reserved for new clothes for Eid. As Stewart notes, the souvenir and the collection are

> ... two devices for the objectification of desire.... The souvenir may be seen as emblematic of the nostalgia that all narrative reveals – the longing for its place of origin. The souvenir seeks distance (the exotic in time and space), but it does so in order to transform and collapse distance into proximity to, or approximation with, the self.[29]

These souvenirs from Baltistan – a place of desire – thus collapsed the physical distance wrought by captivity to an affective proximity.

The relative paucity of poets in Kargil who wrote in refined Balti in comparison to poets in Baltistan, as Balti cultural activists bemoaned, was compensated for by the production of music in Kargil. Those who had visited Baltistan spoke of its stricter religious ambience. Lyrics penned by Balti poets were thus set to music in Kargil as part of the larger endeavour to preserve the Balti language on both sides of the LoC. Kargili travellers would carry cassettes and CDs made in Kargil to Baltistan, forging a shared cultural space through exchange of words and music. In later years, the internet expanded this space. Ruminating on the culture of *qadim* Ladakh one day, Sibte Hasan, a Balti poet from Latoo village, observed:

'Sending songs through the internet is a bit like the old times, when people would send songs to each other in Ladakh and the songs were carriers of hidden messages.' He was referring to the folksongs that I discussed in Chapter 4. The articulation of music and songs as messages collapsed and folded into each other the ancient and modern eras, disrupting the coevalness between time and space sought by post-colonial nation states. As we sat around sipping tea and complaining about the weather during the unseasonal rain in 2014, another friend, who was a member of KASCO, said, 'It's raining like this in Gilgit–Baltistan also.' Virtual spaces that transcend geopolitical closure lend a sense of temporal intimacy to feeling connected to the other side. These affective connections are also sustained through third-places.

For cross-border settlers, pilgrimage (going on Hajj, *ziyarat* and the *arba'in* walk in Iraq) has become an important medium of connecting with kith and kin across the LoC. Besides fulfilling religious obligations, pilgrimage to Mecca, Qum, Mashhad and Karbala offers precious opportunities to get news of those with whom contact has been lost – changing fortunes, births and deaths of family members and friends on either side. If destiny favours, they might also be able to meet there. Among the partitioned communities of Ladakh and Gilgit–Baltistan, identification with the clan (*pa*), defined by common ancestral descent, continues to be an important marker of identity rooted in locale. People identify and locate their extended kin network from the name of the clan. Pilgrims carry photographs and home videos of their own and other families to send to relatives on the other side. Back home, people eagerly await their return, yearning to hear news about the other side; the videos they return with circulate in neighbourhoods and villages. Pilgrims from both sides of the LoC also swap books, music and letters. Third-places are thus nodes that knot together connections but do not always lie along direct pathways. Third-places cannot be barricaded or guarded with checkpoints – infrastructures of 'striated' space erected by states as part of their 'war machine' to extend control and encapsulate territory.[30] In contrast to the striated spaces of state control in the territorial space of the borderland, third-places are 'smooth' spaces that defy state sovereignty, albeit within limited space and time. If cross-border connections between places are materialised through roads and pathways, then third-places reactivate connections through flight, both literally and metaphorically. Third-places mediate the connection–disconnection dynamic and sustain imaginative horizons along this captive borderland.

National Categories and Ethno-linguistic Negotiations of Belonging

Gilgit–Baltistan emotionally resonated not just with the elderly generation of Apo Hasan's vintage, and those who directly experienced the shifting LoC between 1948 and 1971, but also with a younger generation of Baltis. Their desire to maintain connections with the ancestral homeland emanated as much from wanting to reconnect with kin as from an ethnic politics of belonging within India. 'A combination of psychological and political imperatives' led them to explore places lost to them.[31] This 'post-amnesia' was often expressed as a 'thirst for our culture'. A place of direct memories for their elders, Baltistan became a site of cultural politics for Balti youth. It was mobilised to instantiate belonging through national categories of recognition, a condition of belonging that all minorities in India have subscribed to.

Settlement Records, dating to the colonial period, divide the Muslim population of Kargil into three broad ethnic groups: Balti, Brogpa and Kashmiri; there is no mention of Purig. In the view of a prominent Balti cultural activist, this was not incorrect. 'Purig is the name of a region. The Purig-*pa* are not a race. Similarly, Purigi is not a proper language,' he explained. I asked him, why then do people from certain parts of Kargil refer to themselves as Purig-*pa* (people of Purig) even though their official, governmental identity had been subsumed under Balti. With a derisive expression, he reasoned that this was because they were trying to concoct an identity in contradistinction to the Baltis and Brogpas, which were the 'authentic' identities of the region. This dismissal of Purig and Purigi as a language was a crucial strategy deployed by Baltis in their own quest for recognition as a distinct community in post-colonial India. With the drawing up of the LoC, the Baltis settled in Kargil were rendered a minority in numerical terms, which generated a feeling of insecurity. As mentioned in the previous chapter, 'our language' (*gnati skad*) became integral to preserving their identity. The public sphere in Kargil was animated by a rising ethnic consciousness that was reflected in the politics of language, most manifestly in the debates over the authenticity of the Balti versus Purigi dialects. Cultural activism centred on the preservation and promotion of the Balti dialect became a mode of seeking recognition of community identity in ethnic terms.

Both Balti and Purigi are dialects of classical Tibetan. Purigi is the lingua franca of Kargil district, understood by all ethnic groups. Over the years, it liberally absorbed words from Ladakhi, Balti and Urdu. Therefore, Baltis considered it an impure, bastard dialect, merely the 'language of the bazaar'. Based on this, Purig as a region was denied any cultural significance of its own. Sadiq Ali Sadiq, the renowned Balti poet, argued:

Purig absorbed and imitated the cultures of Ladakh, Baltistan and Kashmir. Its own culture got completely lost. They have nothing to show for themselves. And Purig did not influence any other place. This may have been because the rajas of Purig never went outside the region to conquer or wage battles. They always bowed either before the kings of Baltistan or Ladakh.

While this perception of Purigi had been widely internalised in Kargil, some argued to the contrary. Master Hussain from Silmo village, a well-known activist of Purigi, vehemently contended that it is Purigi which is the 'real' language of the region and not Balti:

> I have proof. I know nearly 500 folk songs that have not been adulterated with any Urdu words. Purigi is the *qadim* [ancient] language of the region, as in its original form it was an extremely honorific language. It has been corrupted over the years.

To counter this, a Balti cultural activist retorted:

> Since the ancient times [*qadim zamana*], when Tsering Malik was the raja of Sot and Thi Sultan the raja of Suru [two sub-areas of the Purig region], no new poetry has been written in Purigi. Balti, on the other hand, has moved with the times – to the extent that there is Balti pop music today. It is the Baltis who have made their language and poetry reach the skies.

The preservation of Balti language was also a response to the threat posed by the increasing popularity of Urdu *nauha*s from Pakistan among the younger generation educated in Urdu and English. Elders and cultural activists feared the Balti repertoire would be lost unless actively preserved. Among the various initiatives taken to prevent this, the setting of traditional poetry to modern pop music, as I discussed in the previous chapter, has perhaps been the most popular.[32]

Acknowledging the relative stagnation of Purigi compared to Balti, Purigi activists attributed this to the influence of Islam that led to a forgetting of folk songs. The origin of *majalis* poetry in Baltistan was an important source of legitimacy for the small Balti community's claim to being the upholders of *adab* (refined culture) as compared to Purigi. *Majalis* music is part of the larger repertoire of forms of Persianate poetry, the *ghazal* being the most well-known. The *qasida*, for instance, resembles the *ghazal* in its external form as it 'has a monorhyme and uses the same meters, but extends to a much larger number of verses'.[33] Local historians traced the influence of Persian culture in Baltistan and Kargil through the Kashmir Valley. Under Dogra rule, when Raja Ahmad Shah of Khaplu was taken captive and not allowed to return to Baltistan, his descendants were given *jagir*s (estates) in Kashmir in areas such as Tral and Bandipora.

They are said to have written *marsiya*s, *nauha*s and *qasida*s in Farsi, Kashmiri and Balti.[34] To offer proof of the exalted status of their dialect, Balti intellectuals mentioned Balti *nauha* and *marsiya* in which the first line is in Persian.

Poetry recitation in Kargil was not restricted to religious occasions or formal *musha'ira*. It was a part of daily life. Every Thursday evening (*shab-e-jum'a*), Balti *qasida*s waft through Kargil town relayed from the mosque loudspeaker. The wedding season, usually after the summer harvest and before the onset of winter, announces itself with religious music blaring from homes of those to be betrothed. 'Such is the love of *sha'iri* [the art of poetry] in Kargil that many people start and end their day with poetry,' explained an elder. A *marsiya* is often read along with the Qur'an after the dawn prayer, while the evening prayer is followed by a *qasida*. By reading a *marsiya* and *qasida* every day, a believer remembers Imam Husayn at all times, in times of happiness and times of grief. As Annemarie Schimmel explains, 'In religious *qasida*s God is implored to forgive the poet's sins and the Prophet is asked for his hoped-for intercession at Doomsday.'[35] For many people in Kargil, listening to and reading *marsiya*s imparts peace to the heart. C. M Naim suggests that the *marsiya*, despite being lamentation poetry, leaves believers in a state of exultation rather than despair and dejection. The leitmotif of the *marsiya*, drawn from the martyrdom of Husayn – the cessation of life in death to be followed by the life in the hereafter, which is eternal – imparts a positive emotion that transcends the lachrymose theme. It is 'a prayer that essentially confirms the immortality of the human soul'.[36] Perhaps this explains why a *marsiya* often precedes the recitation of the *fatiha* in a *majlis*. I go into these details to highlight the importance of religious poetry in the emotional and social life of Shi'as. It structures the day for some, offers solace in times of grief and is central to ritual events. Persianate poetic forms in the Tibetan dialect in Ladakh and Baltistan also foreground the encounter between Islam and Tibetan Buddhism in the trans-Himalayan ecumene. The rich history of this encounter is rendered invisible in politics of recognition underlined by pressure to conform to state-formats of ethnic identification.

Linguistic assertions by different ethnic groups in Kargil reflect strategies to garner social and political recognition with a long historical record in the national public sphere. The early years of independent India were witness to a series of movements for linguistic autonomy. This was a time when Nehru and the Congress party had decided to put on hold their commitment to the linguistic reorganisation of provinces for fear that this might prove to be as divisive a force as religion had been during the partition. However, as movements for linguistic autonomy became more vigorous and widespread, they relented, and by the mid-1950s, the old provincial map of India was redrawn along linguistic lines.

The importance of linguistic identity is further attested to by the Eighth Schedule of the Indian Constitution that accords official recognition to twenty-two languages, with a commitment to their promotion through state patronage for arts and culture. At the provincial level, the Sixth Schedule of the erstwhile Constitution of J&K accorded recognition to eight regional languages, including Ladakhi and Balti. The absence of Purigi in this list was accounted for by reference to the 1941 census when Baltistan, Leh, and Kargil together constituted the Ladakh *wazarat*. Linguistic groups were enumerated in the census on the basis of demography. The Purigi population was substantially smaller than the Balti, taking into account the Balti community from Kharmang settled in Kargil town as well as Baltistan itself. As a result, Purigi was subsumed under Balti.[37] This conflation of ethnic and linguistic identity, lingering from the colonial period into the post-colonial state not only led to a relative erasure of Purigi from official records but also meant that it received little state patronage.

The inclusion of Balti in the Sixth Schedule qualified Balti cultural activism for assistance and promotion by the J&K Cultural Academy. If Balti cultural activists argued that it was entirely because of their efforts that their language flourished in its classical form, Purigi activists pointed to the support it received from the state. Radio Kargil became a site that reflected the importance attached to state endorsement and access to state media as sources of ethno-linguistic legitimacy. *Musha'ira*s organised by the J&K Cultural Academy were another important location of state patronage (Figure 5.2).

These became a prominent feature of public cultural life in Kargil since 1964, when *musha'ira*s first began to be organised by the State Information Department. Much respected for their talent, a dozen or so local poets were regularly invited to such gatherings to recite their poetry in exchange for a small honorarium. Such gatherings were prominent events for the literary circuit in Kargil, even though Balti poets felt they did not match the intellectual ambience of Skardu. Over the years, I noticed a sharpening of ethnic identities, with Shina cultural activists of Dard ethnicity also becoming more vocal and prolific in literary production, competing for space in the public sphere with Balti and Purigi. Many scholars started publishing books on the identity and history of their ethnic groups.[38]

Fitting into the Indian state's categories of recognition makes borderland dwellers legible to the state. Legibility creates more avenues for making claims upon the resources of the state but also extends captivity. Kargilis have not resorted to techniques that would render them opaque to the state, a strategy for survival that can be seen among the inhabitants of other South Asian frontiers. Their submission to some of the terms of belonging set by the Indian state came from a considered evaluation of perceived social and political realities in Gilgit–Baltistan.

Figure 5.2 A gathering of poets, 2008

Source: Photograph by the author.

Belonging to India was refracted through the prism of the other side, rather than laboured for in a linear direction of a periphery oriented only to the centre. It was the orientation to Gilgit–Baltistan as a political periphery of Pakistan that also shaped negotiations of belonging to India.

Refractions

Representations of Gilgit–Baltistan specifically, and Pakistan more generally, in Kargil drew upon the narratives of the fortunate few who had the opportunity to travel there, news from pilgrims who interacted with their brethren in third-places, and Indian and Pakistani television channels such as Geo TV. Cross-border settlers' desire to belong to India has been shaped by the arc of post-colonial development in both nation states, rather than being restricted to specific moments of choosing between India or Pakistan in the long partition. Prosaic realities of life in Gilgit–Baltistan – be it the cost of living or infrastructure development or the character of public space – were as much a matter of discussion in Kargil as reveries of poetry gatherings or the sweet water of Baltistan. The longing for people, places and souvenirs from Gilgit–Baltistan was tempered by knowledge of the pragmatic considerations of everyday life and political conditions there, as we saw earlier through Apo's recollections. Inherently plural, their imagination of the other side was imbued with poetic nostalgia, which resisted the realism of history, but at the same time was interrupted by the 'realist' or 'prosaic' definition of the political.[39]

An oft-repeated reaction to quotidian life in Baltistan concerned a comparison of the prices of basic commodities, such as rice and gas cylinders, on both sides of the LoC. Comparing life between Kargil and Skardu, Wafa reflected:

> In Baltistan, everything is very expensive – for example, a gas cylinder costs 950 rupees, and a kilo of rice, 70 rupees. The government is not providing people anything. The people there are struggling. In India, there is government subsidy. People do not have to struggle. Therefore, they [people in Gilgit–Baltistan] are going out, to foreign places.

He added: 'The people there get shocked when they hear how much money the Indian government is spending in Kargil. The government is investing a lot of money here, but despite that development has not taken place.' Another young man, Zakir, on the contrary, waxed eloquently about the quality of 'everything' – the quality of schools and roads as being better in Baltistan. However, he quickly qualified this by attributing infrastructural development in Baltistan to 'foreign funding and NGOs rather than the state'. Master Sadiq echoed this perception of the relative absence of state support: 'The roads there are excellent but have been made by the Chinese. There is a lot of outside money there.' Like Wafa, he too praised the literary culture of Baltistan, but qualified that there was no support for the promotion of culture there in comparison to Kargil, which had the J&K Cultural Academy. All Kargilis, who had visited Baltistan, were keen observers of Pakistan's wider political economy.

On one of the many occasions that Wafa talked of his impressions of Baltistan, he pulled out an Urdu book from his shelf by Yusuf Hussainabadi, a Balti writer from Skardu, titled *Tarikh-e-Baltistan* (*History of Baltistan*) (2003) and read aloud:

> The freedom, which the people living here had dreamt of, was never realised. Instead in the form of the FCR [Frontier Crime Regulation][40] or Agency, an oppressive regime was put into place.... The people of Gilgit–Baltistan put up a massive fight against the Indian forces and made many sacrifices thinking that they were winning their freedom. Despite this, since the beginning we have been disenchanted.

Such literature produced by activists in Baltistan contributed to shaping cross-border settlers' articulations of their location in Hindustan as a 'matter of their good fate'. They were fully cognisant of the post-colonial political history of Gilgit–Baltistan in Pakistan. It therefore merits a summary to situate their negotiations of belonging within India.

Soon after the liberation of Gilgit from J&K on 1 November 1947 – celebrated as *yaum-e-azadi* (Day of Freedom) from the Dogras – the leadership of Gilgit and Baltistan acceded to Pakistan, in the hope that they would benefit from incorporation into a Muslim-majority state, and had resisted incorporation into Azad Kashmir. While accepting the accession of Gilgit, the Pakistani government did not 'formally incorporate the region into its territory due to ongoing tensions with India over the control of Jammu and Kashmir'.[41] Instead, the administration of Gilgit was placed under the purview of a Pakistani political agent through the 'Karachi agreement', signed at the All Jammu and Kashmir Muslim Conference, a process in which the people of Gilgit–Baltistan had no representation.[42] Designated as 'Northern Areas', Gilgit and Baltistan were incorporated into Pakistan via direct rule, with political agents in Gilgit and Skardu. The legal and constitutional status of the Northern Areas also remained undefined in the context of the dispute over J&K.[43] These regions lacked constitutional protection and democratic representation, with no elected assembly or municipal council or rights to vote or appeal in the Supreme Court of Pakistan. Agitations for democratic reform grew over the years. In response to these pressures, a Northern Areas Advisory Council was formed in 1969, renamed the Northern Areas Council in 1971, during the reign of Zulfikar Ali Bhutto. Together, the regions of Gilgit, Baltistan, Hunza and Nagar came to be designated as the 'Federally Administered Northern Areas of Pakistan'.[44] These reforms, however, came to a standstill when Zia-ul-Haq seized power in 1977.[45] It was only in 1994, under the prime-ministership of Benazir Bhutto, that the first party-based elections were held in the Northern Areas leading to the formation of a Northern Areas Executive Council. However, the Council had minimal legislative authority, and real powers of decision-making continued to be vested in the Ministry of Kashmir and Northern Areas Affairs.[46]

Over the years, the Pakistani state lost legitimacy in these areas, and agitation for political rights fomented nationalist movements, calling for the right to self-rule and freedom for Gilgit–Baltistan. Political groups and parties like the Balawaristan National Front, Hunza-Nagar National Movement, Boloristan National Front, and so on became the bearers of a new nationalist discourse.[47] As the discontent against the Pakistani state mounted, the government passed the Gilgit–Baltistan Empowerment and Self-Ordinance Act in 2009, which provided for the formation of a Gilgit–Baltistan Legislative Assembly to which the first elections were held the same year. Nationalist movements, however, contended that these were 'strategic moves to defuse the pressures of rights organizations' as the region continued to be denied representation in the Pakistani parliament and other central-level authorities.[48] As Nosheen Ali argues, these were largely 'symbolic changes that rarely devolved any real powers to the region' and lacked constitutional protection. She also notes that the recent willingness to 'acknowledge the citizenship rights of Gilgit–Baltistanis' is part of the Pakistani government's strategy to 'delegitimize the claims on Gilgit–Baltistan by Azad Kashmir, and, also, of course, by India'.[49]

Interrupting his reading of Yusuf Hussainabadi's book, Wafa reflected upon how Ladakh, in contrast, 'was systematically connected to a chain of national governance after the partition in India, starting from the village *nambardar* right up to the MLA [member of legislative assembly] and then MP [member of parliament] levels'. Besides the Hill Development Council at the district level, Kargil also elected representatives to the J&K legislative assembly and fielded candidates in the national elections. Another day, putting aside his usual euphoric and nostalgic reminiscences of his visit to Skardu, Wafa commented with incredulity that even the '*begari* system' (corvée labour) of the colonial period had not been abolished in Baltistan until 1972, while in Ladakh this had happened soon after independence.

The absence of political representation led to a reversal in the meanings attached to the struggle for freedom against Dogra rule in nationalist discourses in Gilgit–Baltistan. Since 1992, the *jang-e-azadi* of 1947–49 (the liberation of Gilgit–Baltistan from Dogra rule) instead of being celebrated as Independence Day (*yaum-e-azadi*) was marked as *yaum-e-shuhada* (Day of Martyrs).[50] The role of the oppressor was transferred from the Dogra maharajas of Kashmir to the Pakistani government. From the perspective of nationalist activists, the Gilgit agency had, at least, been accorded some representation in the state assembly during the maharaja's reign, a right of appeal in the High Court and protection that the 'state subject' status offered.[51] The nationalists continue to fight for constitutional guarantees of their rights with demands for recognition as a special province with representation in the national assembly. Responses to political alienation in Gilgit–Baltistan have also manifested less overtly through cultural activism that seeks to distinguish the identity of this region from Pakistan. Organisations such as the Baltistan Cultural Foundation (BCF) appropriated tropes of Tibetan authenticity and culture to foreground Baltistan's 'Tibetan' past to extricate the region from the dominant negative representations of Pakistan in the Western world.[52] The activities of the BCF ranged from the promotion of the Tibetan script, the preservation of Buddhist monuments, to the setting up of a heritage museum, resonating with the work of cultural activists in Kargil. Dissatisfaction with the state of affairs in Gilgit and Baltistan acquired an additional dimension for its Shi'i population, with the rise in sectarian violence from the late 1980s.[53]

Zia-ul-Haq's Islamisation of Pakistan led to an imposition of a Sunni interpretation of Islam on the country, reflected, for instance, in attempts to change the curricula of school textbooks.[54] Violence against Shi'as in 1988 marked a turning point for sectarian relations in Gilgit–Baltistan. In alliance with the United States and Saudi Arabia, the Sunni-ised state of Pakistan also felt threatened by Shi'i radicalism in the wake of the Iranian Revolution. Ali argues that the sectarianisation of Gilgit–Baltistan has been a deliberate strategy of the military-intelligence regime to quell the rise of 'secular-nationalist' aspirations in the region.[55] As a Shi'a-majority province, Gilgit–Baltistan is perceived as threatening to Pakistan, which in turn became the rationale for its subordination. Stories of the political struggles of Shi'as in Gilgit–Baltistan since the partition have dominated Kargili representations of the other side. While perhaps unwittingly reinforcing, and even drawing upon depictions of Gilgit–Baltistan as a 'sectarian mess',[56] these representations must be understood in relation to the Indian state's politics of security.

In contrast to Pakistan, rather than seeing the influence of the Iranian Revolution as a threat, the Indian state has mobilised sectarian differences in its politics of security. A Kargili journalist once alluded that the Indian government perhaps even encourages Iran's influence in Kargil in order to counter the perceived threat of Pakistani Islamisation. Especially after the Kargil War, the Indian state has counterposed Kargili Shi'as as peaceful, patriotic Muslims to the violent, threatening Muslims of the Valley to maintain its hold on Kashmir's frontiers through a militarised divide-and-rule strategy. The projection of peace on this frontier of Kashmir rests on a manipulation of sectarian difference.

When Shabir Shah, the founder of the Jammu and Kashmir Democratic Freedom Party (JKDFP), fighting for the self-determination of Kashmiri people, tried to visit Kargil after the Kargil War,[57] he was arrested. Victoria Schofield argues, 'The Indian government also did not want the APHC [All Parties Hurriyat Conference] leaders making political capital out of the Kargil operation.'[58] The arrest of Kashmiri leaders of the popular resistance was a demonstration by the state of considering them to be matter out of place in Kargil. This was likely underlined by the state's fear of separatist leaders in Kashmir mobilising support in Kargil. Such differentiating practices not only seek to deter Muslim unity across sectarian lines but also force the Shi'as of Kargil to participate in this discourse in order to belong to India. They consistently vocalise their distance from radical Shi'i organisations in the Kashmir Valley, such as the Hizbul Momineen.

Kargili Shi'as have quietly resented the discursive and political erasure of their historical, cultural and religious ties with Kashmir that this strategy of rule effects, reaching its zenith in the revocation of Article 370 and the bifurcation of J&K in 2019. However, the invocation of Pakistan in separatist politics in the Valley has necessitated the articulation of a distinct Shi'i political voice. This has resulted in Kargili Shi'as succumbing, to an extent, to the accentuation of sectarian cleavages by the Indian state. The desire, or rather the compulsion, to belong to India also means that calls to open the road to Skardu have not been explicitly articulated in a political language. Instead, the emphasis continues to be placed on 'divided families' and emotional ties even though there is a canny understanding that India might feel threatened by cross-border Shi'i solidarity. Wistful desires for a 'Greater Ladakh' have been sporadically raised by cultural activists in Kargil, who have drawn inspiration from the work of organisations like the BCF, in attempts to reclaim an identification between the Balti language and Tibetan script that has come to be associated with the Leh dialect. These post-partition circulations of cultural and religious forms have, however, scarcely exceeded their symbolic value in Kargil as material and political realties across the LoC have inflected their negotiations of belonging to India.

⚬⚬⚬⚬

Until 2019, cross-border settlers in Kargil were acutely aware of certain privileges of Indian citizenship that they had received compared to their kin in Gilgit–Baltistan. In addition to the status of 'state subject' under the special constitutional provision accorded to J&K, which afforded a measure of socio-economic protection,[59] in Ladakh, they received Schedule Tribe recognition. Besides the material accruements of these constitutional provisions, cross-border settlers' expressions of belonging to India also reiterated the sense of freedom that came from the ability to practise their religion freely and to participate in democratic processes despite narratives of liminal suspension after being incorporated into India. Their articulations of freedom were consistently refracted through the relative absence of constitutional rights in Gilgit–Baltistan. When a Balti interlocutor was leaving Skardu on his first trip in 2007, his heart was heavy. He told a friend of his: 'See you at the Kharul bridge!' The bridge marks the start of the road to Skardu. 'We can at least speak without fear in India, unlike the people of Baltistan,' he proclaimed, recalling that moment. This parting gesture held an emotional proximity that could not be blocked by the closure of the road and other disconnections that have stultified the lives of borderland dwellers. Taken at face value, his statement could simply be read as another expression of freedom within India. Yet its articulation through terms such as fear subtly gestured to the double bind of freedom in captivity.

If freedom is never absolute, neither is fear. For cross-border settlers in particular, and for Muslims in Ladakh more widely, fear too is a relative emotion. They have managed their feelings of fear within India in relation to imagined alternative fates, those that befell their kin in Pakistan. Little did they realise that their fate was once again going to be transformed overnight, with little forewarning, in India.

Notes

1. Zamindar, *The Long Partition*.
2. Rahman and van Schendel, 'I Am Not a Refugee', 558.
3. Malkki, 'National Geographic', 54.
4. Stewart, *On Longing*, xi.
5. Ho, *Graves of Tarim*.
6. Thiranagama, *In My Mother's House*, 18.
7. Feldman, 'Home as a Refrain', 14.
8. Feldman, 'Home as a Refrain', 16.
9. Rashid, 'Theatrics of a "Violent State"', gives an account of the massacre of Muslims in Jammu following their campaign against the Dogras, in Poonch in August 1947.
10. An exception to this is Ibrahim, *From Family to Police Force*, on India's western border with Pakistan in Kutch.
11. For specific insight into society and economy in Hardas in the 1970s, see Rizvi, *The Balti*.
12. One *kanal* of land is approximately one-eighth of an acre.
13. *Residents of Village Latoo Kargil v. State and Others* (2019) ILR 163 J&K, https://indiankanoon.org/doc/107358756/ (accessed on 1 February 2022).
14. Bhan, *Counterinsurgency, Democracy and Politics of Identity*.
15. Gordillo, *Rubble*, 5.
16. Gilmartin, 'Partition, Pakistan, and South Asian History', 1083–84.
17. Ingold, *Being Alive*.
18. Dhawan, 'Zojila Tunnel'. Accessed 8 April 2020.
19. For more on the history of this road, see Jamwal, 'Road to Kashmir'.
20. Bhat, 'Hundreds March in Kargil'.
21. A government of India report titled *Report of the Group of Ministers on National Security* explicitly lays out the need to 'integrate' border populations through new media strategies to serve the state's security 'concerns'. It states: 'The broadcasting time for the programs in local dialects needs to be increased. The difficulties in making programs in local dialects could be overcome by involving local culture groups, NGOs and media professionals' (p. 95). The report also states: 'The Kargil Review Committee (KRC) informed that Prasar Bharati in J&K lacks Balti and other linguistic skills to reach the people across the Line of Control (LoC). It was thereafter brought to the notice of the GoI that the Ministry of I&B would advise Prasar Bharati to ensure daily transmission in each of the local languages comprising at least three bulletins of ten minutes each through individual radio stations' (p. 117). See GoM, *Report*.
22. Reeves, *Border Work*.

23. Feldman, 'Home as a Refrain', 19, notes the references to water and fruit in refrains of home among displaced Palestinians in Gaza.

24. Jackson, *Politics of Storytelling*, 15.

25. Imperial Production Gilgit Baltistan, 'Documentary Film: Ghulam Hasan Hasni: Life, Art, Personality (Part 1)', YouTube video, 0:24:33 hrs, https://www.youtube.com/watch?v=dT8lK3F84qw (accessed on 12 April 2020).

26. Sangari, 'The Configural Mode'.

27. Sangari, 'The Configural Mode', 33.

28. Marsden, *Living Islam*; Ali, 'Poetry, Power, Protest', 16.

29. Stewart, *On Longing*, xii.

30. Deleuze and Guattari, *Thousand Plateaus*.

31. Kabir, *Partition's Post-amnesias*, 26.

32. On Balti pop music, see Magnusson, 'Greater Ladakh'.

33. Schimmel, *Two Coloured Brocade*, 23.

34. Corroborated by Sadiq Ali Sadiq, Balti Bazaar, Kargil, June 2008.

35. Schimmel, *Two Coloured Brocade*, 25.

36. Naim, *Urdu Texts and Contexts*, 12.

37. Paper presented by local Balti historian Sadiq Ali Sadiq at a seminar organised by J&K Cultural Academy, Kargil, October 2008.

38. For instance, 'Gulshani Sheena' by Ab-jabar Chakel and 'Jammu & Kashmir mein Abad Shin Dardon ki Mukhtasar Tarikh' by Reza Ahmed were released in 2014.

39. Chakrabarty, *Provincializing Europe*, 172–79, identifies a similar tension in the imagination of nationalist poets like Rabindranath Tagore.

40. The FCR was a colonial-era law that was finally repealed in 2018.

41. Ali, *Delusional States*, 14.

42. Ali, *Delusional States*, 14–15.

43. The Northern Areas were not considered a part of Azad Kashmir under the Azad Kashmir Interim Constitution Act of 1974. MacDonald, 'Memories of Tibet', 198.

44. MacDonald, 'Memories of Tibet'; Polzer and Schimdt, 'Transformation in Political Structure'.

45. Sökefeld, 'From Colonialism to Postcolonial Colonialism'.

46. MacDonald, 'Memories of Tibet', 197.

47. Sökefeld, 'Balawaristan and Other Imaginations'.

48. For a detailed critique, see Sering, 'Constitutional Impasse', 354.

49. Ali, *Delusional States*, 35; 47.

50. Sökefeld, '*Jang Azadi*', 77.

51. Sökefeld, 'From Colonialism to Postcolonial Colonialism', 964.

52. MacDonald, 'Memories of Tibet', 191–96.

53. On sectarian violence and tension in Pakistan, see Abou Zahab, 'Regional Dimension of Sectarian Conflicts'; Marsden, *Living Islam*; Nasr, 'Islam, the State and the Rise of Sectarian Militancy'; Zaman, 'Sectarianism in Pakistan '
54. Ali, *Delusional States*, 113.
55. Ali, *Delusional States*, 139.
56. Ali, *Delusional States*, 144.
57. In 2001, Shabir Shah had also participated in a seminar in Leh, where he called for unity, when some members of the Ladakh Buddhist Association asked questions about their demand for UT status. Morup, 'Seminar with Shabir Shah', 9.
58. Schofield, *Kashmir in Conflict*, 213.
59. Only those who could prove that their forefathers resided in the state prior to 1942, along with other eligibility requirements, could become state subjects. This status allowed for ownership and transfer of land in J&K and prohibited employment in the state administration to outsiders.

Epilogue

By 2019, Vijay Diwas had become a simulacrum. To celebrate its twentieth anniversary, one of the biggest shopping malls in upmarket South Delhi created an installation that simulated the Kargil War. Visitors, the mall advertised, could soak in the 'Kargil spirit' by visiting a scene, including a big bunker, reportedly conjured from letters sent by war heroes to their families from the battlefront.[1] The installation abstracted the War from Kargil as a place with people and a prior history. It fed into maintaining the strategic importance of Kargil in relation to the 'hyper visible psychic border'[2] that Kashmir represents in the national imagination. Such war memorialisations are also a tactic of distracting a jingoistic majoritarian Indian public from the insecurity that has always haunted the post/colonial state along Kashmir's frontiers. This insecurity could not have been more evident – for those who chose to use their *'aql* – in the manner by which India illegally revoked Articles 370 and 35A of the Indian Constitution in August 2019. This was accompanied by the bifurcation of the state of J&K into the two UTs of J&K and Ladakh (encompassing Leh and Kargil). Along with the Kashmir Valley, Ladakh too was placed under a telecommunications siege, unpredictably oscillated yet again into disconnection from the world. As additional military troops entered the Valley, Hindu pilgrims and Indian tourists were evacuated in the preceding days. Just as Ladakh's destiny had been arbitrarily conjoined with that of Kashmir through Hindu Dogra colonisation, it was overnight decoupled from it with neither warning nor discussion.

The sense of uncertainty that had constituted the ambient atmosphere of the Kargil borderland through the multiple partitions was reactivated. Social activist Sajjad Kargili, speaking of the psychological impact of this rupture, said:[3]

> We have already seen so many divisions in the past seventy years. We have been divided from Baltistan in 1947. Then after that we saw so many divisions in the 1965 and 1971 wars with Pakistan…. We feel the pain of separation and are connected and dependent on the Kashmir Valley.

In administratively and politically severing Ladakh from Kashmir, Indian tentacles of captivity dug deeper and sharper into the region. While Ladakhi Buddhists celebrated the UT declaration, the Muslims of Kargil vociferously and unanimously rejected it. Soon after the announcement, political parties, along with the Islamia School and the IKMT – which continue to mediate politics in the district – came together to form the Kargil Joint Action Committee. It called for a *bandh* (strike) for two days and demanded the restoration of Articles 370 and 35A and the lifting of the curfew and communication blockade. Hundreds of people across the district (excluding Buddhist-majority Zangskar) participated in the protests, defying the imposition of Section 144 of the Indian Penal Code that prohibits large gatherings. They openly denounced the action of the Indian government and clearly expressed their allegiance to Kashmir. Invoking the language of the Indian freedom movement, the people of Kargil termed their strike a 'civil disobedience'. A curfew was imposed to forestall further 'unrest'. Recalling the protests in Kargil in August 2019, a young man told me that the Kashmiri policemen on duty were on the side of the protestors: 'They would hit the road rather than legs of protestors in a show of *lathi* charge. They threw the tear gas canisters over roofs or to the side to prevent hurting the protestors. In contrast, the Kargili policemen were harsh.' He added with a hint of pride that 'the Kashmiri policemen were impressed with the Kargilis – how their stones hit the target … even better than the Kashmiris'. In a more sober vein, he asserted that the youth of Kargil were no longer going to stand injustice.

In the following months, a sense of despair engulfed Kargil. Vocalised as feeling intense *bechaini* (anxiety), it gestured to the acute fear people felt in the face of an ever-more indeterminate future. They were suddenly disinvested of a significant portion of the freedoms that they had extolled India for. With the creation of a UT without a legislature, Ladakh has been denied fundamental democratic rights. Its political representation has been reduced to voting for one member of parliament in the national assembly. In contrast, as part of the erstwhile province of J&K, both Kargil and Leh were also represented by four members elected to the bicameral state legislative assembly. Furthermore, the withdrawal of Article 35A unleashed fears of the Hindu majoritarian state's project of settler colonialism. The security offered by their erstwhile status as state subjects of J&K with regard to land and jobs was lost. As demands for constitutional safeguards remained unmet, 31 October 2020 – the official date of the bifurcation of J&K – was observed as a 'Black Day'. Processions led by the leadership of both the Islamia School and the IKMT took to the streets again, holding aloft black flags, evocative of Muharram. Kargil observed a shutdown for three days. The reported dispatch of a Shi'i cleric from the Valley to Kargil by Indian agencies in September 2020 apparently did not suffice to placate Kargil's leadership into submission. Calls for actively struggling against *na-insafi* (injustice) that had been instigated by reformists over the past three decades acquired a new meaning, scale and urgency. Remaining silent, it seemed, would no longer suffice.

The absence of consultation, leave alone consent, for the inclusion of Kargil within the UT of Ladakh was a historical repetition of its voice being ignored. As a double minority, the Shi'as of Kargil were once again placed in a position of being obliged to play a 'new game of politics' if they were to be counted as political.[4] After the initial strikes in August 2019, Kargil's leadership relented to making an uneasy peace with the new terms of belonging. Even though they did not consent to the UT, their initial politics of refusal withered into triangular negotiations with Buddhists in Leh, political leaders in the Kashmir Valley and the Indian government in Delhi.

By 2020, the real implications of the withdrawal of Article 35A dawned on the Buddhists of Ladakh. They started clamouring for Sixth Schedule status under which the Constitution of India grants special protection to tribal areas. Kargili Shi'as refused to extend solidarity to Leh in this demand. At the time, they supported the Gupkar Declaration made by Valley-based parties demanding restoration of Article 370, which was reported in the Indian press as Kargil being 'closer to Kashmir than to Leh'.[5] Alongside this gesture, Kargili leadership across the political and religious spectrum, excluding members of the local BJP wing, also came together to form the Kargil Democratic Alliance (KDA) in October 2020. The KDA demanded the restoration of Article 370 and, until that happens, also raised a demand for statehood for Ladakh to restore democratic representation. As leadership in Leh received little response from the centre to their demands for Sixth Schedule status, they, too, started advocating for statehood for Ladakh. Forming an Apex Body, they joined hands with the KDA to start an agitation for statehood. The necessity of Kargil's support to meet the demographic and land area requirements for the delineation of a state became clear to Leh's leaders. They could no longer afford to be dismissive of Kargil. In August 2021, the

KDA also independently filed a petition in the Supreme Court (SC) against the nullification of Article 370, following a similar petition filed by the NC party in Kashmir. A young Kargili politician told me, 'The petition made Kashmir also happy – Mehbooba, Omar, etc. – and also gained currency for Kargil all the way to Gilgit–Baltistan. Leh did not publicly comment or raise an objection to the SC petition.' In his view this is indicative of a new understanding between Leh and Kargil to refrain from mutual criticism lest regional solidarity be exploited by the Government of India in a 'kind of policy of divide and rule'. Martijn van Beek's emphasis on analysing the *conditions* for the possibility of representing Ladakhi identity rather than viewing it in entirely communal terms has thus stood the test of time.[6]

The gradual strengthening of regional and sectarian consciousness that this book traces has become ever more clear in the post-August 2019 phase of this frontier's biography. Today, Kargili Shi'as see themselves as equal and no longer inferior political players to their Buddhist counterparts in Ladakh. The social media of Kargili youth are full of sarcasm, expressing their frustrations with the UT administration and reflecting their awareness of the neo-coloniality of Indian rule along its frontiers.

Contrary to portrayals of the development of UT Ladakh in the media by the Indian government, on a brief visit to Kargil in August 2021, I found widespread frustration. People in both Kargil and Leh complained about participatory democracy being replaced by the tyranny of bureaucratic rule in Ladakh. The power of the Hill Councils was being weakened. A friend in Leh commented, 'Since UT has come, we are just spectators. The UT administration has all the power.' The continual release of notifications by the Lieutenant Governor's (LG) office was disorienting.[7] It created chaos and left people confused. As Mustafa Haji, a Kargili lawyer writes:

> The office of the LG and his team have their feet in Ladakh, but their heart is in Delhi. The LG's office has followed a corporate model of working – a majority of the officers are of the Hill Councils, and the rest have been recruited through outsourcing agencies. There is more focus on amplifying on social media the work done rather than actual engagement with people on the ground.[8]

'The LG is like a newly arrived army commander who is trying to plant saplings in the barren land,' an interlocutor in Leh commented, telling me about the inappropriateness of a proposal to install a drip irrigation scheme in this high-altitude region. Ladakhis had always distinguished between the two faces of the state: the civil administration and the military. The comment alluded to the collapse of this distinction through the manner of functioning of the UT administration.

Even as Ladakh gets further entrapped, the disconnect between the frontier and the centre became evident to me on my journey from Leh to Kargil in August 2021. As we drove along the Indus, my fellow passenger in the shared taxi, a quiet non-Ladakhi man, asked the Kargili driver, 'Does this river have a name?' 'Indus,' the driver answered. When this did not elicit any recognition, he said, 'This is the Sindhu *darya*.' 'Oh, *this* is the Sindhu!' the gentleman exclaimed with a flicker of interest briefly animating his otherwise deadpan expression. Hindu nationalists refer to the Indus as Sindhu. A little while later, he asked in Hindi, 'In vadiyon se bhi militant aate honge?' (Militants must be coming through these mountains also?). This question not only betrayed his complete ignorance of Ladakh, it also reiterated the entrenched association of Kashmir's frontiers in the heartlands of India with the spectre of cross-border infiltration. By then I could not contain my curiosity, so I asked him why he was going to Kargil. He cagily replied that he had been sent by the Central Public Works Department (CPWD) in Delhi 'for development of the region'.

In these changed conditions of belonging, you might wonder what, then, we should make of the long process of the awakening of regional and sectarian consciousness, of the articulations of place and self, that this book explores.

My visit coincided with the Independence Day (15 August) celebrations as well as the first ten days of Muharram. Even as Kargilis ran around, following the UT administration's directives to hold events celebrating 'Azadi ka Amrit Mahotsav' (seventy-five years of Indian independence), they also mocked it. 'We have been told to hoist the flag in schools even though the schools are closed due to Covid,' said an irritated teacher-friend. Another confided that the 'Fit India Freedom Run' foisted on them was just another photo-op for the centre. *Azadi*, it seemed, also needed to be branded. In the meantime, Muharram *majalis* were in full swing. I was struck by how clerics narrated the events of Karbala and the martyrdom of Imam Husayn with commentary on freedom in India. In one *majlis*, a shaykh highlighted the *qurbani* (sacrifice) of Muslims – from Tipu Sultan to Maulana Azad – for the *azadi* of Hindustan. He talked about the participation of Muslims in the anti-CAA protests and explained that *kattarpan* (bigotry) had taken hold in Hindustan and that the media was a *gulam* (slave) of those threatening *azadi* in Hindustan. 'It is our responsibility to be aware ... don't forget the *zulm* [oppression] of this *hukumat*.' He reiterated that Hindustan became free from the British because Gandhi had walked on the path of Imam Husayn. A banner strung across the main road of a village in the Suru Valley stated: 'Gandhi said: If I had an army like the 72 soldiers of Hussain I would have won freedom for India in 24 hours.'

Haidar *sahib* (see Chapter 2) retained his scepticism of clerical guidance. When I observed that nearly everyone in Kargil was wearing black clothes for Muharram, unlike the past, he scoffed, 'We have not achieved *fikri azadi* [freedom of thought]. People have changed their clothes, but not their *fikr*.' He was reading Frantz Fanon, and explained that he learnt from him that replacing one set of chains with another on one's feet is not *azadi*. He was not interested in talking about the UT, dismissing it as *waqiat khariji*, an external circumstance, urging instead to think more deeply about right and wrong. Conversations with Haidar *sahib* were, as always, chastening. They were a reminder of the necessity of turning the gaze within to uphold and practise ethical ideals of justice.

In the public arena, the IKMT and the Islamia School continued to compete symbolically and rhetorically, if not ideologically. Representatives from both the Iran Cultural Centre in Delhi and Ayatollah Sistani's office in Najaf had visited Kargil in previous years, reiterating the importance of Kargili Shi'as in constituency building within a transnational Shi'i sphere of competition. These representatives also diplomatically reached out to the other faction and attempted to mediate a reconciliation. Even though people continued to be aligned to either the Islamia School or the IKMT, they were increasingly cynical about the role of religious institutions in politics. It became difficult for the youth to sustain a belief in these as a site of ethical action. One might interpret this cynicism as the limits of the liberatory potential of revolutionary theory in its uncritical and reductive deployment both in its place of origin and in contexts of its adaptation when it becomes a kind of cultural dogma.[9] Yet it seemed to me that revolutionary theory had already done its work. The *inqilabi* spirit among Kargili Shi'as seemed to be stronger than ever before. The younger generation of Kargilis is educated and confident. Together with clerics and politicians, but also independent of them, they are raising their voice against the injustice that is the UT and the daily injustices within the UT. They are not afraid to speak out.

Political consciousness once awakened cannot easily be made to sleep again. People are not fooled by the deceptions of the Hindu majoritarian state. They can see through its histrionics. The inclusion of the weather across the LoC in the bulletin of the Indian meteorological department as a way of laying claim to Gilgit–Baltistan since 2019 does not mean there is a political will to open the Kargil–Skardu road. Kargilis may be happy that the construction of the Zoji-la tunnel has finally been inaugurated. But they know that it is an infrastructure of state security and is not motivated by any concern for their welfare. There is a clear awareness of the fragility of the Indian state with the renewal of conflict with China on Ladakh's eastern frontier.

If 'the raison d'etre of politics is freedom and its field of experience is action', as Hannah Arendt has proposed, how might we interpret Shi'i negotiations of belonging on Kashmir's frontiers?[10] Arendt critiques the identification of freedom with sovereignty, which she argues arises from a philosophical tradition that equates freedom with free will. She also points to the mistaken conflation of freedom with 'liberation from insecurity and external compulsions' in political liberalism.[11] Instead, we need to grapple with how we can 'recuperate the category of freedom' to understand politics that is not directed to sovereignty but is improvisational in nature.[12] From this perspective, Shi'i politics occupies a space between total submission to the hegemonic terms of a majoritarian state and total resistance to its sovereignty. In simultaneously rejecting the revocation of Kashmir's special constitutional status while bargaining for statehood for Ladakh, Shi'i politics in Kargil is sustaining a political space of ongoing negotiation grounded in an ethics of non-violence. In contradistinction to a political theology of suffering, an active politics of rejection rests on the awareness of the ability to withhold the potential to engage in violent resistance. The Indian state is cognisant of this strength. This keeps at bay the spectacles of violence unleashed in the Kashmir Valley. Because this frontier remains so crucial to the politics of state security, negligible freedoms are bestowed upon and embraced by those who dwell in it. The irony of freedom in captivity is not lost on Kargilis. Yet it enables them to imagine and inhabit the more capacious horizons that have always defined their senses of place and self. Only time will tell if these anti-hegemonic imaginaries and horizons will sustain.

Notes

1. Agarwal, 'Shoppers Soaked in Kargil Spirit'.
2. Zia, *Resisting Disappearance*, 11.
3. Bakshi, 'Unseen 2019'.
4. Scott, 'Colonial Governmentality', 208.
5. Zargar, 'A New Alliance Signals'.
6. Pointing to the divisions that existed among the Buddhists and the cooperation between Buddhists and Muslims at different points in the assertion of a pan-Ladakhi identity, van Beek argued that Ladakhi politics needs to be understood 'as a complex process of negotiation, contestation and representation'. See van Beek, 'Public Secrets, Conscious Amnesia', 367.
7. Producing disorientation is a tactic of settler-colonial subjugation. Bishara, 'Driving while Palestinian'.
8. Haji, 'Deeply Insecure Union Territory'.
9. Said, 'Traveling Theory', 247.
10. Arendt, 'What Is Freedom', 151.
11. Wilder, *Freedom Time*, 76.
12. Wilder, *Freedom Time*, 46.

Glossary

Urdu, Hindi and Persian

abaya	a loose-fitting, long full-length robe worn by some Muslim women
adab	discipline; good breeding; literary taste
agha	descendant of Prophet Muhammad's family
ahkām	injunctions for correct Islamic practice
Ahl al-Bayt	the holy family of Prophet Muhammad
akhlāq	morality, ethics
ākhūn	respected teacher
ʿālam	banner; flag; standard
ʿālim (sing.)/ *ʿulamā* (pl.)	learned man in Islamic religious and legal studies
amal	hope; expectation
ʿaqīda	creed; faith
ʿaql	rational soul, intellect
ʿāshūrā	tenth day of Muharram marking Husayn's martyrdom
astāna	shrine
āzād	free
āzādī	freedom
azān	call to prayer
barsi	death anniversary
burqa	full veil
darbār	court
dasteh	procession in Kargil, deriving from 'bunch' in Persian

dil	heart
dīn-i 'ilm	religious education
du'ā	prayer; supplication to God
duniya- i 'ilm	worldly education
falsafa	philosophy
fātiha	the opening sura of the Qur'an
fatwa	legal opinion delivered by an Islamic religious leader
fikr	thought; reflection
fiqh	science of Islamic jurisprudence
girdāwar	inspector
gunāh	sin
gulām	slave
hadith	the sayings and customs of Prophet Muhammad and his companions, or the Shi'i Imams
Hajj	pilgrimage to Mecca
halal	sanctioned by Islamic law
haq	just; right
haram	forbidden under Islamic law
hijab	covering for hair worn by Muslim women
hukūmat	government
ijtihād	procedure in Islamic jurisprudence consisting of creative reasoning in the light of foundational texts to arrive at new rulings
ilāqa	region
'ilm	knowledge
imām-i jum'a	leader of Friday prayers
inqilāb	revolution
insānīyat	humanity; humanness
'izzat	respect
jadīd	modern
jāhilīyat	ignorance
jawān	foot soldier
khānaqāh	Sufi residence
khitta	region; territory
khums	tax incumbent on the Shi'a
madrasa	seminary
mahfil	assembly; congregation
maktab	Qur'an school
majlis (sing.)/ *majālis* (pl.)	assembly; usually religious gathering(s)
marṣiya	elegy sung for Imam Husayn and Hasan

mātam	mourning, lamentation
mātam-sarāi	place for Muharram mourning
mazhab	religion
minbār	pulpit
mohalla	neighbourhood
mu'awaza	compensation
mujtahid	highest authority in jurisprudence
mulāzim	government servant
mushā'ira	gathering of poets
na-insāfi	injustice
namāz	mandatory daily Muslim prayers
nambardār	representative of the village responsible for revenue collection; headman
nauha	rhythmic dirges sung during Muharram
niyāz	an offering
pai'chan	identity
pāk	pure, clean
qadīm	ancient
qaum	community or region
qasīda	poems in praise of the Prophet, his family and the Imams
qissa	story, tale, narration
raja	king
risāla	the prophetic mission; also used as a shorthand in Kargil for *risala 'amaliyya* (legal compendium that a *marji 'al-taqlid* issues for the use of those who emulate him)
ṣadqa	alms given to earn merit; propitiatory offering
safarnāma	travel memoir
saqāfat	culture
salawāt	blessings; benedictions; liturgy in praise of Prophet Muhammad in Kargil
sawāb	reward; a meritorious or virtuous act
sayyid	descendant of the Prophet or the Imams
sharī'a	Islamic law
shā'irī	poetry
shaykh	cleric recognised by white turban
siyāsat	politics
tabarruk	consecrated food
tabligh	to convey; to preach

tahqīqāt	to make an enquiry
tahsīl	revenue jurisdiction of a sub-collector
takbīr	collective chanting to proclaim God is Great
ta'līm	teaching, instructing
taqlīd	emulation of a *mujtahid* or adherence to the established doctrine of one's chosen school of law
taqrīr	speech, lecture
taqwā	fear of God; piety
taraqqī	progress
tarāna	religious song
tawhīd	unity of God
ta'wīz	amulet
vilayat-i faqih	'guardianship of the jurisprudent', doctrine of clerical leadership implemented in the Iranian political system
watan	nation
wazārat	province; the office of the grand-vizier or prime minister
zakāt	obligatory annual alms tax in Islam
zamindār	a collector of land revenue; in Kargil means land tiller
zildār	native officer in-charge of an administrative unit of land comprising several villages
ziyārat	Shi'i pilgrimage to the shrines of the Imams in the Middle East
zulm	oppression, tyranny

Purigi and Ladakhi (Tibetan dialects)

amchi (am ci)	practitioners of Tibetan medicine
api (a phyi)	grandmother
apo (a po)	grandfather
begar	transport labour tax
bakston (bag ston)	wedding
chang	Tibetan beer made of fermented barley
chattu (tse-tu)	Shi'a belief in pollution caused by the touch of a non-Muslim
cho (jo)	king
chorten (mchod rten)	Tibetan *stupa*; reliquary
daman (lda man)	kettle-drum
go (mgo)	head
gonpa (dgon pa)	Buddhist monastery

grong	neighbourhood
gyalpo (rgyal po)	king
hajji mo	woman preacher who has studied in Iran
kacho	male descendants of erstwhile kings of Kargil region
Khachul (Kha cul)	Kashmir
khar (mkhar)	castle, palace, fort
kharpon (mkhar dpon)	regional administrator; governor of castle
khatak (kha btaks)	ceremonial scarf
lama (bla ma)	monk
lha	spirit, deity
Losar (lo gsar)	Ladakhi and Tibetan New Year
nyering (nye ring)	friendship
pa	appended to signify people; community
phalha (pha lha)	spirit of the household
phaspun (pha spun)	group of households worshipping the same *pha lha* who help at life-cycle events
rgyaspa	extensive, vast
sa	earth
schu (bchu)	ten
sherba	collective of men
sherpa (gsher pa)	wet, moist
shukpa (shug pa)	juniper
skad	language
skambo (skam po)	dry
surna (su-rna)	double-reed
tsokpo (btsog po)	dirty
yul	village, country
zanjirzani	shedding blood
zan zos	family

Bibliography

Abou Zahab, Mariam. 'The Regional Dimension of Sectarian Conflicts in Pakistan'. In *Pakistan: Nationalism without a Nation*, edited by Christophe Jaffrelot, 115–28. Delhi: Manohar, 2002.

———. 'The Politicization of the Shia Community in Pakistan in the 1970s and 1980s'. In *The Other Shiites: From the Mediterranean to Central Asia*, edited by Alessandro Monsutti, Silvia Naef and Farian Sabahi, 97–112. Bern: Peter Lang, 2007.

Abu-Lughod, Lila. 'Do Muslim Women Really Need Saving: Anthropological Reflections on Cultural Relativism and Its Others'. *American Anthropologist* 104, no. 3 (2002): 783–90.

Adelkhah, Fariba. *Being Modern in Iran*. London: C. Hurst & Co., 1999.

———. 'Framing the Public Sphere: Iranian Women in the Islamic Republic'. In *Public Islam and the Common Good*, edited by Armando Salvatore and Dale Eickelman, 227–41. Leiden and Boston: Brill, 2004.

———. 'Islamophobia and Malaise in Anthropology'. In *Conceptualizing Iranian Anthropology*, edited by Shahnaz R. Nadjmabadi, 207–24. London: Bergahahn Books, 2009.

Administration of Union Territory of Ladakh. 'CEC Feroz Khan Chairs Meeting Regarding Tourism Vision Document for Ladakh Emphasizes Inclusion of Adequate Data Related to Kargil District to Ensure Holistic, All-Inclusive Vision Document', 30 November 2021. https://ladakh.nic.in/cec-feroz-khan-chairs-meeting-regarding-tourism-vision-document-for-ladakh-emphasizes-inclusion-of-adequate-data-related-to-kargil-district-to-ensure-holistic-all-inclusive-vision-document. Accessed on 24 June 2022.

Agarwal, Rohan. 'Shoppers Soaked in Kargil Spirit at Select City Mall'. *Weekend Leader*, 22 July 2019. https://www.theweekendleader.com/Headlines/32426/shoppers-soaked-in-kargil-spirit-at-select-city-mall.html. Accessed on 12 October 2021.

Aggarwal, Ravina. *Beyond Lines of Control: Performing Borders in Ladakh, India*. Durham, NC: Duke University Press, 2004.

———. 'At the Margins of Death: Ritual Space and the Politics of Location in an Indo-Himalayan Border Village'. *American Ethnologist* 28, no. 3 (2001): 549–73.

Aggarwal, Ravina, and Mona Bhan. 'Disarming Violence: Development, Democracy and Security on the Borders of India'. *Journal of Asian Studies* 68, no. 2 (2009): 519–42.

Aghaie, Kamran Scot. *The Martyrs of Karbala: Shi'i Symbols and Rituals in Modern Iran*. Seattle: University of Washington Press, 2004.

Ahmad, Irfan. *Islamism and Democracy in India: The Transformation of Jamaat-e-Islami*. Princeton and Oxford: Princeton University Press, 2009.

Ahmed, Akbar. 'Islam and the District Paradigm: Emergent Trends in Contemporary Muslim Society'. *Contributions to Indian Sociology* (n.s) 17, no. 2 (1983): 155–83.

Ahmed, Monisha, and Clare Harris (eds.). *Ladakh at the Crossroads*. New Delhi: Marg Publications, 2005.

Ahmed, Shahab. *What is Islam?: The Importance of Being Islamic*. Princeton and Oxford: Princeton University Press, 2018.

Alavi, Seema. *Muslim Cosmopolitanism in the Age of Empire*. Boston, MA: Harvard University Press, 2015.

Al-Hadi, Ja'far. *The Truth as It Is*, translated by Badr Shahin. Tehran: Ahl al-Bayt World Assembly, 2006.

Al-Mustafa International University. 'About Us'. http://en.miu.ac.ir/#aboutus. Accessed on 16 September 2020.

Al-Azmeh, Aziz. *Islams and Modernities*. London: Verso, 1993.

Ali, Nosheen. *Delusional States: Feeling Rule and Development in Pakistan's Northern Frontier*. New Delhi: Cambridge University Press, 2019.

———. 'Poetry, Power, Protest: Reimagining Muslim Nationhood in Northern Pakistan'. *Comparative Studies of South Asia, Africa and the Middle East* 32, no. 1 (2012): 13–24.

Andersson, Ruben. *Illegality Inc.: Clandestine Migration and the Business of Bordering*. Berkeley: University of California Press, 2014.

Antoon, Sinan. *The Corpse Washer*. New Haven and London: Yale University Press, 2013.

Aras, Ramazan. 'Naqshbandi Sufis and Their Conception of Place, Time, and Fear on the Turkish-Syrian Border and Borderland'. *Middle Eastern Studies* 55, no. 1 (2019): 44–59.

Ardener, Edwin. *The Voice of Prophecy and Other Essays*. New York and Oxford: Berghahn Books, 2007 (1989).

Arendt, Hannah. 'What is Freedom?'. In *Between Past and Future: Six Exercises in Political Thought*, 143–71. New York: Viking Press, 1961.

Arjomand, Said Amir. 'History, Structure, and Revolution in the Shi'ite Tradition in Contemporary Iran'. *International Political Science Review* 10, no. 2 (1989): 111–19.

Arkoun, Mohammed. 'Islamic Cultures, Developing Societies, Modern Thought'. In *Expressions of Islam in Buildings*, edited by Hayat Salam, 49–64. Singapore: Concept Media/The Aga Khan Award for Architecture, 1990.

Asad, Talal. *Formations of the Secular: Christianity, Islam, Modernity*. Stanford, CA: Stanford University Press, 2003.

Atwill, David G. *Islamic Shangri-La: Inter-Asian Relations and Lhasa's Muslim Communities, 1600 to 1960*. Berkeley and Los Angeles: University of California Press, 2018.

Bajoghli, Narges. *Iran Reframed: Anxieties of Power in the Islamic Republic*. Stanford, CA: Stanford University Press, 2019.

Bakhash, Shaul. *The Reign of the Ayatollahs: Iran and the Islamic Revolution*. New York: Basic Books, 1984.

Bakshi, Asmita. 'Unseen 2019: What Kargil Wants after Article 370'. *Mint*, 28 December 2019. https://www.livemint.com/mint-lounge/features/unseen-2019-what-kargil-wants-after-article-370-11577464585667.html. Accessed on 25 October 2020.

Bashir, Shahzad. *Messianic Hopes and Mystical Visions: The Nurbakhshiya between Medieval and Modern Islam*. South Carolina: University of South Carolina Press, 2003.

Bayly, C. A. *Origins of Nationality in South Asia: Patriotism and Ethical Government in the Making of Modern India*. New Delhi: Oxford University Press, 1998.

Behera, Navnita. *Demystifying Kashmir*. New Delhi: Pearson Longman, 2006.

Bellamy, Carla. 'Person in Place: Possession and Power at an Indian Islamic Saint Shrine'. *Journal of Feminist Studies in Religion* 24, no. 1 (2008): 31–44.

Benjamin, Walter. 'Theses on the Philosophy of History'. In *Illuminations*, edited by Hannah Arendt, translated by Harry Zohn, 255–66. London: Fontana/Collins, 1973.

———. 'The Work of Art in an Age of Mechanical Reproduction'. In *Illuminations*, edited by Hannah Arendt, translated by Harry Zohn, 1–26. New York: Schocken Books, 1969.

Bhan, Mona. *Counterinsurgency, Democracy and the Politics of Identity in India: From Warfare to Welfare?* New York: Routledge, 2014.

Bhargava, Rajeev. 'Reimagining Secularism: Respect, Domination and Principled Distance'. *Economic and Political Weekly* 48, no. 50 (2013): 79–92.

Bhat, Tariq. 'Hundreds March in Kargil to Demand Opening of Kargil-Skardu Road'. *The Week*, 1 February 2019. https://www.theweek.in/news/india/2019/02/01/hundreds-march-in-kargil-to-demand-opening-of-kargil-skardu-road.html. Accessed on 8 April 2020.

Bishara, Amahl. 'Driving while Palestinian in Israel and the West Bank: The Politics of Disorientation and the Routes of a Subaltern Knowledge'. *American Ethnologist* 42, no. 1 (2015): 33–54.

Bolourchi, Neda. 'The Sacred Defense: Sacrifice and Nationalism across Minority Communities in Post-Revolutionary Iran'. *Journal of the American Academy of Religion* 86, no. 3 (2018): 724–58.

Bornstein, Avram. 'Military Occupation as Carceral Society: Prisons, Checkpoints, and Walls in the Israeli-Palestinian Struggle'. *Social Analysis* 52, no. 2 (2008): 106–30.

Bowen, John. 'Beyond Migration: Islam as a Transnational Public Space'. *Journal of Ethnic and Migration Studies* 30, no. 5 (2004): 879–94.

Bray, John. 'Introduction'. In *Ladakhi Histories: Local and Regional Perspectives*, edited by John Bray, 1–30. Leiden and Boston: Brill, 2005.

——— (ed.). *Ladakhi Histories: Local and Regional Perspectives*. Leiden and Boston: Brill, 2005.

———. 'Readings on Islam in Ladakh: Local, Regional, and International Perspectives'. *Himalaya* 32, no. 1 (2013): 13–21.

Breda, Yael. 'Managing Dangerous Populations: Colonial Legacies of Security and Surveillance'. *Sociological Forum* 28, no. 3 (2013): 627–30.

Bredi, Daniela. 'History Writing in Urdu: Hashmatu'llah Khan, Kacho Sikandar Khan Sikandar, and the History of the Kargil District'. *Annual of Urdu Studies* 26 (2011): 5–20.

Butz, D., and K. I. MacDonald. 'Serving Sahibs with Pony and Pen: The Discursive Uses of "Native Authenticity"'. *Environment and Planning D: Society and Space* 19, no. 2 (2001): 179–201.

Caton, Steven C. 'What Is an "Authorizing Discourse"?' In *Powers of the Secular Modern: Talal Asad and His Interlocutors*, edited by David Scott and Charles Hirschkind, 31–56. Stanford, CA: Stanford University Press, 2006.

Chakrabarty, Dipesh. *Provincializing Europe: Postcolonial Thought and Historical Difference*. New Jersey: Princeton University Press, 2000.

Chatterjee, Partha. *The Nation and Its Fragments: Colonial and Postcolonial Histories*. New Jersey: Princeton University Press, 1993.

Chatterji, Joya, 'Partition Studies: Prospects and Pitfalls'. *Journal of Asian Studies* 73, no. 2 (2014): 309–12.

———. *The Politics of the Governed: Reflections on Popular Politics in Most of the World*. New York: Columbia University Press, 2004.

Cilardo, Agostino, 'A Dispute between Hanafis and Twelvers about Mutʿa (First Half of 2nd c. AH)'. *Journal of Arabic and Islamic Studies* 17 (2017): 299–309.

Cole, Juan. '"Indian Money" and the Shiʿi Shrine Cities of Iraq, 1786–1850'. *Middle Eastern Studies* 22, no. 4 (1986): 461–80.

———. *Roots of North Indian Shiʾism in Iran and Iraq: Religion and State in Awadh, 1722–1859.* Berkeley, Los Angeles and London: University of California Press, 1988.

———. *Sacred Space and Holy War: The Politics, Culture, and History of Shiʾite Islam.* London: I.B. Tauris, 2002.

———. 'The Ayatollahs and Democracy in Iraq'. International Institute for the Study of Islam in the Modern World (ISIM) Paper 7. Leiden, NL: Amsterdam University Press, 2006.

Cons, Jason. *Sensitive Space: Fragmented Territory at the India–Bangladesh Border.* Seattle: University of Washington Press, 2016.

Crooke, Alastair. *Resistance: The Essence of the Islamist Revolution.* London: Pluto Press, 2009.

Crook, John, and Henry Osmaston (eds.). *Himalayan Buddhist Villages.* Bristol: Bristol University Press, 1994.

Das, Veena. 'Moral and Spiritual Striving in the Everyday: To Be a Muslim in Contemporary India'. In *Ethical Life in South Asia*, edited by Anand Pandian and Daud Ali, 232–52. Bloomington and Indianapolis: Indiana University Press, 2010.

Daura, Prasenjit. *Rescuing History from the Nation: Questioning Narratives of Modern China.* Chicago: The University of Chicago Press, 1995.

Day, Sophie. 'Embodying Spirits: Village Oracles and Possession Ritual in Ladakh, North India'. PhD Dissertation, London University, 1989.

de Genova, Nicolas P. 'Migrant "Illegality: and Deportability in Everyday Life"'. *Annual Review of Anthropology* 31 (2002): 419–47.

de León, Jason. *The Land of Open Graves: Living and Dying on the Migrant Trail.* Berkeley: University of California Press, 2015.

Deeb, Lara. *Enchanted Modern: Gender and Public Piety in Shiʿi Lebanon.* Princeton: Princeton University Press, 2006.

———. 'Piety, Politics, and the Role of Transnational Feminist Analysis'. *Journal of the Royal Anthropological Institute* 15, Islam, Politics, Anthropology (2009): S112–16.

Deleuze, Gilles, and Felix Guattari. *A Thousand Plateaus: Capitalism and Schizophrenia*, translated by Brian Massumi. Minneapolis: University of Minnesota Press, 1987.

Deshpande, Satish. *Contemporary India: A Sociological View.* New Delhi: Penguin Books, 2003.

Devji, Faisal. 'Gender and the Politics of Space: The Movement for Women's Reform in Muslim India, 1857–1900'. *South Asia: Journal of South Asian Studies* 14, no. 1 (1991): 141–53.

———. 'Imitatio Muhammadi'. *Cultural Dynamics* 13, no. 3 (2001): 363–71.

———. *Landscapes of the Jihad: Militancy, Morality, Modernity.* London: Hurst & Co., 2005.

———. *Muslim Zion: Pakistan as a Political Idea.* Cambridge, MA: Harvard University Press, 2013.

———. 'Changing Places: Religion and Minority in Pakistan'. *South Asia: Journal of South Asian Studies* 43, no. 1 (2020): 169–76.

Dhawan, Bulbul. 'Zojila Tunnel: Modi Government Working to Complete Asia's Longest Bi-directional Tunnel without Cost Escalation'. *Financial Express*, 16 February 2020. https://www.financialexpress.com/infrastructure/roadways/zojila-tunnel-modi-government-working-to-complete-asias-longest-bi-directional-tunnel-without-cost-escalation/1869693/. Accessed on 8 April 2020.

Digby, Simon. 'Travels in Ladakh 1820–21: The Account of Moorcroft's Persian Munshi, Hajji Sayyid & Quot Ali, of His Travels'. *Asian Affairs* 29, no. 3 (1998): 299–311.

DNA. 'Once a Theatre of War, Kargil Set to Charm Tourists', 27 January 2017. https://www.dnaindia.com/india/report-once-a-theatre-of-war-kargil-set-to-charm-tourists-2296546. Accessed on 18 November 2019.

Doostdar, Alireza. *The Iranian Metaphysicals: Explorations in Science, Islam and the Uncanny.* Princeton and Oxford: Princeton University Press, 2018.

Dresch, Paul. 'Wilderness of Mirrors: Truth and Vulnerability in Middle Eastern Fieldwork'. In *Anthropologists in a Wider World*, edited by Paul Dresch, Wendy James and David Parkin, 109–27. New York and Oxford: Berghahn Books, 2000.

Eickelman, F. Dale and James Piscatori. *Muslim Politics.* New Delhi: Oxford University Press, 1997.

Eisenlohr, Patrick. 'Media, Citizenship, and Religious Mobilization: The Muharram Awareness Campaign in Mumbai'. *Journal of Asian Studies* 74, no. 3 (2015): 687–710.

Emerson, Richard M. 'Charismatic Kingship: A Study of State-Formation and Authority in Baltistan'. *Politics and Society* 12, no. 4 (1983): 413–44.

Esposito, John (ed.). *The Iranian Revolution: Its Global Impact.* Miami: Florida International University Press, 1990.

Ewing, Katherine Pratt. *Arguing Sainthood: Modernity, Psychanalysis, and Islam.* Durham, NC: Duke University Press, 1997.

Fanon, Frantz. *The Wretched of the Earth.* Harmondsworth: Penguin, 1967.

Fassin, Didier. 'Policing Borders, Producing Boundaries: The Governmentality of Immigration in Dark Times'. *Annual Review of Anthropology* 40 (2011): 213–26.

Feldman, Illana. 'Home as a Refrain: Remembering and Living Displacement in Gaza'. *History and Memory* 18, no. 2 (2006): 10–47.

Fewkes, Jacqueline H. 'Living in the Material World: Cosmopolitanism and Trade in Early Twentieth-century Ladakh'. *Modern Asian Studies* 46, no. 2 (2012): 259–81.

Fischer, Michael J., and Mehdi Abedi. *Debating Muslims: Cultural Dialogues in Postmodernity and Tradition*. Madison, WI: University of Wisconsin Press, 1990.

Fischer, Michael J. *Iran: From Religious Dispute to Revolution*. Madison, WI: University of Wisconsin Press, 1980.

Flood, Finbarr Barry. 'Between Cult and Culture: Bamiyan, Islamic Iconclasm, and the Museum'. *Art Bulletin* 84, no. 4 (2002): 641–59.

Flueckiger, Joyce Burkhalter. *In Amma's Healing Room: Gender and Vernacular Islam in South India*. Bloomington: Indiana University Press, 2006.

Fontein, Jan. 'A Rock Sculpture of the Maitreya in the Suru Valley, Ladakh'. *Artibus Asiae* 41, no. 1 (1979): 5–12.

Foucault, Michel. 'What is Enlightenment?' In *The Foucault Reader*, edited by Paul Rabinow, translated by Catherine Porter, 32–50. New York: Pantheon Books, 1984.

Friese, Kai. 'Liver is Not Mutton'. In *Civil Lines: New Writing from India*. vol. 4, edited by Rukun Advani, Mukul Kesavan and Ivan Hutnick, 7–34. New Delhi: Permanent Black, 2001.

Fuchs, Simon Wolfgang. *In a Pure Muslim Land: Shi'ism between Pakistan and the Middle East*. Chapel Hill: University of North Carolina Press, 2019.

Gandhi, M. K. *The Collected Works of Mahatma Gandhi*, vol. 16: *1 September 1917–23 April 1918*. https://www.gandhiashramsevagram.org/gandhi-literature/collected-works-of-mahatma-gandhi-volume-1-to-98.php. Accessed on 17 June 2022.

———. *The Collected Works of Mahatma Gandhi*, vol. 17: *1 May 1919–28 September 1919*. https://www.gandhiashramsevagram.org/gandhi-literature/collected-works-of-mahatma-gandhi-volume-1-to-98.php. Accessed on 17 June 2022.

Gardener, Katy. 'Mullahs, Migrants, Miracles: Travel and Transformation in Sylhet'. In *Muslim in Communities of South Asia: Culture, Society and Power*, edited by T. N. Madan, 1–37. Delhi: Manohar, 2001.

Gellner, David N. *Borderland Lives in Northern South Asia*. Durham, NC: Duke University Press.

Ghamari-Tabrizi, Behrooz. *Foucault in Iran: Islamic Revolution After the Enlightenment*. Minneapolis: University of Minnesota Press, 2016.

Ghosh, Sahana. 'Cross-border Activities in Everyday Life: The Bengal Borderland'. *Contemporary South Asia* 19, no. 1 (2011): 49–60.

Gilmartin, David. 'Partition, Pakistan, and South Asian History: In Search of a Narrative'. *Journal of Asian Studies* 57, no. 4 (1998): 1068–95.

Golkar, Saeid. *Captive Society: The Basij Militia and Social Control in Iran*. New York: Columbia University Press, 2015.

GoM (Group of Ministers). *Report of the Group of Ministers on National Security*, 26 February 2001. https://www.vifindia.org/sites/default/files/GoM%20Report%20on%20National%20Security.pdf. Accessed on 22 August 2020.

Gordillo, Gaston. *Rubble: The Afterlife of Destruction*. Durham, NC: Duke University Press, 2014.

Govindarajan, Radhika. 'Electoral Ripples: The Social Life of Lies and Mistrust in an Indian Village Election'. *HAU Journal of Ethnographic Theory* 8, nos. 1–2 (2018): 129–43.

Green, Nile. 'The Trans-Border Traffic of Afghan Modernism: Afghanistan and the Indian "Urdusphere"'. *Comparative Studies in Society and History* 53, no. 3 (2011): 479–508.

———. *Bombay Islam: The Religious Economy of the West Indian Ocean, 1840–1915*. Cambridge: Cambridge University Press, 2011.

Grist, Nicola. 'The Use of Obligatory Labor for Porterage in Pre-Independence Ladakh'. In *Tibetan Studies: Proceedings of the 6th Seminar of the International Association for Tibetan Studies, Fagernes 1992*, vol. 1, edited by Per Kvaerne, 264–74. Oslo: Institute for Comparative Research in Human Culture, 1994.

———. Local Politics in the Suru Valley of Northern India', PhD Dissertation. Goldsmiths College, London University, 1998.

———. 'The History of Islam in Suru'. In *Ladakhi Histories: Local and Regional Perspectives*, edited by John Bray, 175–80. Leiden, NL: Brill, 2005.

Gupta, Latika. 'Making a Museum: Reimagining Borders'. Paper presented at the Royal Anthropological Institute Conference (Art, Materiality, Representation), London, 2018.

Gupta, Radhika. 'The Importance of Being Ladakhi in Kargil: Affect and Artifice'. *Himalaya (Journal of Nepal and Himalayan Studies)* 32, no. 1 (2012): 43–50.

———. 'Experiments with Khomeini's Revolution in Kargil: Contemporary Shi'a Networks between India and West Asia'. *Modern Asian Studies* 48, no. 2 (2014): 370–98.

———. 'Seeking Knowledge from the Cradle to the Grave: Shi'i Networks of Learning in India'. In *Pan-Islamic Connections: Transnational Networks between South Asia and the Gulf*, edited by Christophe Jaffrelot and Laurence Louër, 195–215. London: Hurst & Co., 2017.

Gutschow, Kim. 'The Politics of Being Buddhist in Zangskar: Partition and Today'. *India Review* 5, nos. 3–4 (2006): 470–98.

Haeri, Niloofar. 'The Sincere Subject: Mediation and Interiority among a Group of Muslim Women in Iran'. *HAU: Journal of Ethnographic Theory* 7, no. 1 (2017): 139–61.

Haeri, Shahla. *Law of Desire: Temporary Marriage in Iran.* London: I.B Tauris, 1989.

Hage, Ghassan. 'Bearable Life'. *Soumen Anthropologi* 44, no. 2 (2019): 81–83.

Haji, Mustafa. 'A Deeply Insecure Union Territory'. *The Hindu*, 22 December 2021. https://www.thehindu.com/opinion/op-ed/a-deeply-insecure-union-territory/article38007564.ece. Accessed on 12 February 2022.

Hansen, Thomas Blom. 'Predicaments of Secularism: Muslim Identity and Politics in Bombay'. *Journal of the Royal Anthropological Institute* 6, no. 2 (2000): 255–72.

Hartman, Saidiya V. *Scenes of Subjection: Terror, Slavery, and Self-Making in Nineteenth-Century America.* New York and Oxford: Oxford University Press, 1997.

Harvey, Penny, and Hannah Knox. *Roads: An Anthropology of Infrastructure and Expertise.* Ithaca, NY: Cornell University Press, 2015.

Hasan, Mushirul. 'Sectarianism in Indian Islam: The Shia–Sunni Divide in the United Provinces'. *Indian Economic and Social History Review* 27, no. 2 (1990): 209–28.

Hassnain, F. M. *Gilgit, The Northern Gate of India.* New Delhi: Sterling Publishers Ltd, 1978.

Hefner, Robert. W. *Civil Islam: Muslims and Democratization in Indonesia.* Princeton and Oxford: Princeton University Press, 2000.

Henig, David. 'Crossing the Bosphorus: Connected Histories of "Other" Muslims in the Post-Imperial Borderlands of Southeast Europe'. *Comparative Studies in Society and History* 58, no. 4 (2016): 908–34.

Hirschkind, Charles. 'The Ethics of Listening: Cassette-Sermon Audition in Contemporary Egypt'. *American Ethnologist* 28, no. 3 (2001): 623–49.

Ho, Enseng. *The Graves of Tarim: Genealogy and Mobility across the Indian Ocean.* Berkeley and Los Angeles: University of California Press, 2006.

Howarth, Toby. *The Twelver Shi'a as a Muslim Minority in India: Pulpit of Tears.* London: Routledge, 2005.

Huq, Maimuna, 'Reading the Quran in Bangladesh: The Politics of "Belief" among Islamist Women'. *Modern Asian Studies* 42, nos. 2–3 (2008): 457–88.

Hussain, Syed Jaleel, and Syed Eesar Mehdi. 'Contours of Shia Political Discourse in Kashmir: Insecurity, Identity and Resistance'. *Economic and Political Weekly* 56, no. 3 (2021): 51–55.

Hyder, Qurratulain. *River of Fire (Aag Ka Darya).* New Delhi: Women Unlimited, 1998.

Hyder, Syed Akbar. 'Iqbal and Karbala: Re-reading the Episteme of Martyrdom for a Poetics of Appropriation'. *Cultural Dynamics* 13, no. 3 (2001): 339–62.

———. *Reliving Karbala: Martyrdom in South Asian Memory.* Delhi: Oxford University Press, 2006.

Ibrahim, Farhana. *From Family to Police Force: Security and Belonging on a South Asian Border.* Ithaca, NY: Cornell University Press, 2021.

———. 'Islamic "Reform", the Nation-state and the Liberal Subject: The Cultural Politics of Identity in Kachchh, Gujarat'. *Contributions to Indian Sociology* 42, no. 2 (2008): 191–217.

Inayat, Hamid. *Modern Islamic Political Thought*. London and New York: I.B Tauris, 2005.

Ingold, Tim. *Being Alive: Essays on Movement, Knowledge, and Description*. London: Routledge, 2011.

Irfani, Suroosh. *Iran's Islamic Revolution: Popular Liberation or Religious Dictatorship?* London: Zed Books, 1983.

Izutsu, Toshihiko. *The Structure of the Ethical Terms in the Koran: A Study in Semantics*. Tokyo: Keio Institute of Philological Studies, 1959.

Jackson, Michael. *The Politics of Storytelling: Violence, Transgression, and Intersubjectivity*. Copenhagen: Musuem Tusculanum Press, 2002.

Jaffrelot, Christophe (ed.). *Pakistan: Nationalism without a Nation?* Delhi: Manohar, 2002.

Jalal, Ayesha. *Self and Sovereignty: Individual and Community in South Asian Islam*. London: Routledge, 2000.

Jamwal, Anuradha Bhasin. 'The Calm and Early Signs of Conflict'. In *A Desolation Called Peace*, edited by Ather Zia and Javaid Iqbal Bhat, 101–10. India: Harper Collins, 2019.

———. 'Road to Kashmir'. *Newsline Magazine*, April 2004. https://newslinemagazine.com/magazine/road-to-kashmir/. Accessed on 8 April 2020.

Jeffery, Patricia. 'Introduction: Hearts, Minds, and Pockets'. In *Educational Regimes in Contemporary India*, edited by Radhika Chopra and Patricia Jeffery, 13–38. New Delhi and Thousand Oaks, CA: SAGE Publications, 2005.

Jenkins, Timothy. 'Fieldwork and the Perception of Everyday Life'. *Man* (New Series) 29, no. 2 (1994): 433–55.

Jina, Prem Singh. *Ladakh: Past and Present*. Delhi: Gyan Publishing House, 2000.

Jones, Justin. 'Shi'ism, Humanity and Revolution in Twentieth-Century India: Selfhood and Politics in the Husainology of 'Ali Naqi Naqvi'. *Journal of the Royal Asiatic Society* 24, no. 3 (2014): 415–34.

———. *Shi'a Islam in Colonial India: Religion, Community and Sectarianism*. Cambridge: Cambridge University Press, 2011.

Junaid, Mohamad. 'Epitaphs as Counterhistories: Martyrdom, Commemoration, and the Work of Graveyards in Kashmir'. In *Resisting Occupation*, edited by Haley Duchinski, Mona Bhan, Ather Zia and Cynthia Mahmood, 248–77. Philadelphia: University of Pennsylvania Press, 2018.

Kabir, Ananya Jahanara. *Territory of Desire: Representing the Valley of Kashmir*. Minneapolis: University of Minnesota Press, 2009.

——. *Partition's Post-amnesias: 1947, 1971 and Modern South Asia*. New Delhi: Women Unlimited, 2013.

Kanth, Idrees. *Seeking Futures, Shaping Pasts: The Fragmented Nature of the Political in Kashmir*. PhD Dissertation. Leiden University, Netherlands, 2019.

Khan, Hashmatullah. *History of Baltistan*, translated by Adam Nayyar. Islamabad: Lok Virsa, 1987.

Khomeini, Ruhollah. *Islam and the Revolution: Writings and Declarations*, translated by Hamid Algar. London: KPI Ltd, 1985.

Khosravi, Shahram. 'What Do We See if We Look at the Border from the Other Side'. *Social Anthropology* 27, no. 3 (2019): 409–24.

Keddie, Nikki R. *Iran and the Muslim World: Resistance and Revolution*. London: Macmillan Press Ltd, 1995.

Krämer, Gudrun. 'Drawing Boundaries: Yūsuf al-Qardāwī on Apostasy'. In *Speaking for Islam: Religious Authorities in Muslim Societies*, edited by Gudrun Krämer and Sabine Schmidtke, 181–217. Leiden and Boston: Brill, 2006.

Laidlaw, James. 'For an Anthropology of Ethics and Freedom'. *Journal of the Royal Anthropological Institute* 8, no. 2 (2002): 311–32.

Lamb Alastair. *Incomplete Partition: The Genesis of the Kashmir Dispute*. Herting Fordbury: Roxford Books, 1997.

Lambek, Michael (ed.). *Ordinary Ethics: Anthropology, Language, Action*. New York: Fordham University Press, 2010.

Lapidus, Ira. 1984. 'Knowledge, Virtue, and Action: The Classical Muslim Conception of Adab and the Nature of Religious Fulfillment in Islam'. In *Moral Conduct and Authority: The Place of Adab in South Asian Islam*, edited by Barbara D. Metcalf, 39–61. Berkeley: University of California Press, 1984.

Luczanits, Christian. 'The Early Buddhist Heritage of Ladakh Reconsidered'. In *Ladakhi Histories: Local and Regional Perspectives*, edited by John Bray, 65–96. Leiden, NL: Brill, 2005.

Malkki, Liisa H. 'National Geographic: The Rooting of Peoples and the Territorialization of National Identity among Scholars and Refugees'. In *Culture, Power, Place: Explorations in Critical Anthropology*, edited by Akhil Gupta and James Ferguson, 52–74. Durham and London: Duke University Press, 1997.

MacDonald, Kenneth I. 'Memories of Tibet: Transnationalism, Transculturation and Production of Cultural Ideology in Pakistan'. *India Review* 5, no. 2 (2006): 190–219.

MacIntyre, Alasdair. 'Is Patriotism a Virtue?' The Lindley Lecture, Department of Philosophy University of Kansas, 1984.

Magnusson, Jan. 'Greater Ladakh and the Mobilization of Tradition in the Contemporary Baltistan Movement'. In *Islam and Tibet: Interactions along the Musk Routes*, edited by Anna Akasoy, Charles Burnett and Ronit Yoeli-Tlalim, 353–75. Farnham: Ashgate, 2011.

Mahmood, Saba. *Politics of Piety: The Islamic Revival and the Feminist Subject*. Princeton and Oxford: Princeton University Press, 2005.

———. *Religious Difference in a Secular Age: A Minority Report*. Princeton and Oxford: Princeton University Press, 2016.

Majidyar, Ahmad. 'Khamenei's Kashmir Remarks Draw Praise in Pakistan, Rebuke in India'. Middle East Institute, 7 July 2017. https://www.mei.edu/publications/khameneis-kashmir-remarks-draw-praise-pakistan-rebuke-india. Accessed on 14 January 2022.

Mankekar, Purnima. 'Women Oriented Narratives and the New Indian Woman'. In *The Indian Public Sphere: Readings in Media History*, edited by Arvind Rajagopal, 135–50. New Delhi: Oxford University Press, 2009.

Marsden, Magnus. *Living Islam: Muslim Religious Experience in Pakistan's Northwest Frontier*. Cambridge: Cambridge University Press, 2005.

Marsden, Magnus, and David Henig. 'Muslim Circulations and Networks in West Asia: Ethnographic Perspectives on Transregional Connectivity'. *Journal of Eurasian Studies* 10, no. 1 (2019): 11–21.

Massey, Doreen. 'Questions of Locality'. *Geography: Journal of the Geographical Association* 78, no. 2 (1993): 142–49.

Mathur, Nayanika. *Paper Tiger: Law, Bureaucracy and the Developmental State in Himalayan India*. New Delhi: Cambridge University Press, 2016.

Mattingly, Cheryl. 'Two Virtue Ethics and the Anthropology of Morality'. *Anthropological Theory* 12, no. 2 (2012): 161–84.

Mayaram, Shail. *Resisting Regimes: Myth, Memory and the Shaping of a Muslim Identity*. New Delhi: Oxford University Press, 1997.

McGranahan, Carole. 'Refusal as Political Practice: Citizenship, Sovereignty, and Tibetan Refugee Status'. *American Ethnologist* 45, no. 3 (2018): 367–79.

Meir, Litvak. *Shi'i Scholars of Nineteenth-century Iraq: The 'Ulama of Najaf and Karbala*. Cambridge: Cambridge University Press, 1998.

Menon, Nandagopal. 'What Do Polemics Do? Religion, Citizenship, and Secularism in South Indian Islam'. *History of Religions* 58, no. 2 (2018): 128–64.

Mernissi, Fatima. *Islam and Democracy: Fear of the Modern World*. London: Virago Press, 1993.

Mervin, Sabrina. 'The Clerics of Jabal 'Āmil and the Reform of Religious Teaching in Najaf since the Beginning of the 20th Century'. In *The Twelver Shia in Modern Times*, edited by Werner Ende and Rainer Brunner, 79–93. Leiden, Boston and Koln: Brill, 2001.

Metcalf, Barbara (ed.). *Moral Conduct and Authority: The Place of Adab in South Asian Islam*. Berkeley, Los Angeles and London: University of California Press, 1984.

———. *Perfecting Women: Maulana Ashraf 'Ali Thanawi's Bihishti Zewar*. New Delhi: Oxford University Press, 2002.

———. *Islamic Contestations: Essays on Muslims in India and Pakistan*. New Delhi: Oxford University Press, 2004.

Mir-Hosseini, Ziba. *Islam and Gender: The Religious Debate in Contemporary Iran*. London and New York: I.B. Tauris, 1999.

Misri, Deepti. 'Showing Humanity: Violence and Visuality in Kashmir'. *Cultural Studies* 33, no. 3 (2019): 527–49.

Mitchell, W. J. T. (ed.). *Landscape and Power: Space, Place and Landscape*. Chicago: University of Chicago Press, 1994.

Mohammadi, Annabelle S., and Mohammadi Ali. *Small Media, Big Revolution: Communication, Culture, and the Iranian Revolution*. Minneapolis: University of Minnesota Press, 1994.

Momen, Moojan. *An Introduction to Shi'i Islam: The History and Doctrines of Twelver Shi'ism*. New Haven: Yale University Press, 1985.

Morup, Tashi. 'Seminar with Shabir Shah in Leh'. In *Ladakh Studies*, 9–10. Leh: International Association for Ladakh Studies, 16 December 2001.

Mostowlansky, Till. 'Development Institutions and Religious Networks in the Pamirian Borderlands'. In *Routledge Handbook of Asian Borderlands*, edited by Alexander Horstmann, Martin Saxer and Alessandro Rippa, 385–95. London: Routledge, 2018.

Motahhari, Mortaza. 'The Fundamental Problem in the Clerical Establishment', with an introduction by Hamid Dabashi. In *The Most Learned of the Shi'a: The Institution of the Marja'i Taqlid*, edited by Linda S. Walbridge, 161–82. New York: Oxford University Press, 2001.

Mottahedeh, Roy. *The Mantle of the Prophet: Religion and Politics in Iran*. Oxford: Oneworld Publications, 2005 (1985).

Naim, C. M. *Urdu Texts and Contexts: Selected Essays*. New Delhi: Permanent Black, 2004.

Najmabadi, Afsaneh. 'Crafting an Educated Housewife in Iran'. In *Remaking Women: Feminism and Modernity in the Middle East*, edited by Lila Abu-Lughod, 91–125. Princeton: Princeton University Press, 1998.

———. *Women with Mustaches and Men without Beards: Gender and Sexual Anxieties of Iranian Modernity*. Berkeley, Los Angeles and London: University of California Press, 2005.

Nakash, Yitzhak. *The Shi'is of Iraq*. Princeton, NJ: Princeton University Press, 1994.

———. 'The Visitation of the Shrines of the Imams and the Shi'i Mujtahids in the Early Twentieth Century'. *Studia Islamica* 81, no. 1 (1995): 153–64.

Nasr, Vali R. 'Islam, the State and the Rise of Sectarian Militancy in Pakistan'. In *Pakistan: Nationalism without a Nation?* edited by Christophe Jaffrelot, 85–114. New Delhi: Manohar Publications, 2002.

Nayar, Mandira. 'Iran's Ayatollah Khamenei Says India Should Stop "Massacre of Muslims"'. *The Week*, 5 March 2020. https://www.theweek.in/news/india/2020/03/05/irans-ayatollah-khamenei-says-india-should-stop-massacre-of-muslims.html. Accessed on 14 January 2022.

Olszewska, Zuzanna. 'Poetry and Its Social Context among Afghan Refugees in Iran'. DPhil Dissertation. Oxford: University of Oxford, 2009.

O'Neill, Kevin, and Jatin Dua. 'A Forum on Captivity'. *History and Anthropology* 30, no. 1 (2019): 491–96.

———. 'Captivity : A Provocation'. *Public Culture* 30, no. 1 (2018): 3–18.

Osella, Filippo, and Caroline Osella. 'Islamism and Social Reform in Kerala, South India'. *Modern Asian Studies* 42, nos. 2–3 (2008): 317–46.

Otterman, Sharon. 'Iraq: Grand Ayatollah Ali al-Sistani'. https://www.cfr.org/backgrounder/iraq-grand-ayatollah-ali-al-sistani. Accessed on 20 August 2020.

Oxford Islamic Studies Online. 'The Origins of the Quit Kashmir Movement, 1931–1947'. http://www.oxfordislamicstudies.com/Public/focus/essay1009_quit_kashmir.html. Accessed on 27 August 2020.

Pandey, Gyanendra. *The Construction of Communalism in Colonial North India*. Oxford: Oxford University Press, 2006.

Pernau, Margrit. 'Space and Emotion: Building to Feel'. *History Compass* 12, no. 7 (2014): 541–49.

———. 'Feeling Communities: Introduction'. *Indian Social and Economic History Review* 54, no. 1 (2017): 1–20.

Petech, Luciano. *A Study on the Chronicles of Ladakh*. Calcutta: Calcutta Oriental Press, 1939.

Pinault, David. *The Shi'ites: Ritual and Popular Piety in a Muslim Community*. London: I.B. Tauris, 1992.

———. *Horse of Karbala: Muslim Devotional Life in India*. New York: Palgrave, 2001.

Pirie, Fernanda. *Peace and Conflict in Ladakh: The Construction of a Fragile Web of Order*. Leiden and Boston: Brill, 2007.

Polzer, C., and M. Schimdt. 'The Transformation in Political Structure Shigar Valley/Baltistan'. In *Mountain Societies in Transition: Contributions to the Cultural Geography of the Karakorum* (Culture Area Karakorum Scientific Studies, vol. 6), edited by A. Dittmann, 179–210. Köln: Rüdiger Köppe Verlag, 2000.

Rabinow, Paul. *Reflections on Fieldwork in Morocco*. Berkeley, Los Angeles and London: University of California Press, 1977.

Rahman, Fazlur. *Islam and Modernity: Transformation of an Intellectual Tradition*. Chicago: University of Chicago Press, 1982.

Rahman, M., and Willem van Schendel. 'I Am Not a Refugee: Rethinking Partition Migration'. *Modern Asian Studies* 37, no. 3 (2003): 551–84.

Rai, Mridu. *Hindu Rulers, Muslim Subjects: Islam, Rights and the History of Kashmir*. London: Hurst & Co., 2004.

Rajaee, Farhang. 'Iranian Ideology and Worldview: The Cultural Export of the Revolution'. In *The Iranian Revolution: Its Global Impact*, edited by John Esposito, 63–80. Miami: Florida International University Press, 1990.

Rajagopal, Arvind (ed.). *The Indian Public Sphere: Readings in Media History*. New Delhi: Oxford University Press, 2009.

Ramaswamy, Sumathi. 'Visualizing India's Geo-body: Globes, Maps, Bodyscapes'. *Contributions to Indian Sociology* 36, nos. 1–2 (2002): 151–85.

Ramazani, R. K. 'Iran's Export of the Revolution: Politics, Ends and Means'. In *The Iranian Revolution: Its Global Impact*, edited by John Esposito, 40–62. Miami: Florida International University Press, 1990.

Ramble, Charles. 'Gaining Ground: Representations of Territory in Bon and Tibetan Popular Tradition'. *Tibet Journal* 20, no. 1 (1995): 83–124.

Rashid, Iffat. 'Theatrics of a "Violent State" or "State of Violence": Mapping Histories and Memories of Partition in Jammu and Kashmir'. *South Asia: Journal of South Asian Studies* 43, no. 2 (2020): 215–31.

———. 'He Who Has Steel Has Everything: Iqbal, Ahmadis, and the Kashmiri Rights Movement'. Paper presented at the Kashmir Symposium, Oxford University and Vidhi Center for Legal Policy, 2 November 2021.

Rashid, Maria. *Dying to Serve: Militarism, Affect, and the Politics of Sacrifice in the Pakistan Army*. Stanford, CA: Stanford University Press, 2020.

Reeves, Madeleine. *Border Work: The Spatial Lives of the State in Rural Central Asia*. Ithaca and London: Cornell University Press, 2014.

Rizvi, B. R. *The Balti: A Scheduled Tribe of Jammu & Kashmir*. New Delhi: Gyan Publishing House, 1993.

Rizvi, Janet. *Trans-Himalayan Caravans: Merchant Princes and Peasant Traders in Ladakh*. New Delhi: Oxford University Press, 2001.

Robinson, Cabeiri deBergh. *Body of Victim, Body of Warrior: Refugee Families and the Making of Kashmiri Jihadists*. Berkeley, CA: University of California Press, 2013.

———. 'The Dangerous Allure of Tourism Promotion as a Post-conflict Policy in Disputed Azad Kashmir'. Society for Cultural Anthropology, Editors' Forum/ Hot Spots, 24 March 2014.

Robinson, Francis. *Islam and Muslim History in South Asia*. New Delhi: Oxford University Press, 2000.

———. 'Islamic Reform and Modernities in South Asia'. *Modern Asian Studies* 42, nos. 2–3 (2008): 259–81.

Roy, Olivier. *The Failure of Political Islam*. London: I.B. Tauris, 1994.

Saad-Ghorayeb, Amal. *Hizbu'llah: Politics and Religion*. London: Pluto Press, 2002.

Said, Edward W. 'Traveling Theory'. In *The World, the Text, and the Critic*, 226–47. Cambridge: Harvard University Press, 1983.

Sajad, Malik. *Munnu: A Boy from Kashmir*. London: Fourth Estate, 2015.

Saldon, Stanzin. 'I Am Saldo I Am Shifa', *Indian Express*, 19 September 2017. https://indianexpress.com/article/opinion/columns/i-am-saldon-i-am-shifah-4850000/. Accessed on 27 June 2022.

Sangari, Kumkum. 'The Configural Mode: Āg Kā Daryā'. In *A Wildnerness of Possibilities: Urdu Studies in Transnational Perspective*, edited by Kathryn Hansen and David Lelyveld, 21–45. New Delhi: Oxford University Press, 2005.

Schielke, Samuli. 'Being a Nonbeliever in a Time of Islamic Revival: Trajectories of Doubt and Certainty in Contemporary Egypt'. *International Journal of Middle Eastern Studies* 44, no. 2 (2012): 301–20.

Schimmel, Annemarie. *A Two Coloured Brocade: The Imagery of Persian Poetry*. Chapel Hill and London: University of North Carolina Press, 1992.

Schofield, Victoria. *Kashmir in the Crossfire*. London and New York: I.B. Tauris Publishers, 1996.

———. *Kashmir in Conflict: India, Pakistan and the Unending War*. London: I.B Taurus, 2010.

Schubel, Vernon J. *Religious Performance in Contemporary Islam: Shi'i Devotional Rituals in South Asia*. Columbia, SC: University of South Carolina Press, 1993.

Scott, David. 'Colonial Governmentality'. *Social Text* 43 (Autumn 1995): 191–220.

Sennett, Richard. *The Fall of the Public Man*. London: Penguin Books, 1974.

Sering, Senge H. 'Constitutional Impasse in Gilgit-Baltistan (Jammu & Kashmir): The Fallout'. *Strategic Analysis* 34, no. 3 (2010): 354–58.

Shaery-Eisenlohr, Roschanack. *Shi'ite Lebanon: Transnational Religion and the Making of National Identities*. New York: Columbia University Press, 2008.

Shahrokni, Nazanin. 'The Mother's Paradise: Women-Only Parks and the Dynamics of State Power in the Islamic Republic of Iran'. *Journal of Middle East Women's Studies* 10, no. 3 (2014): 87–108.

Shams, Alex. 'Revolutionary Religiosity and Women's Access to Higher Education in the Islamic Republic of Iran'. *Journal of Middle East Women's Studies* 12, no. 1 (2016): 126–38.

Sharma, Janhwij. 'Architectural Heritage, Ladakh'. New Delhi: INTACH, 2003.

Sheikh, Abdul Ghani. *Reflections on Ladakh, Tibet and Central Asia*. New Delhi: Skyline Publications, 2010.

Sherman, Taylor C. *Muslim Belonging in Secular India: Negotiating Citizenship in Postcolonial Hyderabad*. Cambridge: Cambridge University Press, 2015.

Snellgrove, David L., and Tadeusz Skorupski. *The Cultural Heritage of Ladakh*, vol. 1. Warminster, England: Aris & Philipps Ltd, 1973.

Sökefeld, Martin. 'Jang Azadi: Perspectives on a Major Theme in Northern Areas' History'. In *The Past in the Present: Horizons of Remembering in the Pakistan Himalaya*, edited by Irmtraud Stellrecht, 61–82. Köln: Rüdiger Köppe Verlag, 1997.

———. 'Balawaristan and Other Imaginations: A Nationalist Discourse in the Northern Areas of Pakistan'. In *Ladakh: Culture, History and Development between Himalaya and Karakoram: Recent Research on Ladakh*, vol. 8, edited by Martijn van Beek, K. Bertelsen and P. Pedersen, 350–68. Aarhus, Denmark: Aarhus University Press, 1999.

———. 'From Colonialism to Postcolonial Colonialism: Changing Modes of Domination in the Northern Areas of Pakistan'. *Journal of Asian Studies* 64, no. 4 (2005): 939–73.

Spencer, Jonathan. *Anthropology, Politics, and the State: Democracy and Violence in South Asia*. Cambridge: Cambridge University Press, 2007.

Stewart, Susan. *On Longing: Narratives of the Miniature, the Gigantic, the Souvenir, the Collection*. Durham and London: Duke University Press, 1993.

Stewart, Tony K. 'In Search of Equivalence: Conceiving Muslim–Hindu Encounter through Translation Theory'. *History of Religions* 40, no. 3 (2001): 260–87.

Stocking Jr, George W. (ed.). *Objects and Others: Essays on Museums and Material Culture*. Madison, WI: University of Wisconsin Press, 1985.

Stoler, Ann L. *Duress: Imperial Durabilities in Our Times*. Durham, NC: Duke University Press, 2016.

Sur, Malini. *Jungle Passports: Fences, Mobility, and Citizenship at the Northeast India – Bangladesh Border*. Philadelphia: University of Pennsylvania Press, 2021.

Tabaar, Mohammad Ayatollahi. *Religious Statecraft: The Politics of Islam in Iran*. New York: Columbia University Press, 2018.

Taneja, Anand Vivek. *Jinnealogy: Time, Islam, and Ecological Thought in the Medieval Ruins of Delhi*. Stanford, CA: Stanford University Press, 2017.

Tayob, Abdulkader. 'Decolonizing the Study of Religions: Muslim Intellectuals and the Enlightenment Project of Religious Studies'. *Journal for the Study of Religion* 31, no. 2 (2018): 7–35.

Tayob, Shaheed. 'Islam as a Lived Tradition: Ethical Constellations of Muslim Food Practice in Mumbai'. PhD Dissertation. Utrecht University, Netherlands, 2017.

Thiranagama, Sharika. *In My Mother's House: Civil War in Sri Lanka*. Philadelphia: University of Pennsylvania Press, 2011.

van Beek, Martijn. 'Identity Fetishism and the Art of Representation: The Long Struggle for Regional Autonomy in Ladakh'. PhD Dissertation, Cornell University, 1996.

———. 'Thoughts on the Ladakh Autonomous Hill Development Act of 1995'. The *Mountain Forum Electronic Conference on Mountain Policy and Law*, The Mountain Forum, 1997.

———. 'Beyond Identity Fetishism: "Communal" Conflict in Ladakh and the Limits of Autonomy'. *Cultural Anthropology* 15, no. 4 (2000): 525–69.

———. 'Public Secrets, Conscious Amnesia and the Celebration of Autonomy in Ladakh'. In *States of Imagination: Ethnographic Exploration in the Postcolonial State*, edited by Thomas Blom Hansen and Finn Stepputat, 365–90. Durham, NC: Duke University Press, 2001.

———. 'The Art of Representation: Domesticating Ladakhi "Identity"'. In *Ethnic and Religious Revival and Turmoil: Identities and Representations in the Himalayas*, edited by Marie Lecomte-Tilouine and Pascale Dolfus, 282–306. Delhi: Oxford University Press, 2003.

———. 'Dangerous Liaisons: Hindu Nationalism and Buddhist Radicalism in Ladakh'. In *Religious Radicalism and Security in South Asia*, edited by S. Limaye, M. Malik and R. Wirsing, 193–218. Honolulu: Asia-Pacific Center for Security Studies, 2004.

———. 'Imaginaries of Ladakhi Modernity'. In *Tibetan Modernities: Notes from the field on Social and Cultural Change*, edited by Robert Barnett and Ronald Schwartz, 165–88. Leiden, NL: Brill, 2008.

van Beek, Martijn, and Pirie Fernanda. *Modern Ladakh: Anthropological Perspectives on Continuity and Change*. Leiden, NL: Brill, 2008.

van Schendel, Willem. 'Geographies of Knowing, Geographies of Ignorance: Jumping Scale in Southeast Asia'. *Environment and Planning D: Society and Space* 20, no. 6 (2002): 647–68.

———. *The Bengal Borderland: Beyond State and Nation in South Asia*. London: Anthem Press, 2005.

van der Veer, Peter. 'Playing or Praying: A Sufi Saint's Day in Surat'. *Journal of Asian Studies* 51, no. 3 (1992): 545–64.

Varzi, Roxanne. *Warring Souls: Youth, Media and Martyrdom in Post-Revolution Iran*. Durham and London: Duke University Press, 2006.

Verdery, Katherine. *Secrets and Truths: Ethnography in the Archive of the Romanian Secret Police*. Budapest: Central European University Press, 2014.

Walbridge, John. 'Muhammad-Baqir al-Sadr: The Search for New Foundations'. In *The Most Learned of The Shi'a: The Institution of the Marja'i Taqlid*, edited by Linda S. Walbridge, 131–39. New York: Oxford University Press, 2001.

Walbridge, Linda S. (ed.). *The Most Learned of The Shi'a: The Institution of the Marja'i Taqlid*. New York: Oxford University Press, 2001.

Wani, Aijaz Ashraf. 'From the Sheikh's Days, a Slice of Kashmir's Troubled Ties with Delhi'. *The Telegraph*, 13 April 2019. https://www.telegraphindia.com/culture/ books/from-the-sheikhs-days-a-slice-of-kashmirs-troubled-ties-with-delhi/ cid/1688714. Accessed on 24 January 2022.

Wilder, Gary. *Freedom Time: Negritude, Decolonization, and the Future of the World*. Durham, NC: Duke University Press, 2015.

Wittgenstein, Ludwig. *Philosophical Investigations*. Oxford: Blackwell Publishing, 1953.

Zakaria, Anam. *Beyond the Great Divide: A Journey into Pakistan-administered Kashmir*. Harper Collins, India, 2018.

Zaman, Muhammad Qasim. 'Sectarianism in Pakistan: The Radicalization of Shi'i and Sunni Identities'. *Modern Asian Studies* 32, no. 3 (1998): 689–716.

———. *The Ulama in Contemporary Islam: Custodians of Change*. Princeton: Princeton University Press, 2002.

———. 'Modernity and Religious Change in South Asian Islam'. *Journal of the Royal Asiatic Society* 3, no. 14 (2004): 253–63.

Zamindar, Vazira F. Z. *The Long Partition and the Making of Modern South Asia: Refugees, Boundaries, Histories*. New York: Columbia University Press, 2007.

Zargar, Safwat. 'A New Alliance Signals Ladakh Is Split Down the Middle, with Kargil Drawing Closer to Kashmir'. *Scroll.in*, 6 November 2020. https://scroll. in/article/977670/a-new-alliance-signals-ladakh-is-split-down-the-middle-with-kargil-drawing-closer-to-kashmir. Accessed on 2 February 2022.

Zia, Ather. *Resisting Disappearance: Military Occupation and Women's Activism in Kashmir*. Seattle: University of Washington Press, 2019.

Zia, Ather, and Javaid Iqbal Bhat (eds.). *A Desolation Called Peace: Voices from Kashmir*. India: Harper Collins, 2019.

Zins, Max-Jean. 'Public Rites and Patriotic Funerals: The Heroes and the Martyrs of the 1999 Indo-Pakistan Kargil War'. *India Review* 6, no. 1 (2007): 24–45.

Zutshi, Chitralekha. *Languages of Belonging: Islam, Regional Identity and the Making of Kashmir*. London: Hurst & Co., 2004.

———. *Kashmir's Contested Pasts: Narratives, Sacred Geographies and the Historical Imagination*. New Delhi: Oxford University Press, 2014.

Index